The Orchestra

The Orchestra

A History by
HENRY RAYNOR

NEW YORK
CHARLES SCRIBNER'S SONS

LONDON
ROBERT HALE LIMITED

© *Henry Raynor 1978*
First published 1978

ISBN 0 7091 6333 9

Robert Hale Limited
Clerkenwell House
Clerkenwell Green
London EC1R 0HT

Library of Congress Catalog Card Number 77-85289

ISBN 0 684 15535 4

Charles Scribner's Sons
597 Fifth Avenue
New York
N.Y. 10017

PRINTED IN GREAT BRITAIN BY
CLARKE, DOBLE & BRENDON LTD.
PLYMOUTH AND LONDON

Contents

Illustrations

Between pages 128 and 129 (continued)

LINE FIGURES

These are based with thanks on diagrams given in *The Conductor's World* by David Wooldridge (Barrie and Jenkins)

PICTURE CREDITS

Preface

The history of the orchestra, like that of any complex organization, is complex in itself. The instruments assembled in any orchestra have their own individual histories, and their invention, improvement and adaptation is part of the history of the orchestra as a whole; the character of the instruments at different times in their development has influenced the ways in which composers have written for them. Composers have made their own individual demands on players and on their instruments in pursuit of their varying aims and ideals. Orchestras play to audiences which have varying national traditions and tastes which composers have considered as they have tried to communicate through music with their hearers.

The history, however, is influenced by more than purely musical considerations and the states of musical taste as composers found it. The auditorium in which a work is heard and for which perhaps it was composed has its own musical character, its own qualities of, for example, resonance and dryness. The acoustics of a cathedral stimulate a composer in one way. Those of a small concert hall in a nobleman's palace prompt him in quite different directions; the shape, design and acoustic quality of a concert hall designed for two or three or more thousand people make different demands upon him. The music Haydn wrote during his London visit was designed for eight hundred people in the Hanover Square Rooms and does not exactly fit into the Royal Albert Hall, designed for audiences ten times greater.

The orchestra began out of the music and social conditions of the Renaissance and has adapted itself to the conditions of each successive century until, by the twentieth century, it can be either a small army of instrumentalists or an almost arbitrary collection of diverse-sounding instruments, capable of the most varied sound colours, the most unobtrusive whisper or of a power of utterance which overwhelms every listener. It is, for most music lovers, the centre of musical experience, loved before they have learned to love the greater sophistications of chamber music or the more restrained music of solo recitals.

This book sets out to tell the story of the orchestra's musical developments. To do so, necessity compels it to attempt to explain its development as an organization and the way in which, as well as the purpose for which, its diverse instruments came together. It needs to study the work of the conductor and perhaps, for the sake of factuality, to dispel some of the mystique with which enthusiastic audiences have invested the conductor's art. It is written with affection and gratitude to conductors and instrumentalists, as well as to composers by whom the writer's life, like the lives of millions of concert goers, has been splendidly enriched.

Henry Raynor

ONE

Foundations

When the translators of the Authorized Version of the Bible were compelled to write about the instruments which called Nebuchadnezzar's people to worship the great golden image he had set up, they admitted defeat and simply anglicized the list. Nebuchadnezzar's herald cried aloud: "To you it is commanded, O people and nations and languages, that at what time ye hear the sound of the cornet, flute, harp, sackbut, psaltery, dulcimer, and all kinds of music, ye fall down and worship the golden image." The reader who has not come into contact with medieval music and the instruments which played it probably thinks of wild, exotic music played by strange instruments to accompany barbaric rites.

Nebuchadnezzar's orchestra, however, is that which we see carved in angel choirs, painted on altar pieces or made gorgeous in stained glass windows. The flutes were probably recorder-type flutes, though they may, by the time the Authorized Version was published, have been modern transverse flutes. The sackbut was an early trombone, the psaltery a dulcimer played with the fingers rather than with hammers. "All kinds of music" includes other medieval wind and string instruments, trumpets, shawms (the forerunners of the oboe), viols and other bowed strings, lutes, their basses, or citterns, and other plucked stringed instruments.

But if we try to imagine the strange blends of orchestral colour and the unusual sonorities created by these instruments when they played together, although they are traditionally associated with heavenly harmonies and the worship of innumerable musically trained angels, we are reading the ideas of later periods into the translator's list. All these instruments played together to call the people to worship, but they were not designed as an organized ensemble. They played together not for the sake of the splendid tone they could produce orchestrally but simply because the more instruments sounded, the louder the sound that resulted; the notion of playing in parts was not a new one when the Authorized Version appeared, but whatever the translators imagined would result from their collection of musical instruments, it was nothing comparable to the sound of an orchestra.

For one thing, the music came from instruments not designed to play together in an organized ensemble and all far less powerful than their modern descendants. The sackbuts, which were made and tuned in the pitch of all four human voices, were subdued instruments compared to the overpowering modern trombone. At the call to worship, this oddly assorted collection of instruments simply—or so it seems most likely—played the same part in octaves, without harmony. The music was simply for every available instrument, and the more instruments available to join in, the better; if any stayed away, there would be no attempt to find substitutes or rescore the music so that any possible gaps were closed. Such ideas, which grow from our conception of the orchestra, cannot have applied.

Instruments had accompanied the singing of the Christian liturgy since the tenth century, at least, when organs found their way into cathedrals and the bigger, wealthier churches. Many Christian authorities objected to any elaboration of service music, but most believed that anything which made worship grander was good and acceptable. By the turn of the eleventh century, Leonin and Perotin, the first composers whom we know by name and who were, apparently, master and pupil in the choir of Notre Dame in Paris in about the year 1180 (Perotin lived until about 1230), had written service music based upon the official plainsong of the day's services. The tenor or tenors in the choir sang the chant very slowly while alto and soprano wove elaborate melodic ornamentations above. The organ and the sackbuts helped to sustain the enormously long notes into which the chant had been slowed, playing note for note with the singers of the choir. Some authorities believe that Perotin added bells of different pitch to his accompaniment; they played to provide a sort of audible punctuation at the cadences. The religious dramas, or 'liturgical operas' sung at Mass on the great feast days in later years seem to have been given a similar orchestra.

But this instrumental support or reinforcement was never conceived in any terms which we would regard as orchestral either in church music or in medieval dances; it was never intended to be more than a means of reinforcing and assisting voices, and whatever instruments were available joined in without regard to any special qualities or characteristics either of the music or of the instruments. It is possible, when several instruments accompanied a strophic song or any metrically written section of a church service, the instruments may have taken it in turn to offer interludes in which each played its own variant between each stanza. Some authorities suggest that much of this music was played over an instrumental drone. Perhaps a more definite step towards the idea of the orchestra came from the town musicians of the Middle Ages. From the mid-thirteenth century onwards, every considerable city and town recruited a group of musicians who were primarily watchmen, using their instruments to give warning of fire, of the approach to the city gates of any inexplicably large band of travellers. The piercing, strident tone of the shawm, a primitive oboe, made it the best available instrument for sounding an alarm, for the town musicians were not, in almost all European cities, allowed to play the trumpet. Town musicians—'waits' in England, *pifferi* in Italy and *Stadtpfeifer* or *Türmer* (from the tower room which had to be their headquarters) in Germany were organized into guilds, like any other medieval craftsmen. The guilds regulated conditions of membership, decided the number of apprentices any qualified man might teach, and the scale of fees they could expect; each player, for example, had to be able to play all the *Stadtpfeifer* instruments —shawm, curtal, cornett, sackbut and serpent; later, the *Zugtrompett* (which in England was called the 'flat trumpet' because it could play in the 'flat' minor keys) which adopted the principle of the trombone slide, and the trumpet itself were added. As the number of civic duties open to them was extremely limited—acting as watchmen, playing at Mass, or after the Reformation, at the Lutheran Sunday service, the *Gottesdienst*, and taking part in municipal ceremonial and banquets—and could not be regarded as a full-time job, they were given the monopoly of public music-making in the town they served and were booked to play at weddings and other private parties. Like all other guildsmen, they served an apprenticeship to qualify as *Gesellen* or 'journey-men' and could hope, in time, to become *Stadtmusiker* or chief *Stadtpfeifer* of the towns which employed them.

It is easier, in this connection, to refer primarily to the musicians of German towns because, though a similar organization prevailed in every European country, including England, the German guilds are the most thoroughly chronicled. Everywhere the shawm was the essential *Stadtpfeifer* instrument because of its loud, piercing sound; Renaissance authorities described it as the loudest of all instruments after the trumpet. It was a primitive oboe, with a double reed, rougher-toned and less agile than its modern descendant, invaluable in demanding attention where a trumpet was not available.

The curtal, an early bassoon, was regarded as singularly sweet and warm in tone, while the wooden cornett, well played, was the sweetest sounding of all their instruments. It developed from the cowhorn which had itself been bored with finger holes to make it a melodic instrument. The cornett had its great days between 1500 and 1650, a curved instrument of hard wood, bored conically from its mouth-piece and capable of playing every semitone of two and a half octaves with a tone which writers compared with a fine, exceptionally well-trained human voice. The serpent was, to all intents and purposes, its bass; alto and tenor cornetts were made, but they seem never to have been satisfactory enough to win popularity comparable to that of the treble cornett itself.

The *Stadtpfeifer* guilds arose in the thirteenth century. In St Gallen, in Switzerland, a group of town musicians existed in 1272. The first mention of a London guild of musicians dates from 1334. There were town musicians in Basel in 1350, and a Nuremberg guild was functioning in 1377. In 1391, the Bristol corporation decreed that the City waits were to be paid five marks for playing at civic banquets; five marks was also the Lord Mayor's allowance for wine at such events. Various miscellaneous duties were handed over to the town players: in Germany it became a custom for them to play the *Abblasen*—anything from a fanfare to a church chorale —every morning and evening from the church tower, and in London, after the opening of the Royal Exchange in 1567, the waits were ordered to play from its balcony every afternoon. In many places, they seem to have been municipal odd-job men. In 1671, fourteen years before the birth of his son Johann Sebastian, Johann Ambrosius Bach was appointed town musician at Erfurt, in Saxony, where one of his duties was that of ringing the church bell which called citizens to pay their taxes.

The musical standards of the *Stadtpfeifer*, waits and town musicians seem to have varied considerably from time to time. There was a period when the Nuremberg musicians were ordered to rehearse regularly in the presence of a member of the city corporation to ensure that they rehearsed at all. Records exist of quarrels between town musicians and cantors, the church music authorities, and of complete neglect of duties by the town players. But at the same time, there were authorities who wrote with great eloquence about the beauty and accomplishment of *Stadtpfeifer* bands in this or that city. Throughout Germany and Austria they played at the chief Sunday services in church, just as similar ensembles played in the private chapels of kings and of the nobility (with the result that organized bands of singers and instrumentalists came to be called a 'chapel', its leader a *Kapellmeister, maestro di capella* or *maître du chapelle*). What part they took in the services before and during the Renaissance can only be guessed; apparently they simply doubled the vocal music to support the choir, even through the complex polyphonic music of the Renaissance. Their secular duties may well have been more adventurous in a musical sense;

much of what they played outside church was dance music, the earliest type of music to emancipate instruments from voices and vocal styles and thus to give them the opportunity to develop personalities of their own.

The Renaissance players' treatment of dance music is largely a matter of conjecture, but the dance music of a few Renaissance composers provides some evidence about their style and practice. Tylman Susato, who died in the early 1560s, seems to have spent his life in North Germany and Holland; the name 'Susato' is the Latin form of Soest, a Westphalian town. Susato was for twenty years from 1529 a trumpeter among the town musicians of Antwerp, after which he took up music printing and publishing. Most of his own work was vocal, much of it for the Catholic Church but some was secular, unaccompanied part-songs and madrigals, it contains among these a number of dances, written with great vitality, especially in the accompanying parts. Susato's music is not precisely scored, in the manner of later music, but his dances sound well on instruments of the type he would have had at his disposal in Antwerp.

It was, however, the early Baroque period which first thought of instrumental music as something autonomous, independent both of vocal styles and techniques and of the inflexible rhythms of the dance. In 1566, the Venetian Andrea Gabrieli, who had worked as a singer and organist in Verona and in the Rhineland, Bohemia and Bavaria, was appointed second organist at St Mark's, Venice; he was forty-six at the time, and sixty-four when he was promoted to the first organ; but by that time he was famous as a composer of great power and originality. Andrea Gabrieli was a pioneer of the Baroque style of composition which developed in Venice from the attempts of composers to exploit the complex, resonant acoustics of St Mark's, with its great central dome and four smaller domes, with their multiple echoes. What had begun in the 1520s as a choral style reinforced by St Mark's two organs became, in Gabrieli's hands, a monumental choral and instrumental style based on the Baroque exploitation of contrast as a structural principle in music.

Nevertheless, when Gabrieli published his settings of the *Seven Penitential Psalms for Six Voices*, he described them as "suitable for all kinds of instruments and for voices", a description which might have been used by a multitude of composers of the period who were not working out a new, 'advanced' style; it indicates that the music is not interested in exploiting the individuality of instruments in any orchestral sense but that they were, to all intents and purposes, simply possible substitutes for voices. It is Andrea's secular music which shows him working towards the idea of orchestral music which owes nothing to voices or to their styles of composition. The 'sonatas' (a term which to him meant simply instrumental music played as distinct from 'cantata', or music sung), are purely instrumental, many of them written for Venetian ceremonial or entertainment, composed for wind instruments but designed to exploit the contrasting tones and colours of the wind band.

It is to Andrea Gabrieli's nephew and pupil, Giovanni Gabrieli, thirty-seven years Andrea's junior, that we owe the survival of most of the elder master's music. Giovanni became second organist at St Mark's in 1584, when Andrea was promoted to the first organ, and he lived on for more than thirty years after Andrea's death in 1586 to extend his teacher's ideas. Among his works are huge motets for voices and instruments which he published as *Symphoniae Sacrae*—'symphonia' to him meant music for choir, often subdivided, vocal soloists and instruments, while 'concerto', a slightly later term, indicated that an equally extensive body of performers was set into action with each group exploiting the possible contrasts in dynamics and colour which it could provide. The richness and power of this music, its contrast between massiveness and simplicity, was typically Venetian and one of the foundations of the style of the entire Baroque period.

Like all successful Venetian composers, Giovanni Gabrieli composed for civic ceremonies and festivities. Like Andrea he wrote *battaglie* (battle pieces) and sonatas for groups of instruments. The *battaglie* was music for a mock battle, often, in Venice, a mock sea battle on the lagoon. Like the sonatas, it contrasted groups of instruments. The most famous composition of Giovanni Gabrieli, perhaps because it is the easiest to fit into modern conditions of performance, is the *Sonata pian' e forte* (the 'soft and loud sonata'), in which the stately utterances of six trombones are contrasted with the softer voices of viols and recorders. Although the numbers involved make a modern listener think of such music rather as chamber music than as an orchestral work, it owed nothing to the highly developed style of vocal composition with which its composer was familiar and depended on instrumental groups to make its effect. A similar *Canzona in Echo*—a soft-voiced group of instruments echoing the cadence phrases of a more powerful group—in this work cornetts echoing trombones—applies the same principle to a more flowing, lyrical composition.

It is in his massive church works, however, like *In Ecclesiis*, a *Symphonia Sacra*, that Giovanni Gabrieli offered most to the future. The Baroque composer was intensely concerned with words and developed a rhetorical style of composition to exploit them with the greatest eloquence and effect; therefore he invented orchestral, or instrumental figurations and phrases to emphasize their effect. The greatest of Gabrieli's pupils, the German Heinrich Schütz, born in 1585, wrote only vocal music; apart from some Italian madrigals, we know Schütz entirely by his religious compositions in German and Latin, many of them with instrumental accompaniments (although Schütz wrote the first German opera, its score is lost), using the instruments to intensify the words, often in a singularly and effective dramatic way. Instruments, composers like Giovanni Gabrieli, Schütz and Monteverdi found, could contribute to a vocal work by other means than simply doubling the voices.

The exploitation of instrumental tone colour, and therefore of the orchestra, took a decisive step forward in 1607, when Monteverdi's opera *La Favola d'Orfeo*, was produced in Mantua. *Orfeo* was not the first opera, for opera had been born in Florence about ten years before, but *Orfeo* is probably the first opera to which an average modern listener can attend with musical pleasure; its predecessors arouse at best their antiquarian interests. The first operas paid little attention to anything beyond the correct declamation and inflection of their texts, but Monteverdi's instinct for dramatic effectiveness led him not only to compose a good deal of lyrical music for his libretto but also to assemble an orchestra to accompany the singers, choosing the instruments he required for their qualities of tone colour and their innate expressiveness. As befits a work designed in part to glorify the Duke of Mantua, Monteverdi's patron, *Orfeo* is planned for sumptuosity. Its orchestra is precisely specified: the composer demands two recorders, two cornetts, five trumpets, five trombones, two violini piccoli (archaic instruments like miniature violins tuned an octave higher than the standard instrument), four violins, four violas, two cellos and two double basses; together with these instruments, he asked for two harpsichords, three archlutes, three bass viols, two archcitterns, two positive organs, one regal and one harp. A cittern is a bass of the guitar family with four pairs of double strings. A positive organ was simply a fixed chamber organ and a regal a small portable organ. Monteverdi did not, however, set out these instruments in score, as a modern composer would; he simply listed them in a score which gives only the vocal line, a figured bass and the instruments which are given an elaborate *obbligato* to play.

The harpsichords, organs, archlutes, archcitterns and bass viols are the *continuo*: one or other of them join together to provide the harmonic background of the music; the composer chooses the instruments from this group which are most appropriate to the dramatic situation of the moment. The trumpets are played only in the fanfare-like Toccata, which acts as an overture and calls the audience to order. The trombones are heard only to give weight and solemnity to the scenes in the kingdom of Hades, where

B

Orpheus travels to rescue Euridice; the recorders are associated with the shepherds of the introductory scene, in which Orpheus and his bride are among shepherds. The main body of instruments is used as selectively as the instruments of the *continuo*.

To assemble so large a group of instrumentalists was possible only under the patronage of a great nobleman who was prepared to spend vastly for the sake of music he loved or the prestige which might accrue to him from so lavish a performance, although it is possible that the trumpeters were also the trombonists and that three of the other string players were responsible for the bass voils; no well-trained player in 1607 would have been at all put out by being asked to double another instrument with that he usually played during the course of a single performance. Despite the lavishness with which the work is planned and was staged, it would be no more, perhaps, than practical common sense for Monteverdi to arrange his orchestra to provide all the expressive tonal varieties he needed from the smallest possible number of players.

The circumstances of Renaissance court opera did not demand the creation of a standardized ensemble which could cope effectively with all the expressive demands a composer might make. While opera existed as a way in which princes celebrated great events and where questions of cost were not allowed to interfere with the splendour of the celebration, the cost of extra instrumentalists needed to make the right effect was negligible when compared with the amount willingly spent on stage settings of the utmost magnificence and the stage machinery which brought gods and goddesses down from the stage flies to earth, carried heroes and heroines to heaven and worked spectacular transformation scenes.

The musical revolution of the seventeenth century, which created the Baroque style and the sumptuosities of opera, developed a doctrine of what came to be called 'affects'. A single musical statement, composers and theorists believed, could express any clear single emotion; emotions could not be mixed or ambiguous, for music could not make two expressions at once, and one emotion could not grow out of another. Thus the Baroque composer treated music in a way which, because it wished to bring out their 'affect', became rhetorical. It was this principle that prompted Italian composers to develop the idea of recitative which at first neglected melody for declamation while their French counterparts, working in a form which admitted spoken dialogue, pieced together songs, choruses and dances in a form closer to the modern 'musical' than to opera.

Italian recitative consisted of declamation, pitched to definite notes, over expressive harmonies which could be noted simply on a single stave of music as the essential bass line on which the harmony was built, with the subsidiary harmonies expressed simply by figures written over the harmonic root note, leaving the player free to interpret the figures in the way he felt to be most effective; that is, if the written root of the needed chord was C and the figures above it 4 and 6, the resulting chord would contain F and A in any position on the keyboard, and in any octave; the actual pitch of the F and the A were not specified. The bass line itself, almost equal in importance to the vocal line in determining the development of the harmony from chord to chord until it reached the necessary cadence, eventually not only occupied the essential keyboard player or lutenist but also a cellist and a double-bass player, and, it may be, a bassoonist to give the root bass sufficient definition and emphasis; until the time of Bach and Handel, in the first half of the eighteenth century, the lute and the cittern remained possible alternatives for 'realizing' the figured harmony, but increasingly composers left this duty to the keyboard instrument, a harpsichord or organ. The elaborate varieties of *continuo* groups specified by Monteverdi for *Orfeo* were not developed because it was possible for composers to obtain the expressive power they needed and the contrasts of effect in which they delighted from the use of the general orchestral body. Orchestration became a matter of selecting the right expressive instruments over an invariable *continuo* of keyboard, cello and double-bass.

The trumpets of Monteverdi's opera orchestra were not drawn from among the normal body of court musicians. The trumpet had a special role in court life and almost a special mystique until the seventeenth century. It was associated with kings and the nobility, and with war; it was the instrument of heralds (socially notable people) who did not themselves play the trumpet but who were attended by trumpeters who belonged to a special guild of their own, socially superior to the other instrumentalist guilds of town musicians. In war time, they gave signals in battle, a function they also performed at military manœuvres and any ceremonial involving the military; in peace time some of them, especially in Germany, were expected to play in ensemble with other musicians as *Konzert-trompeter* or *Kammertrompeter*; a *Kammertrompeter*, or group of *Kammertrompeter*, was expected to open the main midday and evening meals of their patron with a short, fanfare-style piece in which they were joined by drummers, for timpani and trumpets went together as essential partners. They played at great birthdays or any other special court ceremonial, but their involvement in general music-making rarely went any further than this. As late as 1754 one authority, Johann Heinrich Zedler, in his *Grosses Voll-*

ständiges Universal Lexicon, was still insisting on the special status and duties of a trumpeter:

> No honourable trumpeter or kettledrummer shall allow himself to be employed with his instrument in any way other than for religious services, emperors, kings, electors and princes, counts, lords and knights and nobility, or other persons of high quality: it shall also be forbidden altogether to use a trumpet or a kettledrum at mean or despicable occasions.

The trumpeters' guilds, like the socially less exalted *Stadtpfeifer* guilds, fought savagely to preserve their privileged status against gradual but inevitable erosion as the guild system in general became increasingly irrelevant to society. The trumpeters struggled vigorously to keep their instruments out of the hands of town musicians; their trumpets were unkeyed trumpets restricted to the notes of the harmonic series in which they were tuned, so that it was only high in their register that they were capable of playing a melody; the sensational style of trumpet music from the Baroque period, exploited by Handel and Bach, was the result of techniques developed, and styles of mouthpieces designed to allow the player to climb high in his instrument's register with comparative security of effect.

The development during the Renaissance of the slide trumpet became the subject of ceaseless attacks by the trumpeters' guilds because it seemed likely to break their monopoly. But there were cities, notably the Imperial Free Cities of Germany, like Augsburg and Nuremberg, where the guilds' monopoly had never been effective; they and the Baltic Hanseatic ports adopted trumpeters into their town musicians so that by the end of the eighteenth century the trumpet had been taken up by *Stadtpfeifer* everywhere, and it was town musicians in such cities as Leipzig who preserved the technique which made possible the flamboyant high-pitched *clarino* trumpet parts of Bach and his contemporaries.

The rise of the violin family brought the various possible instrumental groups of the Renaissance and the early Baroque period closer to the idea of the orchestra. The violin seems to have emerged as we know it round about the year 1550, slowly ousting the viol family. By 1604 an English composer, John Dowland, was writing for "viols or violins", according to the title page of his *Lachrimae, or Seven Teares Figured in Seven Passionate Pavans,* music which he based on his phenomenally popular song *Lachrimae.* As such works were written for amateur performance by players in their own homes, the suggestion that violins could be used as an alternative to viols seems to indicate that English music lovers had already began to find the violin attractive. The viola was soon to follow: Gasparo de Salo, who was born in 1540 and became a violin maker in Brescia—some of his instruments from the 1560s have survived—also made violas. The pitch and tuning of violins and violas had been established by this time, and later adjustments to the actual shape and dimensions of the violin dealt only with details. The viola, however, was more often altered; to achieve richness of tone for an instrument lower pitched than the violin, but played in the same way as the violin and limited by the reach of human arms, created problems which still troubled the great violist Lionel Tertis in the twentieth century. After a great career in which he showed that the viola was as worthy a solo instrument as the violin or cello, Tertis designed violas slightly longer and fractionally deeper than violins or than earlier violas, which had varied between fifteen and sixteen inches in length. Throughout most of its history, the viola was regarded as a necessary utility, needed to act as tenor in the string choir to the soprano and alto of the violins and the bass of the cello, which, like the viola, came into the world immediately after the violin; so too did the double bass, tuned an octave lower than the cello, usually equipped at first with five strings and never regarded as a solo instrument (though virtuoso players on the double bass have been heard), but intended simply to give solidity and strength to the lower reaches of the string choir.

The importance of the string instruments in the development of orchestration was that they constituted the closest and most effective parallel to a vocal choir; the nature of harmony itself suggests, if it does not prescribe, four-party harmony filling the depth of rather more than three octaves from a low bass to a high treble. Other instruments, like the trombone or the recorder, were designed and tuned to act with the four voices of a choir, usually in the support of voices; a consort of viols or of recorders provided other possible choirs; the shawms, with their own tenor (bombard) and bass (pommer) were another, with a possible alternative bass; the new transverse flute, often at first known as the 'German flute', and the trumpet fitted into none of the families because the Renaissance ideal was homogeneity of tone and the 'broken consort', in which contrasts of instrumental colour were admitted, seemed imperfectly balanced to Renaissance ears, accepted only because the correctly voiced instrument was not available. The violin family spoke with homogeneous tone and great adaptability, qualities not shared by any of their rivals; they had, too, the power to provide a discreet background to voices and other instruments which they could throw into prominence, a quality of great importance in the early days of opera.

The rise of the violin family seems to have been rapid, though it was probably less rapid than some dates suggest. The Leipzig *Stadtpfeifer*, for example, found their monopoly of social music challenged in 1595 by fiddlers who began to take over some of the official musicians' engagements with the support of the Leipzig citizens. Apparently listeners began to find string tone more enjoyable in their domestic music than the sound of woodwind and brass. By 1607 the encroaching string players had won an official position and were recognized as *Stadtgeiger* ('town fiddlers'); Leipzig employed three of them, giving them lower pay than the *Stadtpfeifer* and a subordinate position; they were employed on the condition that they learned to play the *Stadtpfeifer* instruments and trained themselves to fill gaps in the ranks of the senior musicians.

Opera naturally extended to orchestral vocabulary of the composer because it demanded special effects to match the drama, and like film audiences of the twentieth century, listeners found that musical effects which would strike them as inexplicable in the abstract became not only reasonable but eloquent and impressive when embodied in a dramatic situation which they illustrated.

So long as opera was a diversion for wealthy courts, composers could expect that any instrument they chose to accompany singers and to illustrate the action of a work. But in 1637 the first public opera house was opened in Venice as a commercial venture; its proprietors were a group of Venetian noblemen, and their venture was so successful that in thirty years Venice had eight public opera houses and by 1700 there were sixteen. In 1646, John Evelyn noted in his *Diary* that an opera composed, designed and produced by the architect Bernini had been seen in a public theatre just before his arrival in the city. Crema, a town in Venetian territory, opened a municipal opera house in 1696, and Hamburg, which liked to think of itself as 'the Venice of the North', opened its opera house in 1678. French opera, beginning as a court entertainment fostered by Cardinal Mazarin as a means of keeping the French nobility occupied with unpolitical activities, was naturalized into an individual French style in the reign of Louis XIV and was played in public theatres as well as at Louis's Versailles. Italian opera, too, had its French adherents and was regularly to be seen in Paris.

Thus it became necessary for works to travel from one opera theatre to another, and while the seventeenth century had few scruples about adapting a composer's score to new requirements and the capacities of a theatre the composer had never seen, certain basic orchestral essentials appeared, so that the standardization of the orchestra was accelerated by the demands of the European opera house. Instruments which were not generally available tended to disappear from opera scores because of the need to make any work as effective as possible. The habit of simplifying any score to the vocal part and a figured bass continued, with the instruments required simply listed before each 'number' of the opera. In addition, orchestral music, in the form of overtures, dances and entr'actes, came more frequently from the opera house than from any other source. Monteverdi's operas for the commercial opera houses in Venice were less ambitious in their orchestral demands than the orchestra he assembled for *Orfeo*; but each of them needed—as *Orfeo* did not—a basic group of strings, first and second violins, violas, cellos and double bass. The demands of drama, in Monteverdi's scores, led to an enormous increase in the expressive vocabulary of the orchestra. When Orpheus pleads with Charon, the infernal ferryman, to be conveyed across the River Styx, he does so in the most elaborate virtuoso solo Monteverdi could contrive for him, and each stanza of his song is accompanied by *obbligato* instruments; two violins, two cornetts and a harp join in his pleading, and all are given music requiring unprecedented speed and agility as well as asking for the utmost exactitude of rhythm and timing; the speed of the violin's florid decoration of the vocal line must have seemed all but impossible to violinists in 1607. For dramatic purposes, Monteverdi exploited what he called the *stile concitato*, agitated style, rapidly repeating a string *tremolo*, with notes of unchanging pitch played as rapidly as a bow can scrub across the strings, or characteristic rhythms hammered out repeatedly as horses gallop or swords clash together; both these rhythms appear in *Il Combatimento di Tancredi e Clorinda*, a dramatic cantata composed in 1624. Monteverdi was, too, apparently the first composer to write *pizzicato*, exploiting the effect of plucked strings in the violin family.

Seventeenth- and eighteenth-century strings, however, must have sounded noticeably different from the strings of a modern orchestra. The upper registers were hardly exploited, for even in the time of Mozart it was rare for a player to be asked to move up into the fourth position, which enables him to reach an octave above the note of the string on which he is playing; there was much more movement from string to string, and therefore less homogeneity of tone than a modern player would think desirable. Gut strings, tuned with less tension than the strings have required since the late eighteenth century, produced a more relaxed, less intense tone than later audiences recognize.

Tied notes, played in succession with a single movement of the bow, were rare, for the bow remained shorter than that modern players use, with thicker wood and a far less pronounced inward curve, so that it was heavier and less well balanced than the type of violin bow developed by François Tourte in the second half of the eighteenth century. The idea of *legato* playing, with a succession of notes sounded by each bow movement, was not beyond the players of Monteverdi's day—in fact, there is no other way in which they could tackle such music as the rapid scale passages which accompany Orpheus's pleading. But for a long time only passages of such rapidity appear in violin parts without the slurs which indicate unchanged bowing.

The string orchestra, with a *continuo* instrument, usually a harpsichord or organ, sometimes a lute or bass lute, became the essential foundation of orchestral style. Louis XIV's orchestra, for example, was 'The Twenty-four Violins of the King' (the word 'violins' including the deeper-voiced instruments of the violin family), and Charles II, after his restoration to the English throne, created an identical ensemble at his court. Other instruments were added at need for their special effects. Purcell's arrogantly swaggering trumpet parts, or pastoral flutes and oboes, were added to the strings when they could contribute some particular effect of expression or atmosphere, not because they belonged in some way to a conventionally organized body regarded as 'the orchestra'. In a sense, the Baroque orchestra began to exist when the string ensemble became the most effective available ensemble.

Monteverdi's pupil and greatest successor, Pietro Francesco Cavalli, who died in 1676 after composing a vast number of operas for the Venetian theatres and producing one of his works in Paris to assist Cardinal Mazarin in popularizing opera, scored his works in the simplified manner of Monteverdi but seems to have taken it for granted that wherever an opera was produced, the standard string ensemble would be available and that the other popular instruments—flute, oboe, bassoon, trumpet, drums and, occasionally, horns—would be available with harpsichord, lute and bass lute to hand whenever they were needed. So far as Cavalli was concerned, the string orchestra of first and second violins, violas, cellos and double-basses was a facility any composer could expect wherever he was invited to work. The other composers for the Venetian opera houses, too, employed the string orchestra as the basis of the accompaniment and the essential ensemble for the non-vocal music of overture, entr'actes and incidental dances.

The development of the string orchestra as the invariable necessity influenced church music both in Italy and Germany, in Catholic and non-Catholic countries. Heinrich Schütz, the first of the great German masters, born in 1585, precisely a hundred years before Bach and Handel, had been sent as a young man from Cassel by his patron, the Landgrave of Hesse-Cassel, to study under Giovanni Gabrieli in Venice and had risen to be *Kapellmeister* to the Elector of Saxony at Dresden, where he had been empowered to reorganize court music on Italian lines. In 1625, as a result of the spread of the Thirty Years War towards Saxony and the death of his wife, Schütz had returned to Venice to study the new style of Monteverdi. Little of his music has survived except a mass of eloquent church music more restrained than Monteverdi's in its instrumental accompaniment but making the same demands as Monteverdi's and working according to the same principles; the orchestral and choral style of the early Italian Baroque composers thus became international. Giovanni Legrenzi, who was born in 1626, came from Bergamo, worked in Ferrara and in 1672 had become director of one of the Venetian Conservatories, which began their lives as orphanages training their inmates, boys or girls, as musicians, apparently in order to provide them with a possible career that did not prove too expensive in the fees and indentures demanded by their training. In 1685 Legrenzi became Director of Music at St Mark's, where he reorganized the orchestra; he gave it eight violins, eleven violettas (by which he probably meant a now obsolete instrument with sympathetic as well as bowed strings; the name was also used for the viola), two violas, two old-fashioned violas da gamba, a double-bass, three trombones, two cornetts, a bassoon and four theorbos (bass lutes).

In Legrenzi's day, however, an orchestra at St Mark's, Venice, not necessarily identical with an orchestra anywhere else except in the importance attached to the members of the violin family. The Church of San Petronio, in Bologna, designed to be the largest church in Christendom but never completed, had become a centre of elaborate music towards the end of the sixteenth century though it never employed composers of the consequence of the Gabrielis and Monteverdi. Like St Mark's, San Petronio had two organs, one on each side of the choir and therefore played antiphonally and employed in the dynamic contrasts, echo-effects and other Baroque devices. In 1657, Maurizio Cazzati was appointed *Maestro di Capella* at San Petronio, where the music on feast days was on a grander scale even than that of St Mark's; at Mass on such days the liturgy was interrupted between the *Gloria* and *Credo* by instrumental music, and another interruption separated the *Credo* and *Sanctus*; these interruptions took the form of concerto-like works, which Cazzati called 'sonatas'; they required string orchestra and solo trumpet with organ *continuo*; the trumpet naturally was asked to undertake great feats of agility and to exploit its upper range; but Cazzati was satisfied with a string orchestra of the violin family, and when he published his Trumpet Sonatas in 1665, he allowed the use of theorbo as an alternative to the organ and suggested that the solo part could be played by a violin.

Until the late eighteenth century, the interruption of the Mass by instrumental music was taken for granted, especially in Catholic Italy and Austria. Although there is little or nothing intrinsically religious about the music of all the composers from Cazzati to Mozart which was heard between the Epistle and the Gospel at High Mass, it was designed to fill the time occupied by the ceremonies with which the reading of the Gospel is prepared.

The early Baroque orchestra, with its collection of instruments we now regard as obsolete, and its collection of mixed timbres, established one thing—the basic string orchestra as a source of four-part harmony underpinned by the double-bass sounding an octave lower than cellos and bassoons. Oboes and trumpets were the most frequent additions to the string texture, and bassoons often appeared to add a characteristic bite and definition to the bass line. Other instruments—the various types of viols, the small, high-pitched violino piccolo, the various members of the lute family, cornetts and trombones—might at times be available to offer effects not provided by the essential strings, but such instruments were occasional extras whose participation in instrumental music could not be taken for granted.

TWO

The Baroque Orchestra

The string orchestra was established in the second half of the seventeenth century, but one problem remained to be solved: did it constitute a three-part or a four-part choir? With double-basses reproducing the cello line at an octave's distance, did the violas play an independent tenor part of their own, or did they simply duplicate the alto harmony of second violins, either in unison with them or an octave below them, or did they work with the cellos? There was no immediate answer to this, and no principle was established to solve the problem. A viola with no independent harmony of its own would thicken and enrich the ensemble even if it did not add to its harmonic complexity and, even until the time of Handel's later operas, there are passages in which the strings drop into three-part harmony. One reason for this may, of course, simply have been the less than mellow and eloquent tone produced by many viola players. The viola was so often regarded as a mere utility that its players were more often than not simply unsatisfactory violinists, not sufficiently effective to make the most of musical independence either from cellos or from violins.

With the string orchestra, however it was used, every composer demanded a *continuo*, the essential bass of which continued to be doubled by cello and double-bass, and often with the extra incisiveness of a bassoon which composers by and large took so for granted that they did not specify it on their scores. The use of a group continued beyond the middle of the eighteenth century, until its original purpose of providing full harmony no longer existed, the orchestra having itself grown to the point at which a keyboard filling-in had become unnecessary.

The string orchestra, by this time, had become the all-purpose ensemble to which, in opera scores, other instruments were added for the sake of appropriateness and effect. In the enormously influential court of Louis XIV, which came to mean in all European courts greater and lesser, it was the ensemble needed for dance music and for social music in general. Jean Baptiste Lully—the Italian composer taken to France as a servant at the age of ten or twelve (he was born in 1632), who rose to become Louis XIV's favourite composer and virtual dictator of French music—is not a composer whose music is familiar to the twentieth century. He composed some twenty operas between 1660 and his death in 1687. These were printed in score (an unusual luxury for composers of his period), so that his orchestral style is open to study in detail. As musician in charge of all music in Louis's court, Lully was responsible not only for the string orchestra—*Le Quatre-vingt Violons du Roi*—and the smaller string orchestra *Les Petites Violons du Roi* which Louis created for him before he was twenty, but also the military music played by the *Grande Ecurie*, the wind players who were responsible for regimental marches and military ceremonial music. The *Grande Ecurie* consisted of woodwind instruments played, apparently, with a high degree of virtuosity, and the woodwind group, especially flutes, oboes and bassoons, was co-opted by Lully into his opera and ballet orchestra; trumpets and drums, and horns in hunting scenes, were also enlisted in the opera band. But the basic Lullyan orchestra remained the strings; possibly woodwind instruments doubled the voices in Lully's often monumental choruses, but if they did so, he did not invariably note the doubling in his scores, and otherwise they appear, like trumpets, horns and drums only when they are appropriate to atmosphere or situation. Lully's flutes are rarely old-fashioned recorders; most of the time he specifies the new, more penetrating transverse flute, or 'German flute', as it was often called, which players came to prefer because a skilled instrumentalist could vary not only its volume but its tone through lip movements. Lully made few demands for old or unusual instruments, and rarely left the woodwind to make any extensive contribution to the music without the support of the strings. The restriction of trumpets and horns to the notes of their harmonic series means that he uses them only to contribute to the splendour when splendour is required. Seventy years after Lully's death, J. S. Bach was ready to demand instruments which Lully seems to have regarded as archaic.

Lully's principles of orchestration, which had a great influence outside France, had little to do with blends of orchestral colour to exploit Baroque principles of contrast. With his enriched woodwind style, he composed for the orchestra largely in a style of dialogue between woodwind and strings, the strings acting as initiators of the conversations and the woodwind repeating, in their own manner and with their own accent, what the strings have told them. His dances—and the dance was an essential feature of French opera—are graceful, stylish and rhythmically varied but they are orchestrated sensibly and straightforwardly; it is his marches, with trumpets and drums, which achieve splendour and panache.

Orchestration was, of course, a new department of any composer's work, and Lully did much to stabilize a method which
persisted throughout the late Baroque period; the dialogue of
woodwind and strings, sometimes turned by trumpets into a three-
cornered discussion and sometimes, by Bach and Handel, made
colourful by the coupling of flute and strings conversing with oboes
(as in the 'Pastoral Symphony' which introduces Part Two of
Bach's *Christmas Oratorio*), remained a principle of orchestration
throughout the Baroque age.

When colour demanded exceptional attention, Lully would
supply it no less whole-heartedly than any other composer of his
period; his penultimate ballet, *La Triomphe d'Amour*, of 1681,
contains a *Prelude pour l'Amour* for four flutes (soprano, alto,
tenor and bass) using instruments mostly obsolete now, and there
are points at which he adds guitars to *pizzicato* strings and castanets
to the percussion. His instructions are always precise; the strings
are directed when to use and when to remove mutes, and all the
details of the new art of orchestration which create problems for
instrumentalists unaccustomed to orchestral style are made as clear
as they can be. But ultimately the orchestra is always subordinated
to voices. Even the massive choral and orchestral *chaconnes* which
are his favourite way of ending an act in triumph use the instruments only to double and enrich the music of the chorus.

The orchestral horn was not entirely Lully's innovation. In 1639
Cavalli introduced the horn into a hunting scene in one of his
operas, and Lully followed suit in 1664; this was, originally, less
the adoption of a new instrument than the use of a new and
appropriate effect. The instrument was at first used only in this
limited way because of its restricted range and its roughness of
tone; it was to all intents and purposes a development in brass of
the animal horn pierced with finger-holes, less manageable than
the wooden cornett; it was restricted, at the beginning of the seventeenth century, to the lower-middle notes of its harmonic series,
like the bugle, so that it existed only as an instrument useful for
transmitting signal calls. In the middle of the seventeenth century
French horn makers narrowed the bore of the instrument, slightly
lengthened its tube and curved it into a large single coil. In this
form, with the possibility of a less restricted utterance, horn players
learned to master the upper register in which it can act as a
melodic instrument, and in this form it became popular in France,
and the Francophile Charles II brought it to England at his restoration. By 1691 it was differentiated, in this new form, from instruments of the same type by the name 'French horn'.

This new instrument, though its technique was anything but fully
developed and its resources clearly understood, so fascinated a

Bohemian nobleman, Count Anton von Sporck, that in 1681, when he returned from his Grand Tour, he took several French horns with him and insisted that his own domestic musicians learned to play them. In eighteenth-century scores, horns seem to go by several names. They could be set down in Italian as *corni*, or *corni da caccia*, or in German as either *Waldhörner* or *Jagdhörner*, or in French as *Cors de chasse*. Bach's use of the instrument in his earlier works Italianizes the name; he first wrote a horn part in one of the court cantatas he composed at Cöthen, *Was mir behagd*, where two *corni da caccia* make their appearance. In later works, horn parts are simply noted as *corni*, though the German terms *Waldhorn* and *Jagdhorn* appear in his scores. It seems to be impossible to tell whether these varieties of name indicated some slight difference of form or technique or whether the single instrument was subject to so many names.

Horns appear in a variety of keys in eighteenth-century music but trumpets are rarely found in any key but D major. The horn's versatility was due to the ease with which a crook, an extra coil of tube, could be inserted between the mouthpiece, itself detachable, and the main coil of the instrument to lower its fundamental note. Trumpets, when they were coiled, could be treated in the same way, but trumpets were usually restricted to the more familiar curved oblong shape; they became ill-balanced if crooks were added and the trumpet guilds exerted all their power to preserve the instrument unchanged. The precise shape of trumpet or horn has little influence on the tone it produces, for tone is the product of the length of the tube, the width of its bore, the straightness or conical expansion of the tube and the type of mouthpiece through which air enters it. A trumpet mouthpiece has a shallow, thick-walled cup directing air into a narrow but widening cylinder; air reaches the tube of a horn through a thin-walled, deep cup mouthpiece opening into a cylinder which narrows before it expands. The adaptability of the horn, and its mellower, less penetrating tone, rapidly won the instrument acceptance into the orchestra.

The use of the orchestra as two or three families of instruments engaged in conversation and combining together only for climaxes was an obvious and effective method of using new resources. When Purcell set the woodwind in contrast to the strings, he found that was not the widest contrast available to him; the combination of trumpet and oboe—for the oboe's often pastoral voice can be changed by the player into a bold sound like that of a wooden trumpet—and a sort of orchestral chiaroscuro could be gained by opposing trumpet and strings to a group of oboes and bassoons though Purcell seems either not to have known or to have taken no interest in the deeper-voiced members of the oboe family like the oboe d'amore, the alto, or the oboe da caccia, the tenor. Purcell, in addition, like his contemporary Alessandro Scarlatti, was not content simply to use the orchestra as a back-drop against which voices displayed themselves. Purcell's orchestral accompaniments are often based on figurations in the instrumental parts which add a new dimension to songs, operatic arias and oratorio settings; Lully kept his orchestra in subjection to the voices, but the following generation increasingly gave the orchestra its independent contribution to the matter in hand, often basing the orchestral parts on a musical figure suggested by the words, just as the Second Tenor's description of Spring in *The Fairy Queen* sings "I dart forth my beams to give all things a birth" and the strings at once find a figure of their own which suggests the idea of "darting" and stabbing.

Trumpets, of course, remain still in reserve for moments of special pomp or excitement. Eighteenth-century trumpets, using a very shallow, conical and not cup-shaped, mouthpiece, developed a technique for playing with security at the top of the instrument's range, where it is not only capable of playing complete melodies but of doing so with the utmost brilliance. Purcell naturally used slide trumpets for music of great, solemn pomp, as in the powerful march in the music for the Funeral of Queen Mary in 1694, but his delight in the florid, spectacular music of natural trumpets in the hands of a virtuoso player provides the musician with some splendidly inspiriting and heartening music.

The scale of London music-making, from which Purcell's scores for the theatre and for occasional works were able to benefit, grew from a variety of causes. The Puritan closure of the theatres in 1642 meant that for eighteen years theatre musicians had to earn what money they could from performances in inns and taverns. In 1660, after the Restoration, Charles II reorganized his court music, but his various financial difficulties made it impossible for him completely to maintain the string orchestra of twenty-four players and the separate chamber group of twelve which he had founded in emulation of Louis XIV's organization; in 1668 the two groups coalesced into a couple of orchestras, each taking its turn to do duty at court for alternate months, while the 'resting' orchestra found itself free to work elsewhere. The London theatres were one source of employment for the King's under-employed, underpaid and sometimes unpaid musicians. But it was John Bannister, the leader of the Twenty-four Violins (whom Charles had sent to study in France), who decided that money might be made by the organization of regular concerts for the general public.

In January, 1672, Bannister announced that at four o'clock every afternoon, there would be a concert "by the most excellent masters" at Bannister's house, "now called the Music School" in White-friars. The public seems to have been so used to listening to tavern music that Bannister furnished his small auditorium to look as much as possible like the music room of a tavern. Bannister found his concerts so profitable that he not only continued them to his death in 1679, when his son took over, but also moved them to larger and more fashionable premises in Chandos Street, Covent Garden, in 1674.

A few weeks after Bannister's death, a rival series of concerts began in the Fleet Tavern, St James's, and yet another in 1679. By this time a group of musicians had arranged for a music room to be incorporated in York Buildings, a fashionable new development more or less on the site of the modern Charing Cross Station. Admission to the concerts in the Fleet Tavern was "a shilling for the best places, sixpence in the other". The Concert Room in York Buildings, specially designed for music and a fashionable audience, took the lead in these developments, and Purcell's *Ode on St Cecilia's Day* was sung there early in 1693, only a couple of months after its first performance.

Concerts designed for profit settled in the more fashionable parts of London and in that way became part of the social life of the wealthy. The programmes seem to have been extremely mixed, including solo songs and sonatas as well as ensemble pieces. In 1697 Thomas Hickman, who owned a dancing school in Panton Street, behind the Haymarket, began to give concerts featuring the stars of the opera and foreign virtuosi, accompanied by the orchestra of the opera from the King's Theatre in the Haymarket. Hickman, having enlarged his original premises in 1700, moved his concerts to Brewer Street, Soho, another fashionable newly-built area, in 1739, and the infant prodigy Mozart played there in 1765; a year later, "Hickman's New Rooms" became for a time the home of the concerts given by J. C. Bach and his partner Carl Friedrich Abel.

While the public concerts naturally performed music by Purcell, his theatre works, which ranged from isolated songs with harpsi-chord accompaniment to the elaborately scored masques which are often called 'semi-operas', had the benefit of players from the 'King's Musick' released by Charles's eccentric organization from much of their court duty and recruited into theatre orchestras on the strength of their standing as fine instrumentalists; Charles's inability to make full use of their services worked to the advantage of the aristocracy and the middle class who were, unlike their king, anything but chronically short of money. A few of the players involved in Purcell's music when it was new were reputable composers in their own right, and he had the services of the cream of England's performing talent. The most celebrated of them all was probably John Shore, youngest of three brothers who were all 'Trumpeters in Ordinary' to the King. Matthias and William were appointed by Charles II and John by James II, just before his fall in 1688. It was for John Shore that Purcell wrote his most spectacular and eloquent trumpet *obbligati*.

The D major tuning of trumpets at the same time gave players, especially violinists, their own opportunity for brilliance. The most grateful keys for any string instruments are the major keys of the notes in which it is tuned, which in the case of the violin are G, D, A, and E. The coincidence of a Baroque trumpet's normal tuning in D with the brilliance of D major for the strings is one of music's happiest accidents; the Renaissance trumpet was tuned in C and consisted of some seven feet of brass or silver tubing curled on itself for ease in playing. In the seventeenth century, pitch rose by a tone, so that Renaissance C became Baroque D in characteristic Baroque pursuit of splendour and brilliance; the effectiveness of strings in the key of D major probably deterred composers from making any great demand for trumpets in other keys.

With trumpets went, as a matter of course, drums. The tabor, the folk musician's rhythmic accompaniment to the melodic pipe and the ancestor of the modern side-drum, was not an orchestral instrument, just as the effectively dry rattle of the side-drum itself did not reach the orchestra until the nineteenth century except in the last movement of Handel's *Firework Music*. Baroque drums were kettledrums or timpani, two instruments, tuned to the tonic and the dominant (the key note and the fifth above it) of the music. They were smaller than modern concert drums, remaining at the size which could conveniently be slung over a horse's neck for the use of a cavalry band; Handel often borrowed a pair which had been kept in the Tower of London since they had been captured from the French at the Battle of Malplaquet in 1709. Though they were regarded as unusually large in their day, their size made them quieter than modern drums, and the types of drumstick used gave a more distinct, incisive sound than modern drums and drumsticks achieve unless the composer specifies it. The *tremolando* roll favoured by composers since Berlioz was, of course, in the drummer's repertoire of effects—Bach asks for it on occasions—but most eighteenth-century drum parts mark the rhythm and precise notation of what is required of the instrument.

To describe the orchestra in the Baroque age is to be compelled to return, time and again, to the opera house and developments in it, for the orchestra, except in London, as an autonomous musical entity, separated from the opera and church music, was in little

c

demand. Music for orchestra outside the theatre and the church was chiefly provided by music clubs and other amateur groups in which, very often, the undomesticated and less socially graceful instruments were played by local professions, waits, *Stadtpfeifer* and music teachers; such professional backing was co-opted from official bodies whose members played with the amateurs either for a fee or for the prestige of honorary membership. From the dance music which had been the town musicians' mainstay as providers of music for social events grew the suite of contrasted dances, at first assembled by the players themselves from the items in their repertory but later taken over by composers and given a more abstract character by the more ambitious. From the music of the diverse participants in church music grew the concerto as a purely orchestral form exploiting the contrasts within the range of available orchestral tone or, as taken up by Arcangelo Corelli, idealized into a *concerto grosso*, with a contrasting group of solo instruments —violin, viola and cello—set against the main body of the string orchestra; the solo concerto, for a single instrument and orchestra, developed from the orchestral concerto later in the seventeenth century.

Outside the church, orchestral music could be heard in the *Collegia Musica* or similar amateur organizations in Germany and the *Accademia* of the Italian towns. Of these, the *Accademia* probably provided the most effective music, for they were clubs not simply of instrumentalists eager for an opportunity to make music but of the minor nobility and wealthy middle-class citizens, not only musicians or music lovers but devoted to the arts in general; they welcomed professional musicians into membership after such candidates had qualified themselves by a test for membership; Mozart was elected to membership of the *Accademia* of Bologna as a boy of fourteen, during his tour of Italy. The German *Collegia Musica* do not seem to have achieved specially high musical standards in most places; traditionally, the name belonged to music societies formed within the universities, but it was later adopted by music clubs with no academic affiliations, in place of the old-fashioned title *Convivia Musica, Musikkränzlein* and many others; later, the title *Musik Gesellschaft* became the favourite name for such organizations. Like the music clubs in provincial English towns, they met to perform music for their own pleasure rather than to learn and rehearse it. German music societies had the advantage of a trained local musician—often the cantor of the city church—as a professional director and composer in residence, but apart from local music teachers, the English music clubs were entirely amateur bodies which, for example, permitted any visitor to their meetings to take an instrument and join in the performance; thus they tended to build a repertory of music in a familiar style. The fact that they had no regular contact with a local composer and therefore depended on published works was one of the main causes of the rapid development of music publishing in England during the first half of the eighteenth century, and it was for music clubs rather than for his own professional performance that Handel wrote his set of Concerti Grossi op 6. As all Handel's oratorios and operas reached print shortly after their first performance, many of the music clubs seem automatically to have subscribed to sets of printed orchestral parts. The public concert played and sung by professional musicians had been familiar in London since the last quarter of the seventeenth century; the provinces made their own music, and it was not until the early years of the eighteenth that German societies, often very tentatively, began to make themselves responsible for public performances to paying audiences.

The other source of public performance was the *Conservatorios*, or orphanages, of the larger Italian cities. The title 'conservatory' for a college of music owes itself to the fact that orphans and illegitimate children in the main Italian cities were brought up in 'conservatories' or orphanages which trained them for a musical career, often in a rather haphazard way, because music in Italy seemed to offer them the chance of a career which could be entered fairly easily and fairly cheaply. Many of these institutions were attached to hospitals—Venice had four 'conservatories', each known by the name of the hospital to which it was an annexe; older than these were the four 'conservatories' of Naples.

From time to time, the music of an orphanage was put under the care of some musician of great consequence; in Venice, Legrenzi was director of the Conservatoire dei Mendicanti for some ten years up to 1681, and from 1704 to 1740 Vivaldi was in charge of music at the Conservatorio dell' Ospedale della Pietà. The children in such institutions learned singing and all the orchestral instruments, and gave regular concerts to public audiences. The vast number of *concerti* for which Vivaldi was responsible are a result of his work organizing the teaching of his orphans and teaching them himself, though in his own days Vivaldi was better known as a composer of opera and church music. In 1770 Charles Burney, the English historian of music, set out for Italy to undertake research for his *General History of Music*, and in Naples he visited the Conservatorio of S. Onofrio:

On the first flight of stairs was a trumpeter, screaming upon his instrument until he was ready to burst; on the second was a French horn, bellowing in the same manner. In the common practising room there was a Dutch concert, consisting of seven or eight harpsichords, more than as many violins, and several voices, all performing different things, and in different keys. . . . The violincellos practise in another room, and the flutes, hautboys, and other wind instruments, in a third.

Haphazard though the system was—for Burney's account of his travels, *The Present State of Music in France and Italy*, describes similar proceedings in other Italian conservatories—it was one of the causes of the Italian domination of Europe in music in the eighteenth century; there were simply more Italian musicians than musicians of any other nationality. The primary commitment of the composer was still to music with words, sung in church or in the opera house; the wider his interest in vocal and choral music became, the more the orchestra grew. In the nobleman's chapel, as in the opera house, a group of trained professional musicians provided whatever music was needed. The Lutheran Church was equally devoted to music, not only in the services as part of the liturgy but as a general aid to devotion, so that, during the latter part of the seventeenth century, many churches in Protestant Germany took up the idea of the church cantata, a work for soloists, choir and orchestra usually linked to the Gospel or the Epistle heard at Mass that day, adding anything up to forty-five or fifty minutes' music to the already long *Gottesdienst* service, but the most widely discussed and most fully recorded Lutheran music in the generation before Bach was provided by Dietrich Buxtehude, the city Cantor and organist at Lübeck between 1678 and his death in 1707. The *Abendmusik* concerts followed the evening service, normally on the five Sundays before Christmas; the programmes consisted of religious music on a grander scale than the average cantata performance. St Mary's Church, the chief church of the city, had a fine organ, but Buxtehude, with the support of the city council, had the organ gallery, in which choir and orchestra assembled, enlarged to accommodate the extra number of players he wished to occupy. His orchestra consisted of the city *Stadtpfeifer* and a subsidiary guild of *Rollbrüder*, an amateur society formed to take part in the church music; several northern cities had similar guilds of amateurs competent to play in the church services and, by qualifying as guildsmen, entered on the roll of church musicians. With these was the choir of the principal school, of which the Cantor was *ex officio* music master and which provided the entire choir. Thus Buxtehude could make use of what for the late seventeenth century was a remarkably large force of musicians; altogether, he wrote for a choir and orchestra of about forty. Apart from the normal strings, with two first and two second violins, Buxtehude wrote for a viola da gamba; he had two trumpets and two cornetts, and as well as the organ there was a cembalo (the term for keyboard instruments in this connection seems to imply a harpsichord) to play the *continuo* with cello, double-bass and bassoon. But for his more ambitious works he called in separate groups of trumpets and drums, two groups of *Waldhorns* and oboes, and twenty-five strings. In 1692 he had eight town musicians and sixteen *Rollbrüder* in his orchestra, and no particular record was made of the source of his extra forces; probably they were drawn from the better musicians in the school and other town amateurs who had not been enlisted in the *Rollbrüder* guild. Apart from strings, oboes and trumpets, his orchestra was not a formalized or conventional ensemble; from time to time he wrote for flutes, bass trombone and the almost archaic shawm with its tenor, the Pommer. These musical riches were deployed in 1692 in a performance of his largest work, *Templum Honoris*. After his death, the *Abend-musiken* concerts continued in the hands of his successors, but none of them was as capable as Buxtehude of composing works which justified the effort such events demanded.

THREE

Bach, Handel and their Contemporaries

The Town Cantor, *ex officio* composer of whatever church music was needed, wrote for whatever orchestral forces were available to him. As a municipal employee, he could not write for a conventional, standardized orchestra like that of an opera house unless it already existed. He could not expect such an orchestra to be assembled for him. Johann Sebastian Bach, much of whose greatest music was written for the Lutheran Church, wrote little which suggests a standardized, invariable orchestra. At Arnstadt, when he was eighteen, he was appointed organist of St Boniface's Church, able at times to write music which needed the services of the town musicians. At Mühlhausen, in 1707, four years after his appointment at Arnstadt, he decided that his duty was to bring church music up to date along the lines of Buxtehude, whose *Abendmusiken* had attracted him to Lübeck, where he had extended a month's leave to three months and earned his subsequent dismissal.

We can confidently assign only one major work by Bach to his period in Mühlhausen as organist of St Blasius's Church. It is the cantata we know as No. 71, *Gott ist mein König*, in which, perhaps, he set out to show conservative Mühlhausen the splendours they could expect from a young composer who had learned from Buxtehude how to compose church music in the grand style. *Gott ist mein König* is scored for two choirs (one, apparently, of doubtful reliability, trusted with nothing beyond loud interjectory shouts), with an orchestra of strings, two drums, three trumpets, with drums, two oboes and two bassoons with organ *continuo*. Naturally, this use of unusually large forces is explained by the occasion which called for a major effort. The cantata was composed for the Sunday on which a newly-elected town council attended service, so that Bach was able to enlist the services of Mühlhausen's *Musikalische Societät* as well as the town musicians and whatever local amateurs took part in the church music; the *Musikalische Societät* provided him with his second choir and an unspecified number of instruments, and his normal choir—trebles, altos, tenors and basses—was drawn from the pupils of the town grammar school, which also probably provided him with additional instrumentalists.

Bach's instruments, like those of Buxtehude, function in groups, laid out in Bach's score as four choirs; trumpets and drums are inseparable; the flutes, when any are required, play with a cello, and the oboes with the bassoons, while the fourth choir consists of the strings, which often consisted of no more than two violins, viola, cello and double bass, so that when the cello is needed by the flutes, the strings lose his services. The figured bass of the *continuo*, however, probably presupposes that another cello and double bass were available for this special duty

The Town Cantor in any German city was necessarily a composer of church music, but his orchestra was simply the group of players available for his use, not a recognized ensemble; the Cantor of Town A, appointed to a new post in Town B, could not be sure that his previous music would be usable unaltered in his new post. Bach spent the last twenty-seven years of his life, after 1723, as Cantor of St Thomas's Church, Leipzig, a city which had a notable musical history before his arrival. As Cantor, he was responsible for all the church music—that is, settings of the words of the service to be sung on every Sunday and feast day, a morning cantata to be sung in the middle of the *Gottesdienst*, which needed orchestral accompaniment; the evening service, too, demanded music in the form of an often resplendent orchestral setting of the *Magnificat* and a one movement motet, often with orchestral accom-

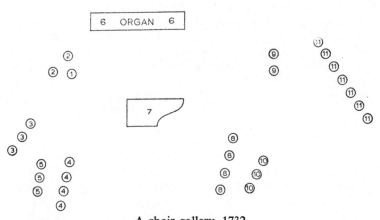

A choir gallery, 1732

1, conductor; 2, continuo; 3, bass and drums; 4, strings; 5, woodwind; 6, organ; 7, harpsichord (cembalo); 8, sopranos; 9, altos; 10, tenors; 11, basses (*see* Plate 1).

paniment. As music and Latin master of the grammar school attached to the church (out of which he had to organize the choirs for five Leipzig churches), he had not only to teach his subjects but also to rehearse the week's church music. In addition, the Cantor was necessarily involved in any local amateur society or *Collegium Musicum*, not only expected to supervise its rehearsals but also to ensure that it had music to rehearse.

Bach's church orchestra in Leipzig consisted of the eight *Stadt-pfeifer* and the subordinate group of 'town fiddlers', who had acquired the grander title of *Kunst Geiger* ('violin artists'). As *Stadt-pfeifer* were not qualified according to Guild regulations unless they could play several instruments "both wind and percussion", the position of the *Kunst Geiger*, as candidates for vacancies in the *Stadtpfeifer* band mean that the bulk of them could be used in any department of the orchestra; in addition, the Cantor could expect the regular help from amateur players in the town and could, if he needed to do so, augment the orchestra with any players from the school who could be expected to play effectively, but this meant the loss of boys who might be an asset to his choir. In 1730, Bach wrote an irritable letter to his employers, the Leipzig Town Council, who wanted bigger and better music at St Thomas's but were not prepared to pay for it. He said that the town musicians provided him with two trumpeters (who could also be trusted with horn and trombone parts), two oboists, a bassoon player (an apprentice) and two violinists. This meant that he had a professional orchestra of seven players. The rest of his orchestra—two more first and two more second violinists, two violists, two cellists and a double-bass player and two flautists—were ideally competent amateurs from the University *Collegium Musicum*. But as the Council had discontinued the gratuity which used to be allowed to University players, the undergraduates were unenthusiastic about playing in the church orchestra, so their places had often to be taken by schoolboys whose presence in the orchestra weakened the choir, which consisted only of Foundation scholars, admitted to the school as charity boys because of the quality of their voices.

Probably Bach's music was often far beyond the reach of both his singers and his instrumentalists. The cast of his mind was polyphonic, so that the bulk of his work is a texture of interwoven lines of equal, or almost equal, melodic importance, and the aim of his orchestration was to achieve this interweaving with the greatest possible clarity, so that the individual strands could be followed through the texture. But to Bach colour is one of the means of securing clarity; he never seems to have felt that colour was unimportant: when, in the *St Matthew Passion*, the crowd howls for the execution of Jesus, Bach's flutes almost snigger with sadistic glee at the idea of a crucifixion. (*See* Appendix 2, No. 1.) While all the rest of the orchestra, in particular the strings, are simply part of the furious hubbub, the flutes, lying above the *tutti*, can make their own personal comment without allowing it to be lost in the excitement of the moment.

The *St Matthew Passion* was first performed on Good Friday, 1729, the year before Bach's statement to the City Council. The huge work, which occupied all the school's choir, usually divided between five churches of a Sunday, and all the instruments he could find, so that as many as fifty or sixty may have taken part. Bach's letter ends with his requests to the authorities: he needed two "or even three" more first violinists, two "or even three" more second violins, two or three oboists, one or two bassoonists, three trumpeters and a drummer. This means that he was asking the Council to provide him with eighteen professional players in place of seven, and that the authorities would have to make themselves responsible for the extra salaries. His requests were not met. "Since church music needs flutes," he continued, "at least two flautists are needed." In other words, he believed that the city should provide him with a professional orchestra of twenty players. Even with such an orchestra, he could score for trumpets or trombones or horns, not for any two or three of the instruments: Bach's trumpets, his horns and his trombones are used as polyphonic groups of three, often in trumpet parts which chase themselves in a spectacular way through glories of florid figurations.

Bach's orchestra on great occasions stretches his resources beyond their apparent numerical limits. With the necessarily versatile town musicians as the basis of his orchestra, he could write for trumpets or horns or trombones in the groups of three which were his ideal. His two oboes could grow, in those movements in which the brass was silent, so that while he continues to employ orchestral families in sharp contrast, he apparently uses more than the available instruments so that each family contributes not only to the colour but to the polyphonic structure of the music. The six Christmastide cantatas of 1734 which have been grouped together as the *Christmas Oratorio* begins ebulliently with an orchestra grouped into choirs of trumpets and drums, oboes and flutes, and strings, each given its individual contribution to the rejoicing.

The second of the six parts of the *Christmas Oratorio* begins with a 'Pastoral Symphony' which takes the form of a dialogue between flutes and violins in two parts on the one hand, and two oboes d'amore (alto oboes) and oboes da caccia (tenor oboes) on the other; this probably means no more than that Bach's two normal oboists were joined by two of his brass players whilst their normal instruments were silent, or that his bassoon player forsook his normal instrument to take on other duties. The four oboes make it possible to reveal aspects of the nature of the music which flutes and violins, treating it simply as a beautiful pastoral tune, never think of exploring.

Limited as Bach felt himself to be by the poverty of his resources (as well as by the poor ability of some of the professional players; this was a point, he told the Council, on which he preferred not to dwell), he could nevertheless employ his professional instrumentalists, trained to a rough and ready proficiency at least in several instruments to undertake parts for whatever instruments they could handle. The basis of his orchestra was the *continuo*, to which he added first strings and then whatever other instruments provided the tone colour or special qualities of expression which he felt that he needed. A big chorus will naturally call for the strings; the woodwind will be added for the sake of their special contribution, like the sniggering flutes of the *St Matthew Passion* chorus. In solo arias, various old instruments—the recorder flute (flute-a-bec), the cornett, the oboe da caccia, the oboe d'amore, the violino piccolo, the violetta, the viola da gamba and the violoncello piccolo or the viola pomposa appear in Bach's Leipzig scores, as does the lute as a *continuo* instrument. The viola da gamba and the viola pomposa seem to have been called into service as possible soloists in the bass of the string orchestra and possibly more capable of handling difficult solo passages than the official cellist. The other archaic and semi-obsolete instruments were always adopted for the sake of their tone colour.

Bach's orchestration is built on the *continuo* of a keyboard player whose part lays out the entire harmonic framework of whatever music he is writing, whatever the number of instruments or voices involved. The orchestra above the *continuo* may be divided into contrasting but complementary instrumental families or may weave an orchestral web as a single body. Trumpets, almost invariably employed in a group of three, mean jubilation; oboes can be pastoral or can remember their development from the watchman's pipe; flutes ripple meditatively; the strings can take part in a musical hubbub like the choruses at the condemnation and the crucifixion in the *St Matthew Passion*, but Bach regarded them as versatile enough to be given most of the great lyrical melodies and emotional intensities.

The full orchestra is usually employed only when the chorus is active, but the church chorales which Bach uses to secure the co-operation of his congregation can be interrupted after each line by an instrumental enrichment, as the violins comment on the chorale "Sleepers wake", and the oboe on "Jesus joy of man's desiring". Solos and duets are usually enriched with an elaborate polyphonic *obbligato* part for a solo instrument, the rest of the orchestra silent and the *continuo* subduedly filling in the harmonies. The *Laudamus Te* of the B minor Mass, for example, is a delightful duet between contralto and solo violin, each working out the theme according to its own nature; the same combination is given the beautifully moving aria *Erbarme dich*, which comments on Peter's betrayal of Christ in the *St Matthew Passion*; the tenor aria in the *Passion*, *Ich will bei meinem Jesu*, the scene in the Garden of Gethsemane with Jesus praying while the disciples sleep, is a duet between oboe—a watchman's instrument—and tenor. The interweaving of two lines of melody in such arias often inspires Bach to compose ravishingly beautiful, sensuously appealing music.

It is part of the professional composer's duty to write what is practical, to know his singers and instrumentalists and to tailor his work to their abilities: it is hard to believe that Bach, with a choir of adolescent boys and soloists drawn from his choir, always remembered the duty of practicality. But the part played by his orchestra, though it must have strained his players to the utmost, never forgets its practical duties. It remembers, for example, the small choir at his disposal for the usual Sunday cantata, so that the vocal lines of the chorales are always given weight by instrumental doubling to encourage the participating congregation. Bach's traditional manner of treating the orchestra as a set of separable choirs, his polyphonic outlook and his habit of drawing inspiration from those texts which permitted him to evolve a musical symbolism for their treatment was a style which led to great musical richness; the *Sanctus* of the B minor Mass, with its suggestion of swinging censers and the tumultuous worship of all the glorious company of heaven is Bach at his most powerful, richly detailed and brilliantly clear, forgetting the problems of personnel and individual capacities for achieving the effects at which he aims.

Because the B minor Mass is a work apart from his other great choral pieces, it has, perhaps, the right to move away from the practicalities of music-making in St Thomas's Church. The first two movements, the *Kyrie* and the *Gloria in Excelsis*, were written to be sung in Leipzig in the service commemorating the death of August II, Elector of Saxony, and to celebrate the accession of his son Augustus III; they were sung in the Leipzig service on 21st April 1733. The *Credo*, another huge group of movements, were sung on 5th June 1733, at the inauguration of the reorganized *Thomasschule*. The other movements of the Mass, though some of them were remodelled from earlier cantata movements, were written in the hope that the work might be sung as Augustus III's Coronation Mass, so that they were written without reference to Leipzig's conditions, and the *Sanctus*, the work's musical climax, could reach for the greatest splendour the composer could imagine because, should he succeed in arranging a performance at the coronation, he could expect everything he needed in the way of musical resources.

Bach's career and problems as a church composer are typical of those of his contemporaries among German musicians. Johann Philipp Telemann, four years older than Bach (he was born in 1681 and lived to be eighty-six) made his musical mark on Leipzig while he was a student at the University there, qualifying himself, as many musicians did, for a career outside music should he fail as a musician. Telemann founded the *Collegium Musicum* at Leipzig University (Bach directed the citizens' *Collegium*) and composed operas for the small company which worked in the Leipzig theatre. Telemann had a great enthusiasm for French music, with a lighter rhythm and innate grace; in consequence, he developed a far less complex style than Bach. Furthermore, he could compose anything that was required of him at high speed and with great effectiveness; his catalogue of compositions is far longer than the apparently inexhaustible supply of works composed by Bach.

Telemann worked at minor courts and in small towns to establish himself, and in 1712 he was appointed to the post of Director of the Frauenstein Society, a club of the town's aristocracy and successful business men, at Frankfurt-am-Main, where he was also organist of the Bärfusser Kirche and, at the same time, *Kapellmeister* to the Prince of Bayreuth. His appointment at the Frauenstein Society seems not to have been primarily musical, but he arranged, among other things, regular public concerts for members and their guests at a time when, in Germany, public performances of music of any kind outside the church and the opera were hardly known. Naturally, his concerts depended largely on the music he wrote for them. In 1721 he became Cantor of St John's Church in Hamburg, where his duties paralleled those of Bach, in Leipzig, with the music of five city churches to organize weekly cantata performances to arrange in the Sunday morning service and a *Collegium Musicum* to run and direct. The incredible amount of music Telemann poured out to satisfy the conditions of his post— twelve sets of church music for the entire year, forty Passions for Holy Week, music for the installation of Hamburg clergy and the commissioning of sea captains, ordination services and music for important weddings and funerals, would have been enough work for any man, but Telemann, a pioneer of public concerts, wrote prolifically for the Hamburg *Collegium Musicum*, which had been established in 1660 and which he turned into an organization, the *Grosses Konzert*, giving regular subscription concerts in the drill hall of the Hamburg Militia.

Like Lübeck, Hamburg was one of the cities where a guild of *Rollbrüder* had been organized to take part in the church music, and unlike Leipzig, Hamburg was a wealthy city which survived the wars of the seventeenth and eighteenth centuries not only undisturbed but able to profit from its position as the greatest port of northern Europe, so that the Council, realizing that the *Grosses Konzert* was a genuine amenity in a town which could afford to encourage amenities (Hamburg had its opera house and an efficient company, for which Telemann somehow found time to compose) gave its musicians all the encouragement it could. In 1761, six years before Telemann's death, the Council built a hall for the subscription concerts.

The bulk of the music heard at Hamburg concerts was naturally composed by Telemann, though probably his programmes contained the work of other composers when he could find copies or parts for his players, and probably he included overtures, incidental dances and entr'actes from Hamburg operas. Bach, at Leipzig, cannot have depended entirely upon his own compositions to keep the *Collegium Musicum* busy. In the days when little music was printed in Germany, Bach's fourteen Leipzig concertos are all the works which we can definitely associate with his amateur instrumentalists, together, possibly, with his two last orchestral suites, which belong to the years between 1727 and 1736, when he was active with the *Collegium Musicum*; the demands of the two suites, with their passages of brilliant trumpeting, were within the scope of the combined *Collegium Musicum* and the *Stadtpfeifer*, who seem to have been *ex-officio* members of the amateur organization; there is, however, no evidence to show that the third and fourth suites were written for the *Collegium* except the unlikelihood of Bach's finding time to compose such works for pleasure in the endless activity of his Leipzig duties. As it was, several of the keyboard concertos (possibly written for his sons to play at meetings of the *Collegium*) are adaptations either of earlier music of his own or of concerti by other composers such as Vivaldi; possibly it seemed to Bach that he could make more than the original composer had done of their material but his borrowings suggest that additional music was wanted from him while he was working at extraordinary pressure.

Between his departure from Mühlhausen in 1708 and his arrival in Leipzig in 1723, Bach was employed in musical posts in minor German courts. Court musicians in the major cities where there was court opera lived with and could make use of great musical resources; at Weimar, when he took up his duties there in 1708, he was at first merely an orchestral violinist, but he seems quickly to have become Court Organist; his duties did not include composition until 1714, when he was appointed *Konzertmeister* (leader of the orchestra), a post which included the duty of writing a monthly cantata for the Duke of Weimar's chapel. Here he had a choir of twelve (six boy sopranos and two each of the lower voices); the orchestra included three violinists, one of whom, apparently, was a violist, a cellist and a bassoonist. There were six trumpeters whose duties were not exclusively with the Duke's regiment, and with them a drummer. One of the violinists was the Duke's secretary; the cellist combined his musical duties with those of the Superintendent of the Ducal Art Gallery. One of the trumpeters was also Groom in Waiting, another was Palace Overseer, and the adult singers also had official duties in the Court. The combination of musical and other posts in this way was a familiar way of organizing court music economically, and the Duke of Weimar, a deeply and rather puritanically religious man, had reduced his musical establishment before Bach arrived, disbanding his theatre company and keeping in service only those musicians necessary for chamber music and his chapel services; with such limited orchestral forces in his new official post Bach naturally composed more for the organ than for orchestra or choir during his Weimar period.

The cantatas which he wrote for the Duke's chapel are scored only for strings and woodwind; probably the trumpeters were capable of coping with oboe and flute parts. Easter Day 1717 was celebrated by the cantata *Ich Weiss, dass mein Erlöser lebt* (*I know that my Redeemer liveth*, No. 160) simply with tenor, bassoons, violins and *continuo*, and with no Bachian glory of trumpets, instruments which appear in only five of the Weimar works. But one, *Ich hatte viel Bekümmernis* (No. 21) demands three soloists, choir, oboes, bassoon, three trumpets, four trombones and drums, outrunning the capacity of the Duke's orchestra, completely and probably defying the acoustic qualities of a long, narrow, over-lofty chapel; but this cantata seems to have been a favourite of its composer, who repeated it more than once in Leipzig, and the score which we have was probably an adaptation of a Weimar work for the new conditions of St. Thomas's.

At Cöthen, where Bach was *Kapellmeister* from 1717 until his appointment to Leipzig in 1723, he was exclusively concerned with instrumental music. Prince Leopold of Anhalt-Cöthen, his patron, was a Calvinist, so that for the only time in his life Bach was not concerned with church music as the Cöthen chapel had no musical establishment and rejected the idea of music to adorn divine worship. On the other hand, the Prince himself played the violin, the viola da gamba and the harpsichord at least competently and apparently very well. In addition, he kept a Kapelle of sixteen instrumentalists, eight chamber musicians and four players described merely as "musicians", subordinate to the chamber players and apparently local *Stadtpfeifer* co-opted by the court whenever their assistance was needed. There were also two trumpeters and a drummer, members of the Prince's own musical establishment. The eight chamber musicians included three violinists, one of whom also played the viola da gamba, an oboist, two bassoonists and a cellist. The only cantatas Bach composed at Cöthen were, because of the Prince's religious convictions, secular court works accompanied by an orchestra of woodwind and strings; apparently the Cöthen oboists could also be used as flautists.

The Cöthen orchestral works—the Suites in C and B minor and the six Brandenburg Concertos—lie within the resources available inside the Cöthen court, except that the first Brandenburg Concerto has parts for two horns; these instruments help us to date the work to June 1722, when two Waldhornists visited Cöthen and played at court. The first, third and sixth of the Brandenburg Concertos look back to the old Venetian style with the orchestra divided into more or less evenly balanced choirs, with themes passed from one group to the other and back again. The other three works divide the orchestra into a *concertino* group of soloists and an orchestral *ripieno*, but they are not Corellian in the mixed voices which Bach chooses for his *concertino*—violin, flute, oboe and trumpet in No. 2, violin and two flutes-a-bec (recorders) in No. 4, harpsichord, violin and flute in No. 5: No. 4 was one of the works which Bach turned into a Clavier Concerto in Leipzig. The small orchestra at Cöthen cannot have put much weight on tone as a counterpoise to the *concertino* group in any of these works. The viola da gamba part in No. 6, and all the keyboard solo parts, were probably written to be played by Prince Leopold himself, but the size and membership of the Cöthen orchestra suggests that they were played at Cöthen with no more than a single instrument to each part; whether Bach regarded that as the ideal method of performance, of course, is something we do not know, but such strictly chamber-music performances have been known to be very effective in their exactitude of balance and the audibility they give to fine polyphonic detail.

Nevertheless, it was the demands of vocal and choral music which did most to extend ideas of orchestral sonority and technique, and to encourage the use of the orchestra as a contributor to the effect instead of a merely subordinate accompaniment to the all-important voices. The need to comment effectively in sinfonias and entr'actes on a dramatic situation prompted the composer continually to make new demands on the technique of his players and to work out new ideas of orchestral texture and expression. Therefore the opera orchestra, often containing admired virtuoso players in its ranks, not only finally standardized the orchestra but also tended to regulate the effects of which it was capable. Of the standard orchestral forms, for example, only the concerto did not evolve from the opera; the eighteenth-century classical symphony, with its structure of opposed keys characterized by opposed themes eventually reconciled at the end of a movement evolved from the overture, which grew from a preliminary fanfare demanding attention to a self-sufficient commentary on the character of the work to be performed; it was also influenced by the formal operatic aria, which grew up in the opera house in Naples as a manifestation of the Baroque doctrine of affect; it offers a stanza in its main key, a complementary stanza in a different but related key and then, after a *da capo* sign (directing a return to the beginning) repeats the first stanza, so that it provided both a satisfactory musical form and also a demonstration of the belief that a single stretch of music should manifest only a single emotion; the doctrine of affect laid it down firmly that a character in a single aria could not develop from one emotion or one state of mind into another.

At a period when a composer was almost invariably a court or municipal functionary, composing the music that was needed from him for specific occasions and more or less immediate use, Handel's determination to write operas (until even his stubbornness was convinced that opera would be his financial ruin) and his later development of English oratorio—opera, so to speak, without settings, costumes or acting—set him apart from the generality of his contemporaries. The catalogue of his works contains singularly little purely orchestral music for a composer who held court appointments and might thus have been regarded as in duty bound to provide music for a court orchestra. The *Water Music* of 1717 and the *Fireworks Music* of 1749 apparently were enough to discharge his court obligations in that direction. The six *Concerti Grossi* of op. 3, the 'Oboe Concertos', seem to have been written during his association with the Duke of Chandos, to be played first of all at the Duke's palace at Cannons, and eventually published in 1734, when Handel had apparently realized the profitability of such works because of the demand for them among English music clubs. It was, apparently, this demand that prompted the publication of the twelve *Concerti Grossi* of op. 6 in 1739: Handel continued the tradition of publishing such works in sets of six, and the three sets each of six Organ Concertos were published in 1738, 1740 and 1769 (ten years after his death). The Organ Concertos were primarily written to be played between the 'acts' of his oratorios, just as the famous *Concerto Grosso* in C major was played before Act II of the very successful *Alexander's Feast*; another concerto, which did not catch the attention to the same extent, was played between Acts II and III.

There remains a handful of other works to which no precise date or purpose can be assigned. Nineteen cantatas for solo voice and string orchestra, to Italian texts, come from the time of his travels in Italy. One of these asks for trumpet, three for flutes, four for oboes; one cantata of the same period rejects the string orchestra for guitar. As a professional composer exploiting an accepted style and using the instruments available to him, Handel was in a sense proving his competency in these works, and they are never less than melodious, expressive and effectively composed; Handel's combination of almost inexhaustible lyrical gifts with his great musical intelligence ensure that even these barely known works are music which, once known, are unlikely to be neglected again.

The 'Oboe Concertos' are in the Corelli style, the form most popular in England, but with oboes, bassoons and at times two flutes added to the string orchestra. The oboes are not solo instruments taking the lead in the musical discourse but are almost invariably part of the orchestra; in certain movements, however, the first oboe is given the leading role. The first concerto calls for two flutes in its slow movement; a flute is offered as an alternative to the oboes in the third (which does not demand a bassoon to strengthen the bass). The fourth movement of the second concerto is laid out as a *concerto grosso*, with a string trio as a *concertino*, separate in function both from the oboes and bassoon and from the *ripieno* body of strings, while the two-movement sixth, which asks for organ instead of harpsichord as its *continuo* instrument, makes the organ and not the oboe the hero of its lively finale, with a cadenza of its own to assert its authority. At any point, the violins are as prominent as the oboes, and some of the most beautiful lyrical movements in the set, like the second movement of the first concerto, sets a solo violin again the first oboe in a long-breathed duet. Having found his instruments, Handel is not bound by doctrine to any particular method of exploiting them but simply distributes the score as he thinks most effective in the context of themes and movements, satisfying the need for both contrast and agreement as well as the demands of orchestral colour.

In many ways, this set of concertos is more adventurous in its orchestration than the later *Concerti Grossi* for strings, and in some ways it exploits orchestral colour with more adventurousness than much in the operas and oratorios. The first of the op. 3 set, with its movement of elaborate filigree work from solo violin and solo oboes against the gentle accompaniment of flutes and strings, is not an attempt to find a new way of deploying contrasting families of instruments but the use of all the instruments involved as a

D

single body capable of colour combinations rather than simple colour contrasts. While the characteristic sound of the Bach orchestra is that of the *continuo* group underlying the activities of whatever instruments are playing, Handel's characteristic sound is that of the string orchestra, at times combined with the woodwind, oboes and violins, cello and bassoons, doubling each other's music. Handel took this combination of instrumental tones so much for granted that at times he forgets to mention the co-operation of the woodwind until a change of texture, signalled by the direction *senza oboi* or *senza fagotto* indicated that although these instruments have not previously been mentioned, their participation in whatever has gone before has been necessary. As very often, first and second oboes play *colla parte* with first and second violins; this practice presupposes that sufficient oboes will be used to colour the tone all the time they are playing, for they are equal partners to the violins, the chief melodic instrument of the woodwind family. Handelian orchestra balance demands that when the two instruments play together, the oboes are as much in the lead, giving as much weight to the tone, as the violins.

Throughout his career, Handel worked with entirely professional orchestras with anything up to ten or fifteen violins; the orchestra which took part in his performances at the Foundling Hospital at the end of his life had twelve violins, three violas, three cellos, two double-basses, four oboes, four bassoons, two horns, two trumpets and drums; probably on most occasions his oboists were double-handed and played the flute—for flute and oboe are rarely heard together in Handel's scores. He was never, like Bach, forced to cut his coat according to a limited supply of cloth. At Cannons, before the formation of the Royal Academy of Music in 1719 and his official post as musical director of London's major opera company, there was an orchestra of six violinists, a fiddler, a viola player, two cellists, a harpist, an oboist, a flautist, a bassoonist and a trumpeter as well as a harpsichordist and a choir of nine.

As a composer of ceremonial state music from 1713 (the *Utrecht Te Deum*) he could score as he wanted within the conventions of the day, asking for three trumpets and all the necessary strings and woodwind to balance them on the basis of the idea that an oboe could balance three or four violins. For the rest, his opera orchestra, or any equivalent body of professionals with whom he worked, was at his disposal for all his later music. This, of course, meant a greater degree of standardization than Bach ever expected. Handel's *continuo* group of keyboard, cello and double-bass is always in demand, but the foundation of Handel's orchestration was the string orchestra which, in both opera and oratorio, was the staple accompanying body of his arias and which he used as a two-, three- or four-part ensemble according to the material he used or according to his need, in the dramatic context, for variety. Oboes double violins and bassoons double cellos, but are withdrawn when the texture needs to be varied or lightened. In the overture to *Serse* (1738) for example, the viola, the weakest of the string instruments in all but the size of its tone, has no support from the woodwind, but the cellos are left unsupported only in some bass entries in the fugal second movement; there was, of course, no obvious and totally reliable supporting instrument which could match the oboes by reinforcing the violas. Handel's bassoons could not climb high enough in their tenor register to support violas in their upper-middle register.

Serse, a reasonably light-hearted and delightfully melodious work —it includes the Largo which has always been one of the most dearly beloved of Handel's slow melodies—comes from the time when he was gradually moving away from opera in the direction of his own type of dramatic oratorio, and it was closely followed by *Saul*, a masterpiece on any reckoning and possibly the most lavishly scored of all his works. Its overture grants the oboes far more independence than they were given in any of his operas; for much of the first movement they double the violins, but they are given brief exchanges with violins in dialogue and invent their own answers instead of simply repeating the violins' ideas. The second movement sets them in counterpoint to the violins, and the third movement, though it opens frugally, turns almost into an oboes' concerto.

In *Serse*, trumpets or horns, each in two parts, are added to strings in all the choruses except the last, but trumpets and horns never play together. Flutes, in two parts, play in the Sinfonia (Handel's term for an entr'acte) in Act I, which is interrupted by recitative and a moment of dialogue, and they are prominent in the following aria, but they have no other duties, not even that of adding a top line an octave above the oboes in the choruses, although by 1739 they were mechanically equipped to do so. All other arias are accompanied by strings, often used with maximum richness in four parts with the double-bass adding a fifth part an octave below the cellos. In other arias, first and second violins unite to form a three-part texture; in some, violas are rested and the accompaniment becomes a duet between unison violins and the *continuo* bass line.

The move from Italian opera to his own style of dramatic oratorio in English makes no difference to Handel's dramatic principles or his employment of the orchestra in what, in English, he calls 'airs'; their accompaniment remains primarily the business of the strings, in two, three or four parts. In some half-dozen arias oboes join the first and second violins when Handel thinks their tone and bite appropriate; airs with oboes are usually active and vigorous—oboes do not indulge in meditation or contemplation. The High Priest's address to David and Merab, at their betrothal, is a strophic song, three stanzas to the same repeated melody; at the third repetition, strings and voice are joined by an *obbligato* flute in counterpoint to the voice's melody, offering not only a variation in colour but also commenting appropriately on words which had turned from the consideration of the boy David's greatness to dwell on his goodness. Saul's demented jealousy is characterized by bassoons, which remove themselves from the general bass line to follow an independent musical course when the King expresses his hatred for his one-time protégé. There are a large number of recitatives with orchestral accompaniment—accompanied recitative marks a dramatic high point in the operas, too—and the use of two bassoons in duet when the Witch of Endor calls up the spirit of the dead prophet Samuel achieves eeriness.

The setting of David's lamentation over Saul and Jonathan after the death in battle, opened by the Dead March, is a series of linked arias and choruses; the airs are accompanied by strings until, at the core of the tragic outpouring, David's voice is left with the *continuo* alone; his grief is most profound, for another air, fully accompanied, follows before he is left again to lead the chorus in the final lament, his voice still alone but for the *continuo*, as though mourning is at its most intense when it is most simple.

In several arias, a group of third violins plays with the violas, who therefore never descend to their lowest string and silence their companions; in these passages, the string orchestra is a four-part accompaniment, and the violins, perhaps, are intended to add confidence as well as sonority, as though the composer was doubtful about both the viola and its players, who were often drawn from the less proficient violinists. If the new subdivision of the violins is a device to offer support for weak instrumentalists, it at the same time strengthens the colour of the orchestra.

Trumpets, trombones and timpani support the oboes and strings in the grander choruses which deal with David's martial exploits, but the trombones—two tenors and a bass—were apparently soon regarded as optional. The work was only two years old when a performance of the Dead March was advertised as "to be performed with the sackbutts". as though the performers were offering a special treat. The rejoicing over David's killing of Goliath calls for a Carillon in F, which in Handel's score has a range of one and a half octaves from the F below middle C; in a 'Symphony' (Handel's anglicization of the familiar term 'sinfonia') its peals are accompanied by first and second violins, and it continues to tinkle throughout the following chorus. The carillon was entirely Handel's innovation, demanded by dramatic appropriateness.

Oboes, trumpets, trombones or violins from time to time double the voices in the chorus, but selectively, often in opening phrases or in the separate entires of fugal choruses, as though to ensure that Handel's major premises are declared with all possible vigour and emphasis. The trumpets are melodic instruments, usually riding over a great mass of sound, but the trombones are used to strengthen the harmony of the ensemble and never take up a leading melodic function though they can give the panache of brass to melodies in the middle register where trumpets cannot play a connected melody because of the gaps in their harmonic series. With this large orchestra to which Handel adds a harp for a single 'symphony', with carillon and organ as well as the harpsichord of the *continuo* (the organ takes over the figured bass and the harpsichord is silent in the passages of solemnity and mourning) Handel was obviously eager to achieve the greatest diversity of colour and effect an eighteenth-century orchestra could provide. The admission of trombones into the orchestra perhaps owes something to the use of a biblical story; trombones had never been associated with opera.

Apart from the use of harp and carillon in the mid-act sinfonias, that in Act II is music for which 'heterogeneous' might well be a better term than 'contrasted'. The first of its three movements is a Largo for oboes, trombones and strings with the bassoons given an independent part while oboes double the violins, first, seconds and thirds all having really independent parts and not engaged in octave doublings of any other instrument. Organ, oboes and violins, in two parts, share the music of the second movement, which is to all intents and purposes a fugal movement from an organ concerto, and the third movement is a gavotte for organ alone.

The 'Symphony' in Act III represents the battle on Mount Gilboa in which both Saul and Jonathan are killed; the orchestra turns traditionally into three choirs—woodwind, brass and drums, and strings, each choir discussing in turn a vigorous two-bar phrase which comes to each of them twice before they combine in a final statement by the orchestral *tutti*. (*See* Appendix 2, No. 2.)

Only a recitative and aria where the angry David condemns Saul's killer to death (with oboes and strings in angry unison on a spiky, jerking figure) followed by a tragic postscript, are heard before the orchestra—two flutes, bassoon, trombones, timpani and strings—plays the Dead March again in the old, 'separated-families' orchestral style; the brass and strings making a statement to which flutes and organ reply; the organ is silent when brass and strings are heard; again, the separated choirs combine for a final statement.

It is sensible to discuss *Saul* in some detail because it is the most lavishly scored of all Handel's works and shows his orchestral technique involved in handling a large body of instruments for the sake of the greatest varieties of colour and dynamic contrast. *Messiah*, which English listeners know better, perhaps, than any other music, is known in a variety of orchestral treatments by later composers, and Handel himself was responsible for various adaptations of the score devised to match changing conditions of performance. In *Messiah*, trumpets are heard in four choruses, bringing the music to spectacular climaxes, and in the brilliant *obbligato* to the bass air "The trumpet shall sound"; the work does not explore orchestral colour and effect; it is contemplative and not active, unlike the dramatic oratorios where the orchestra is used to make dramatic effects. In his operas, when occasion demands, Handel wrote spectacularly; recorders sometimes take the place of flutes when their warbling tone is appropriate; he was one of the first composers to co-opt the clarinet into his orchestra; at different times he demands lute, theorbo, mandoline and the alto flute which he called a 'bass flute'. In *Rinaldo* he needs four trumpets, in *Giulio Cesare* four horns, for his purpose is always the creation of an atmosphere of dramatic excitement. The great oratorio arias with trumpet *obbligato* are among the great, dramatically effective glories of his work, not only "The trumpet shall sound" but "Let the bright seraphim", with soprano solo, in *Samson* and "Sound an alarm" from *Judas Maccabeus* produce a powerful excitement.

Handel's operatic contemporaries and rivals, unjustly forgotten though such composers as Bononcini and Hasse are, never used the orchestra to produce anything of comparable physical excitement though they wrote for an orchestra more or less identical with Handel's and could, like him, call for unfamiliar colours and sonorities. They were more willing to subordinate orchestra to voice and to think of instrumental accompaniment rather than of the orchestra's power to enter into expressive partnership with the singers. Handel and Bach lived at the end of a period in orchestration, and by the time they died their younger contemporaries had begun to reject the idea of the orchestra as a group of separable families combining only in passages which require great power.

In France, to all intents and purposes, it came to an end with the triumph of Jean-Phillipe Rameau's *Hippolyte et Aricie* in 1733, when the composer was already fifty years old and widely known only for his keyboard works. *Hippolyte et Aricie* was his fourth opera; his earlier stage works had won no recognition because the first two were regarded as insufficiently serious—humour was not welcome at the royal opera, the *Académie Royale de Musique*—and the third, *Samson*, suffered an automatic veto because of its Biblical subject. In 1733 the *Académie* decided to produce *Hippolyte et Aricie*; in 1740, Rameau's *Dardanus* was a tumultuous success.

Though Rameau was attacked by his contemporaries as a wild revolutionary, his operas were typically French, following in the footsteps of Lully, with scenes of impressive spectacle, with dances and ballet, and stories based on mythology. His tendency to compose entire acts without a single break was, apart from his orchestration, his only innovation; Rameau's early difficulties were his departures from precedents set by Lully, for only strict observation of Lully's forms was acceptable to French audiences. The real triumph of *Dardanus* was that it gave composers a new convention to observe, and the new convention was first and foremost orchestral, apart from its demand for greater musical continuity. Rameau's greatest innovation was that of orchestral colour. His music and his aims were otherwise entirely French—he never seemed to have wished to create real human beings instead of mythological beings—and it came to mean little to the rest of Europe. Restoration England, with a monarchy close to the French in its style and its ambitions, had been deeply influenced by Lully, and composers like Telemann had found from Lully the way to rhythmic vitality and lightness of texture, but neither England nor Germany was much influenced by Rameau, whose music really completed the search for a studied magnificence of presentation which Lully had begun. The glowing colours of Rameau's scores were lavished on a style which the rest of Europe had left behind.

The orchestra of the *Académie Royale de Musique* had, since 1713, consisted of forty-six players; in *Dardanus*, in 1756, Rameau asked for two flutes, four oboes, five bassoons, one trumpet, sixteen violins, six violas, four cellos (*due petit choeur*), eight basses "*de grand choeur*", and a harpsichord; one of the violinists was also drummer, one of the violinists also played the musette, a type of bagpipe developed in the seventeenth century; another musette was played by one of the cellists.

It would be possible to regard Rameau as the first composer who composed orchestrally as distinct from simply distributing his music to instruments which happen to be in the right register and to have the correct, appropriate power of penetration. Themes and melodies in Rameau's music are, so to speak, conceived in terms of a particular instrumental timbre, and accompanimental figures seem to have the same close relationship to the instrument which plays them. Violins and the high woodwind, for example, are often set to weave brilliant filigree passages in semiquavers round a melody (Rameau's learned contemporaries were shocked at extended passages in very rapid notes) but the figurations of the woodwind differ from those of the violins whenever their voices or the players' fingering does not suit the notes suitable for a violinist.

Rameau's operas contain a good deal of purely orchestral music: dawn, bird song, magic gardens, streams; wars, riots, tempests, monsters rising from the depths of the ocean; the comings and goings of gods and goddesses—all these are treated imaginatively, and Rameau from time to time finds that they demand a richer texture than a five-part string orchestra can provide and therefore further subdivides his strings. The sense of colour in his orchestra is inseparable from themes he invents to characterize these moments of stage spectacle, and it was not until the coming of Berlioz that music produced another composer with Rameau's attitude to the orchestra.

It was through Rameau that the clarinet began to become an indispensable member of the woodwind. The instrument was invented by a Nuremberg instrument maker, J. C. Denner, round about 1700. Apparently the clarinet developed from an older instrument, the chalumeau (a word with the same root as shawm) which Denner set to work to improve, which he did to such effect that although it had a range of only eight notes, it appeared in a few opera scores round about the turn of the seventeenth century. Its eight notes were in the tenor register, and the clarinet, with a much larger range, which Denner developed from the chalumeau, kept the name of the smaller instrument for its often rather melancholy low register; the lowest of its three octaves tends to be sombre and plangent but it is strong and almost pert in its upper reaches. Its extensive range and its dependability in its high register, where the oboe is unreliable, as well as its tone colour, made it an asset to the composer who not only knew how to use it but also had a reliable player or two available.

FOUR

The Eighteenth-century Court Orchestra

It is easy to think of the development of music as a string of separable periods each following its predecessor after a decisive change of style. Many historians encourage us to think of a later Baroque style reaching its final flowering in the music of Bach and Handel and reaching its end in the 1750s, the year of their deaths; it then changed into the classical style, the greatest glory of which is the work of Haydn, Beethoven and Mozart. It is easy for historians of music to forget that the rise of the new musical style was in progress before either Bach or Handel died, and that it accompanied a general change in European thought and society which influenced not only music but the other arts as well.

To the generation which grew up while Bach and Handel were in their maturity, their style, often great and impressive but equally capable of great sweetness, tenderness and gentleness, was overcomplex; its contrapuntal textures were triumphs of skill and learning and it matched the way of thinking of the age that began in religious tumult. The classical age set out to return to simplicity and naturalness of utterance if not to simplicity of subject. The idea of nature and the natural as invariably good, direct and honest, beyond the process of corruption which is the inevitable consequence of abandoning whatever is natural. In place of the great fugal choruses of Handel and those movements by Bach in which themes treated by a master of counterpoint are dressed in an elaborate musical symbolism to provide a commentary on music already complex, composers set out to simplify their music to the most straightforward presentation which would not falsify their intentions by over-simplification. They set out to express direct emotions directly; they did not reject the idea of emotional intensity, but they distrusted anything that seemed to aim at overpowering greatness through skilful elaboration. All Bach's sons were thoroughly trained composers and practical musicians of more than some consequence. Although their father had trained them in his art of contrapuntal eloquence, the two greatest of Bach's children, Carl Philipp Emanuel, born in 1714, and Johann Christian, born in 1735, made no effort to write in Johann Sebastian's style; both were pioneers of the new type of symphony and sonata, which depended on the opposition of two keys, each characterized by a theme or subject for development, and their eventual reconciliation in the key of the first subject. Naturally, any effective technique which contributed to the exposition and final reconciliation of the two keys had a place in the new-style symphony, so that passages of counterpoint appear even in quite early symphonies by Haydn, written less than ten years after Handel's death, but the orchestral treatment of the early symphony naturally aimed at simplicity and directness of statement. In a sense, the enjoyment of the new symphony depended on the cultivation of a new type of musical memory. The listener would not make complete sense of the work unless he could recognize the return of the main key at the culmination of the movement, and hear any intervening keys only as stages on a musical journey or new situations in a musical drama.

Such a style of composition meant that its composer must orchestrate his work in such a way that themes, and all the melodic material, must be presented with complete clarity and considerable emphasis. The music progress from key to key, too, must be scored to mark each stage in this harmonic evolution. This at first meant the creation of far lighter textures than the great Baroque composers had normally employed; in place of the interweaving of equally important lines of material, the composer needed to keep one all-important line of music stretched out to the necessary degree of tension over harmony that is entirely necessary but entirely subordinate to the theme from which the harmonic changes gain their motive power.

The early symphony to the time of Haydn's maturity regards the strings as the essential melodic section of the orchestra, with the woodwind and horns (and trumpets whenever they were employed) as primarily responsible for the harmonic texture. Although composers continued to write a figured bass and use a keyboard instrument to 'fill in' the harmonies, the real binding agents in the harmony were the horns, two or four of them, usually both tuned in the same key and playing in the centre of their register where any scale would be incomplete; their limited range restricted the number of keys in which the composer wrote for orchestra.

Two oboes or two flutes, rarely both, with two bassoons and two horns, added to the strings, were an orchestra; on occasions of particular importance or festivity, two trumpets and drums began to be added in the 1760s. The number of strings was far smaller than would have satisfied any early nineteenth-century composer,

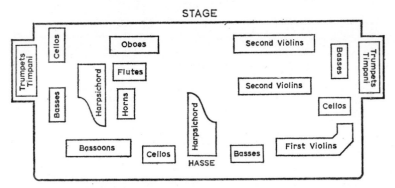

The Orchestra of the Dresden Opera under Hasse, 1713–71

and throughout the eighteenth century the orchestra was made to balance strings and woodwind on the principle that an oboe balanced three or four violins, not more, in volume; six violins were therefore an absolute minimum, as violins were either firsts or seconds and each part had to balance. In Salzburg, in 1777, the Archbishop's orchestra, of which Mozart was a member, had from twelve to sixteen violins, with six oboes, two bassoons, two flutes and two horns. The court orchestra in Vienna, in the same year, had from twelve to fifteen violins and from two to five oboes according to the requirements of the score. But the Milan orchestra, occupied in La Scala opera-house, had two oboes to twenty-eight violins, six violas and two cellos. The Vienna orchestra, with its six or seven first and second violins, had four oboes and three cellos. In 1756, in the Mannheim orchestra, the first great virtuoso orchestra, four horns were available if they were needed, as in Milan fourteen years later, but most orchestras were satisfied with a couple of flutes, a couple of oboes, a couple of bassoons and a couple of trumpets, far more frequently used in the opera-house than in the music room of an aristocratic patron who wanted music for the entertainment of his family and guests. Even the strings, to our way of thinking, were essentially unbalanced. As late as 1813, as conductor of the Prague Opera, Weber had four first and four second violins, with a couple each of violas, cellos and double-basses; this was a well-balanced ensemble though small for its purpose. But Salzburg, with six or eight first and second violins, had only four violas, three cellos and three double-basses.

The Baroque idea of the oboe as the principal melodic instrument of the woodwind department, began to disappear as composers began to think of the orchestra as a single united instrument, and composers distributed melodic parts as seemed to them most effective. The doubling of flutes with first violins an octave below them seemed more effective and pleasanter on the ear than the traditional coupling of oboe and violin. The oboe was needed, too, for most of the time, to sustain the upper line of the harmonies picked out from the figured bass by the harpsichord, with its lack of any sustaining power, but this was a duty they could relinquish to become melodists when its particular colour was needed to bring out the essential thematic, melodic line. Bassoons in France were instruments independent of the general bass, but elsewhere they belonged to the *continuo*, where their participation was so much a matter of course that many composers—Haydn among them in his early works—did not usually bother to specify them.

It was in German-speaking Europe that orchestral music was energetically developed for its own sake. Central European composers were more concerned about the actual substance of their music than about colour and effect; while Rameau was developing new ways in which to communicate the mythological excitements of opera, his German contemporaries were beginning to build the forms through which the orchestra developed. Opera demanded new and ingenious musical effects; in this way it continually increased the expressive vocabulary of music. At the same time, the symphony, the concerto and the various forms of 'abstract' instrumental music were creating an autonomous art which owed nothing to the need to illustrate settings, situations and actions. In the German courts, no less than in cities and churches, music was a social necessity; opera and concert music were required as a matter of course in the house of a nobleman, so that the nobility created for themselves the largest and most effective musical organizations they could afford. In 1760, when Haydn entered his service, the palace of Prince Esterhazy at Eisenstadt had a theatre, a large music room for orchestral concerts, an opera company to use the theatre and sing the music of the chapel, and an art gallery. A few years later a new Prince built Esterhaz, a new palace in his remote Hungarian estate, with even greater amenities including a puppet theatre for which Haydn wrote marionette operas.

Early in the eighteenth century, standards and tastes varied considerably. Frederick the Great of Prussia, released when he reached his majority in 1734 from the tyranny of a father whose tastes hardly moved beyond military display, began at once to create the musical establishment which he expanded splendidly when he became King in 1740. Frederick was an industrious composer whenever leisure allowed, and a flautist whose ambitions may have outrun his powers; at any rate, his audiences declared that in slow movements he was a masterly player but that quick music betrayed him into uncertainties of rhythm and dubieties of fingering. ("What rhythm," cried a sycophantic courtier after one of his performances. "What rhythms!" said his court accompanist, C. P. E. Bach, not quite inaudibly.)

Frederick's repertoire was based upon three hundred flute concertos, written for him by Joachim Quantz, his teacher and probably the most highly paid composer in Europe; apart from a salary of 2,000 thalers, Quantz was paid twenty-five ducats for every concerto he wrote for his master, and a hundred ducats for every flute he made. Quantz died while writing his three hundredth flute concerto, and his illustrious soloist completed the manuscript. The Quantz concertos were played over and over again in chronological order; when the vast cycle of works was completed at the rate of four or five concertos an evening—the rate of production dropped to three as the King began to age—Frederick immediately began again with the first concerto.

At enormous cost, Frederick built a new opera-house in Berlin, and opened it in 1742. It was equipped with every possible scenic device including cascades and waterfalls pumped from a huge tank in its cellars placed there as a precaution against fire. Frederick created an orchestra of sixty players for the Opera, and the musicians, when not required in the theatre, were on duty in the palace for concerts whenever there was no performance in the theatre; this was sometimes as often as five evenings in a week; he himself supervised rehearsals as stringently and with as much insistence on discipline as he used when he commanded his army.

The opera was his own; citizens of Berlin and visitors to the city were admitted so long as they were respectably dressed; it was never very difficult for 'gentlemen' to gain admission to Frederick's concerts. As the King paid for everything, no taste was consulted but his own. The musicians he employed were the best he could find. Carl Philipp Emanuel Bach, who seems to have been determined to remain as far as he could from Leipzig to escape his father's overpowering influence, was court accompanist and harpsichordist, but Emanuel Bach was a 'modernist' of the latest school and to our twentieth-century minds the greatest of all Frederick's musicians, but as a composer he received little or no encouragement from his master. Johann Sebastian visited Berlin at Frederick's invitation in 1747; his sons disrespectfully referred to the ageing composer as 'old peruke' (thus history records the nickname though perhaps 'old wiggy' conveys their meaning better) but he was treated with a respect which Emanuel never won from his employer. The composers whom Frederick valued were the conventional but always tasteful and grammatical Quantz, Carl Heinrich Graun, Frederick's *Kapellmeister* from 1735 until his death in 1759 (a composer of operas in the old-fashioned style of Handel and

Hasse), J. S. Bach and Handel; Graun, however, provided the greater part of the Berlin operatic repertoire for nearly a quarter of a century.

Frederick's orchestra contained several other notable composers; among them were the Benda family; Franz Benda, born in Bohemia, was a fine violinist whose playing attracted Frederick's attention and was in Prussian court service from 1740 until his death in 1786. Franz Benda was joined by his brother, George, who left Berlin to become *Kapellmeister* at Gotha in 1750, and by his son Wilhelm, born in 1745. All three Bendas, and George's son who was never in Frederick's service, were composers of some quality though Franz, who was Frederick I's favourite colleague in sonata performances, wrote almost exclusively for the violin. They were typical of Bohemian musicians in that they all took posts outside Bohemia, where the aristocracy neglected their estates in order to spend as much time as possible in Vienna, the centre both of power and of fashion. Frederick's taste for the style of the beginning of the century largely dictated what his domestic composers wrote, and Emanuel Bach (who to the generation after Frederick's was the greatest of the Bach family because of the expressive intensity and 'modernism' of his music) received little official recognition until he resigned his court appointment in 1767 and succeeded his godfather, the famous and prolific Telemann, as Cantor in Hamburg. Official music in his new post was rough and ready, but Hamburg had a public opera-house and regular concerts, and Emanuel Bach's intensely expressive, revolutionary symphonies and even more startling harpsichord sonatas won a devoted audience from the wealthy, cultured, music-loving bourgeoisie. Emanuel's symphonies demand a concentration on the strings and use the rest of the orchestra almost exclusively as harmonic background; some of them are simply for string orchestra, and while his powerful, expressive but sometimes undisciplined style did much to shape the later development of the symphony and the concerto, it did little to expand and consolidate the orchestra.

In 1742 the Elector Palatine engaged Johann Stamitz (another Bohemian musician better known by the German form of his Christian name than by its national equivalent 'Jan') to be *Kapellmeister* of his court music at Mannheim. Stamitz used his authority to build the first virtuoso orchestra that Europe had ever heard. It was based on the excellence of the strings which Stamitz collected from Germany, Austria, Italy and Bohemia, for Stamitz imported a number of his compatriots, and the Bohemians were as celebrated for their quality as strings players as they were for their proficiency on the French horn and the more recent clarinet. Stamitz composed symphonies, concertos and chamber music in the new style of key-

and-subject contrast, and his achievements almost overwhelmed visitors to the Electoral court. Listeners of its own period claimed that the Mannheim orchestra had invented the *crescendo* and the *diminuendo*; they could maintain a true *pianissimo* throughout a lengthy passage of music, and this was a feat apparently beyond any other orchestra of the time. In addition, it played with precision and complete responsiveness to the music and its *Kapellmeister*'s direction and was notable for the fire and unanimity of its attack. These qualities stayed with it after Stamitz's death in 1757, and it lost nothing of its outstanding character under Stamitz's sons Philipp and Anton, both of whom remained with the orchestra after Johann's death, when Christian Cannabich became *Kapellmeister*.

The Stamitz family and Cannabich composed music that had no great profundities of emotion but which paraded its composers' skills. Their musical ideal was orchestral sensationalism designed to exploit the quality of the orchestra, and it was served by the group of composers in the Mannheim band—the Italian Toeschi, and the Germans Anton Filz, Holzbauer, Franzl, Cramer and Franz Beck (who fought an ill-advised duel and was compelled to flee from Mannheim; he settled in Bordeaux and conducted opera and orchestral concerts there). Cannabich himself was a composer rivalling Telemann in the extent of his output, and like his subordinate composers in the orchestra followed so devoutly in the style of the first Stamitz that the Mannheim composers really present a 'school' united in style and aims. The tours of travelling virtuosi and the natural comings and goings of orchestral players to new posts spread the works of the Mannheim school round Europe.

Because its greatest men were specialist string players, music composed for the Mannheim orchestra notably followed the eighteenth-century convention of giving the meat of the work to the strings, set the bassoon to follow the general bass line entrusted to the cellos and double-basses (a method of composition growing increasingly outmoded which composers were oddly reluctant to discard), used the horns to underpin the harmony and the oboes to fill it except at special moments when the pitch of the melody and the course of the movement compelled them to demand a thematic statement in their special tone of voice. Trumpets appeared only rarely in concert music, in works written for occasions which demand special celebration, and then to add their brilliance of colour in fanfare-like passages at a climax. As the Baroque age ended, the old clarino technique of trumpeters and horn players began to be forgotten; the disappearance of the old trumpeter guilds in the eighteenth century left the musical world with few players who had mastered the techniques of the old guildsmen. Therefore trumpets, rarely able to play complete melodies in their accessible upper middle register, became harmonic instruments, like the horns. In addition, the strength and penetration of trumpet tone necessarily meant that they were used sparingly. A court music-room, rarely holding as many as a hundred people, with a relatively low ceiling and walls which did not (at least in most palaces) absorb sound, naturally discouraged the composer from using trumpets too frequently; in the larger spaces of a church or an opera-house, trumpets, like trombones, needed fewer inhibitions, but trombones, except in Paris, were exclusively church instruments, used most frequently to support voices as they had been in the past. In Paris they were accepted into the opera orchestra.

The restrictions on the activities of the woodwind, too, are easily understandable. The instrument was capable of playing in most keys by the middle of the eighteenth century, but the boring of sound holes along the pipe, and the width of its bore, were matters demanding the utmost mathematical accuracy, and many of a chromatic oboe's semitones were to a greater or lesser degree bored slightly, or less slightly, out of tune. The same is true of the flute. Therefore, although their basic tube length insisted that their natural tuning was in D, they were capable of a range of keys but not always, or perhaps not usually, with perfect accuracy of intonation. According to Dr Burney, during his visit to Mannheim, the one weak spot in the orchestra was its upper woodwind; it was "an army of generals, as capable of planning a campaign as of fighting a battle", but the poor intonation of its oboes and flutes disturbed him, and the playing of woodwind instruments was something he learned never to take for granted; he seemed to go round Europe with unquenchable enthusiasm but repeatedly noting the inferiority of the woodwind wherever he went. Probably Mozart's dislike of the flute, for which he wrote solo music only when it was commissioned from somebody too important to be neglected, was due to its often uncertain intonation. The fault was less in the players than in the difficulty of making the instruments effectively. The adoption of the clarinet as a permanent member of the Mannheim orchestra may be due not only to its extended range and qualities of tone but also to the fact that its longer pipe helped makers to voice it more precisely.

The rare orchestras formed to play to city audiences were, on the whole, less adventurous than court musicians because they needed to please an audience by deciding for them what music would be most pleasing; fear of failure made them conservative. The court musician had the advantage of immediate contact with his audience; if he was lucky enough to have a patron whose tastes were educated and highly developed, he might find himself encour-

Cantata performance
in the choir gallery of a
German church

A *Collegium Musicum* rehearsing a cantata

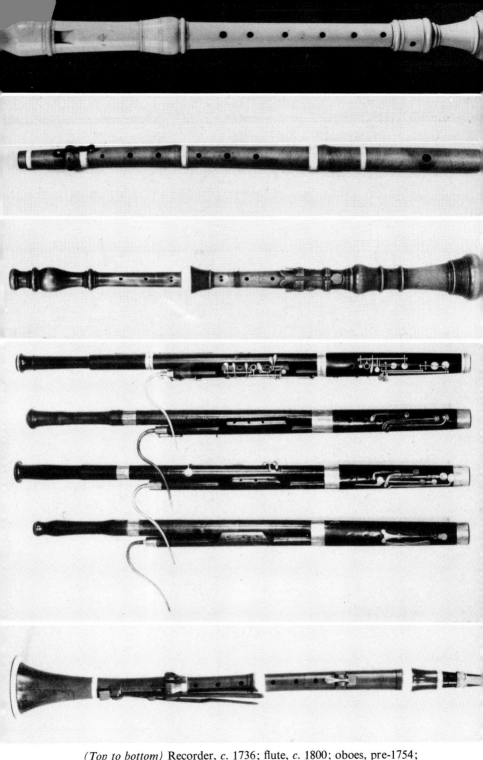

(Top to bottom) Recorder, *c.* 1736; flute, *c.* 1800; oboes, pre-1754; four bassoons, eighteenth century; clarinet, English *c.* 1810

Modern woodwind instruments: flute, oboe, cor anglais, clarinet,
bassoon

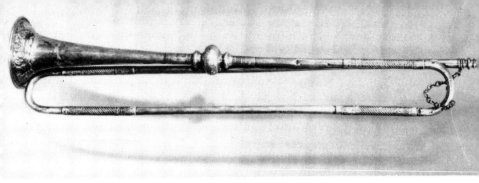

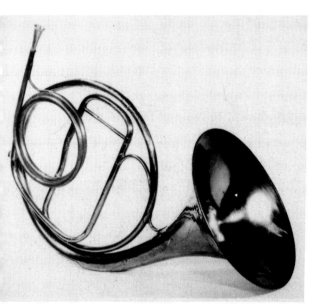

(*Above*) Natural trumpet, early nineteenth century

(*Left*) Natural horn, early nineteenth century

(*Below*) The five Nuremberg *Stadtpfeifer*, sixteenth century

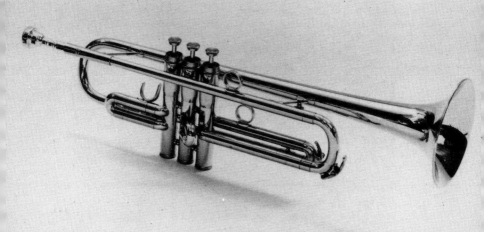

Modern brass instruments (*top to bottom*): bass trombone, valve horn, valve trumpet

The Hanover Square Rooms, opened in 1774. This illustration dates
from 1843

The Odeon Concert Hall in Munich, opened in 1825

The original *Gewandhaus* Concert Hall in Leipzig, engraved in about 1840

The interior of the Queen's Hall, London, 1893

A Handel Festival in the Crystal Palace, London, in 1859

Royal Festival Hall, London

aged to experiment. The public audience normally asked for something familiar in style to that which it was used to, but the court musician was usually engaged in playing what was new not only in the actual notes it used but often in the style it exploited. The *Collegium Musicum* which Johann Sebastian Bach had directed turned, after his death, into a concert society financed by the subscriptions of its supporters and to a lesser extent by takings at the box office and succeeded in prospering, bringing up an audience prepared to listen attentively to new music in new styles. As a concert society, it had played originally in an inn, the *Drei Schwanen,* but the town council, recognizing the value of public concerts as an amenity and their popularity among the townspeople, made the hall of the *Gewandhaus,* the clothiers' guild, available to it in 1781, and the *Gewandhaus* has given its name to the two concert halls which have taken the place of the original concert room as well as to the orchestra itself. The orchestra contained professional musicians— the Leipzig *Stadtpfeifer* and local music teachers—with a number of competent amateur musicians, so that in 1781 it had six first and six second violins, three violas and four players sharing the cello and double-bass parts. Four years later it amalgamated with the totally professional orchestra of the Leipzig Opera, in danger from a management which was seeking to cut costs, making possible the production of more ambitious operas and thus winning a more enthusiastic public, while the standards of the orchestral concerts apparently rose.

The original *Gewandhaus* held close on eight hundred people, nearly two-thirds of them sitting in seats facing towards the centre gangway, as though in the choir stalls of a church, simply because only a church provided the designers of the auditorium with any precedent for the seating of a large audience. The Leipzig audience was ready for new music, and expected to hear it, but the concerts were dependent for their programmes not, like a court orchestra, on new music specially composed for them (for the *Gewandhaus* had no *Kapellmeister* employed to direct it), but found the music they needed from other orchestras or from publishers. From 1760 onwards Emmanuel Breitkopf, whose firm eventually became Breitkopf and Härtel, issued regular catalogues of the works he had available in print or in manuscript, indicating the growing amount of music available in Germany for mere purchase, so that the few organizations like the *Gewandhaus* orchestra, as well as the numerous amateur concert orchestras, could find the music they needed to keep them reasonably up to date.

In London, where public concerts of one sort and another had been familiar entertainments since 1672, the number of instruments involved had originally depended on the performance of pro-

E

grammes so miscellaneous that Roger North, the contemporary amateur musicologist, whose writings provide a disenchanted view of London's early concert life, mentioned the disorganized pushing and shoving of musicians on to the platform at the end of every item, but the popularity first of Italian *concertì grossì* and then of Handel's concertos and orchestral pieces in his operas and oratorios, set out for organized and co-ordinated orchestral forces, made concerts a business for balanced and effective orchestras. In 1762 the youngest of Bach's sons, Johann Christian, had been brought to London as composer for the Italian opera. J. C. Bach had gone to Italy, become a Roman Catholic and spent some years as organist of Milan Cathedral, succeeding as an opera composer both in Milan and in Naples. Unlike his elder brother Emanuel, whose urgency and forcefulness of expression sometimes disregarded formal symmetry and grace, Johann Christian was beyond everything else a '*galant*' composer, insisting on beauty and grace of style and sound and firmly rejecting what often seemed to be the emotional extravagance of his elder brother.

Opera in London was still, as it had been in Handel's day, an entertainment for the wealthy, who demanded the brightest available stars supported by a fine orchestra and good stage designers much more than originality of musical style; it was therefore at best both expensive and financially hazardous. Economic necessity compelled Johann Christian Bach to find a second string to his bow, and he augmented his earnings from the opera, and survived the years in which opera was silent, by entering into partnership with another German musician, Carl Friedrich Abel, an ex-pupil of his father's at the Thomasschule, in Leipzig, as a concert promoter. It was J. C. Bach and Abel who, in their concerts, brought the new symphonic style, with the new symphonically motivated solo concerto, to England; the two won a devoted audience which followed them from one fashionable hall to another until, in 1775, they opened the Hanover Square Rooms in partnership with Giovanni Andrea Gallini, ballet-master at the opera. The Hanover Square Rooms remained London's leading concert hall until 1874, occupied by events which combined great musical value with the adherence of a rich 'society' audience. The hall held about eight hundred people and, at its opening, was considered to be the last word in fashionable elegance of decoration.

Whether it was because he could find more reliable woodwind, better instruments, or both, than were generally available on the Continent, or simply because he submitted to the apparently inevitable imperfections of intonation of the flutes and oboes of his period we cannot say, but both in operas and in his concert music J. C. Bach used the woodwind with greater freedom than his contemporaries even in Mannheim, and, consequently, with a richer sense of colour. His music has an ease and naturalness of expression which makes its neglect extremely unfortunate, and he is perhaps remembered best as one of the greatest influences on the music of Mozart. The young Wolfgang Amadeus Mozart met the expatriate composer during his long stay in London as a child prodigy; the two became extremely fond of each other and the boy wrote his first symphonies in emulation of those of his elderly friend. The elegance of form and beautiful finish which Mozart infallibly achieves come, perhaps, first and foremost from the influence of J. C. Bach.

But in the second half of the eighteenth century the further development of the orchestra really depended upon the formal and harmonic development of the symphony and the concerto and on the growth of less conventionalized styles of opera. The demand for new musical effects to match the events and situations in opera scores has always been a rich source of new orchestral ideas, but the sheer conventionality of operatic subject matter and the pre-dominance of the voice between Monteverdi and Mozart meant a diminution in the new demands made on composers. Thus, towards the end of the eighteenth century, it was the evolution of the sym-phony and the concerto, and of those light-music forms like the serenade and the divertimento, which expanded the orchestra's expressive capacity. The serenade, in particular, because it was out-door music and therefore depended more on wind instruments than on strings and could not employ a keyboard instrument to 'fill in' from a figured bass, effectively turned composers towards the idea of a more expressive woodwind band and away from the traditional figured bass towards orchestral self-sufficiency. Like the sonata and the symphony, the serenade and the divertimento rested always on the opposition and reconciliation of music in opposing but related keys; the reconciliation is effected through the developments of themes which characterize and identify the keys involved, and it is a process which inevitably demands reference to other keys beyond the structural ones.

Trumpets, outside the limited range of keys in which they were tuned (their tuning depending on the length of the brass pipe which gave no sounds beyond the harmonic series of the tube's keynote, each note reached by lip movement and breath control), were silent whenever the music moved beyond their strictly limited range. Pas-sages in the minor keys were out of a trumpet's range until valve mechanism in the nineteenth century gave the trumpet as much versatility as any other instrument; they were possible when trum-peters were trained in the high clarino technique of the Baroque trumpeters; a trumpet in D can play the essential notes of a D major chord—D, F sharp, A and an upper D—but they cannot, except in the difficult high register which gives them a real chromatic scale in continuous semitones, make an equal contribution to music in D minor—the F natural which gives D minor its essential character is outside the natural trumpet's range—and while a trumpet in D can make some contribution to music in A major, it has little to give to music in C or in G. The considerable length that must be added to a brass tube to deepen its voice by as much as a semitone meant that trumpets were made to speak only in a limited number of keys; a trumpet tuned, for example, in G or F might well be too unwieldy for its player.

Horns were less inhibited, but the addition of extra lengths of piping, crooks, between the mouthpiece and the main tube of the instrument, though not impossible to apply to trumpets, seemed to add difficulties for the player and never proved really satisfactory. As the horns had become the most useful instruments for sustaining the harmony, horn players developed a technique to deal with new demands; additional notes can be added to those of the series in which they are tuned by closing or partly closing the end of their tube by thrusting the left hand into it; the left hand used in this way can effectively raise the pitch of a note. The method was unsatisfactory because it created a wide disparity of tone between the natural 'open' notes and the rather husky, almost choked sound of the 'closed' additional notes, but handstopping enabled horns to contribute far more continuously to the harmonic development which was the essential action of the symphony, and to a small extent it helped to solve the composer's problem of finding ways in which the horns could act as continuous bearers of the harmonic structure.

While the first movement of a symphony involves two structural keys and the last movement is in the main key of the opening, the second movement, usually until late in the nineteenth century the slow movement, is in a different key for the sake of contrast; the structural keys of a first movement are the main key and its dominant, a fifth up; a movement in C major, like the first movement of Beethoven's First Symphony or Mozart's 'Jupiter' Symphony, moves to G major for its structural contrast, but a movement in C minor, like the first movement of Beethoven's Fifth Symphony, moves to E flat, its 'relative major' (that is, the major key which uses the same key signature). The second movement chooses a key only one step less closely related than the keys of the first movement and is usually in the subdominant, a fourth away from the keynote; in the C major symphonies, the slow movement would choose to be in F. The third movement is usually in the main key, as is the last, with a relapse into the subdominant for its trio. Thus, in Haydn's Thirteenth Symphony, for example, written in 1763, the main key is D major and its contrast key in the first movement is its dominant, A major. The slow movement is in G major, its minuet third movement in D major with a trio in D, and its finale, inevitably, in D major. The work is scored for flute, two oboes, four horns in D, timpani and strings, with bassoon sharing the bass line with cellos and double-basses, and the still obligatory harpsichord *continuo*. The four horns lay down the essential D major harmony but can contribute only detached chords to the harmony in A major, and as the music develops through a circle of keys to reach D major again, the harmony moves in a way that silences the horns. They have nothing to say in the second movement, in G, but they are back in their element in the minuet and finale though the G major trio again silences them, not simply because a trio was normally more lightly scored than the rest of a symphony.

Horns were made in a variety of keys and could be crooked into others; it was also possible to use diversely tuned horns. Haydn's *Farewell* Symphony (No. 45), is in the outlandish key of F sharp minor, which means that the contrasting key in the opening movement is A major; he scored the work for two horns, one in A and the second in E, so that they are able to make a fuller contribution to the harmony. The second movement, in A major, asks both the horns to play in A major, though they sound only for five consecutive bars, holding an E in octaves. For the minuet and trio, in D sharp minor, the horns are in F (each player, one assumes, did not bring several instruments but one instrument and several crooks). For the fourth movement, they return to the original tuning, and as the symphony ends with all the players leaving the platform one by one as their contribution ends, leaving only two violinists still in action, each contributes a fanfare figure as its last word.

In this work, Haydn is concerned with the horns primarily as harmonic instruments; Mozart, in his earlier G minor Symphony, composed in 1774, when he was eighteen, demanded horns tuned in B flat and G, so that between them they could play the melody of the minuet of the third movement. (*See* Appendix 2, No. 3.)

Haydn was appointed Assistant *Kapellmeister* to Prince Paul Esterhazy in 1761; before that he had held the parallel post for Count Morzin, a minor nobleman who had dismissed his orchestra, and Haydn with it, a year before because he could no longer afford to support it. Before his post with Count Morzin, he had looked after the music of Baron von Fürnberg when the Baron was at home in his country house for the summer, but the musical establishment which the Baron employed was simply a string quartet.

Haydn's first real orchestral works come from his period with

Count Morzin, whose orchestra had six violins, one viola and one double-bass, two oboes (or flutes, as apparently the oboists could play both instruments), two bassoons and two horns. One of the bassoonists seems to have been a cellist, as the works written for Count Morzin have a cello part. There was, too, a cor anglais available, though Haydn did not use it in his symphonies. Prince Paul Esterhazy, an Austro-Hungarian nobleman of vast wealth, employed an orchestra of five violins, or violas, one cello, one double-bass, one flute, two oboes, two bassoons, two horns and a timpanist. Haydn gained the confidence of the Prince sufficiently to be encouraged to increase the size of the orchestra and to experiment with varieties of scoring. Much of Prince Paul's year was spent in his palace at Eisenstadt, where the musicians of his chapel —two violinsts and a double-bass player could be used to augment the court orchestra. The local church at Eistenstadt had its own musicians, who could be co-opted into the court establishment if they were needed. The church musicians would include the Eistenstadt *Stadtpfeifer*, and the trumpeters and drummers of the Prince's regiment were at the *Kapellmeister's* disposal when they were needed. Performances were directed by Haydn from the harpsichord at which he played the *continuo*—it was not until 1768 that he began to feel that, the cello and bass excepted, the *continuo* players had no real contribution to make to the performance. Haydn apparently expected the participation of a bassoon, or two bassoons, in the *continuo* group, and this seemed still to be so much a matter of convention that Haydn often neglected to mention them in his scores.

When the Prince moved to his palace in Vienna, there was an abundance of freelance players to satisfy any of the *Kapellmeister's* demands for supernumeraries. Haydn's first symphonies for the Esterhazy orchestra were Nos. 6, 7 and 8—*Le Matin*, *Le Midi* and *L'Aprés-midi*, a cycle of works. Each requires one flute; *Le Midi* demands two. All three are scored for two oboes, bassoon, two horns and strings with, of course, a harpsichord for the *continuo*. Perhaps to ingratiate himself with an orchestra which did not know him, Haydn not only wrote a number of concertos—notably for violin, cello and horn—but he also laid out movements of his symphonic cycle, and of other symphonies during his first few years in Esterhazy service, almost in the old Baroque concerto form, with occasional solo instruments. At the same time, he was ready to experiment not only with the form of the symphony but also with its orchestration. The Twenty-second Symphony, composed in 1764 and called 'The Philosopher', is an example. It begins with a slow movement in the style of a Protestant church choral prelude, and its orchestra dispenses with flutes and oboes but uses two cors anglais in their place, so that the music has a sort of sombre, glowing richness.

The Esterhazy princes collected together a notable orchestra and allowed Haydn to enlarge it. Several of the players were well known as virtuoso players. Luigi Tomasini, the leader or 'concert master,' nine years younger than Haydn, joined the Esterhazy orchestra in 1757 and became leader in the year of Haydn's appointment. His style of playing had some influence on Haydn, who wrote his string quartets in the expectation of Tomasini playing the first violin parts, while the concertos written for Tomasini to play ask for exceptional grace and elegance as well as agility. Tomasini was notable enough to be asked to join the orchestra of the *Tonkünstlersocietät* in Vienna, an organization of professional musicians which every year gave public performances, usually of oratorios, in Vienna, devoting the profits to charity. Tomasini composed a number of concertos, quartets and works from the baryton (an archaic instrument in the cello register with a number of sympathetic strings) for Prince Nikolaus, the second of Haydn's princely patrons, to play.

The leading cellist from 1778 until 1790 was taken into the orchestra by Haydn, who heard him playing in Vienna. Kraft was himself a not inconsiderable composer, and for some years Haydn's Cello Concerto in D was attributed to him, but authorities have again decided that Kraft was its player and not its composer.

When Haydn first went into the service of the Esterhazy family, he could count on the services of four brilliant horn players. Symphony No. 31, composed in 1765, and Symphony No. 72, probably composed in 1763 (the order in which Haydn's symphonies are numbered is not that of their composition), are hunting symphonies demanding four horns, and these are given passages of hair-raising difficulties. In No. 31, the *'Horn Signal Symphony'* or *'Auf dem Anstand'* (the *'Anstand'* is the point at which huntsmen wait for the first cry of the hounds or the first notes of the huntsmen's horn), not only gives the four instruments passages of melodic substance but also sets them to deal with passages in which, settling into their highest register, they have music of startling, athletic exuberance. Eventually Haydn seems to have decided on a standardized orchestra of flute, oboes, horns, timpani and strings, adding trumpets for special occasions until, in 1786, he was invited to compose the six 'Paris' Symphonies (Nos. 82–87) for a public concert organization in Paris; trumpets are essential to his orchestra in these works and in the twelve 'London' Symphonies composed between 1791 and 1795, also intended for performance in public. It seems that he found this combination of instruments to be the most versatile and most effective in music of all types and all moods after trying out various alternatives among the woodwind. When, in 1762, Prince Paul Esterhazy died and was succeeded by his brother Prince Nikolaus, Haydn found himself with a patron who was not only an enthusiastic chamber-music player but also a musician whose sympathies seem to have been wide enough if not to encourage Haydn's experiments at least not to prevent them. Prince Nikolaus apparently disliked Vienna and was bored by the palace at Eisenstadt; he built himself a new palace at Esterhaza, where the family had a hunting lodge, draining a marsh in southern Hungary to do so. His opera-house, his puppet theatre, his concert room and his delight in chamber music kept Haydn almost exhaustingly active but isolated him from other composers and forced him, in his own phrase, "to be original". With an orchestra, chorus, solo singers and incessant demands for new music to cope with—everything from operas and masses to sonatas for the Princess to play—Haydn had to exploit his originality in every direction as well as that of the orchestra.

The commission for the 'Paris' Symphonies, brought about by the popularity of his music in published editions, gave Haydn his first opportunity to write for a larger orchestra and a public audience in a larger hall, but this did not suggest to him that new instruments be added to his orchestra or that his music should alter its texture; the greater size of his orchestras in Paris and London did not even suggest to him that he should exploit a wider range of tone colour. He still linked woodwind with strings, with oboes and flutes reinforcing violins, flutes often delectably an octave above, and bassoons reinforcing cellos, with the horns—for Haydn's virtuoso horn parts came to an end in the 1760s and he never attempted them in his works for orchestras other than his own—sustaining the harmony. But the 'public' symphonies written for Paris and then for London demand trumpets and drums as a matter of course. The 'London' Symphonies also demand clarinets. This final development of Haydn's orchestral style was the fruit, it seems, of his meeting with Mozart and their friendship after Mozart had left the service of the Archbishop of Salzburg in 1771.

Despite Mozart's dislike for Salzburg, of the city itself as well as of his work there and its conditions—as Court Organist he ranked with the valets and ate at their table, finding their conversation and attitudes depressing—the musical staff there was impressive. His father, Leopold Mozart, a fine violinist and author of an impressive book of instructions for would-be virtuoso violinists, no mean composer both of rather severe church music and of charming, high-spirited entertainment music, was Vice-*Kapellmeister*; Haydn's younger brother, Michael, who in his adolescence had been regarded as more promising than his genius brother, joined the Salzburg staff as *Conzert-Meister* (leader of the orchestra) in 1762 and stayed there until his death in 1806. Among the instrumentalists was the horn player Ignaz Leutgeb, who left the Archbishop's service shortly after Mozart and settled in Vienna, combining his career as a noted virtuoso player with the running of a cheese shop. Mozart's horn concertos were written for Leutgeb and thus demonstrate his abilities as a player and his apparently unvarying command of a long-sustained *legato* line, as though he needed never to breathe at all, just as the abusive jocularities scribbled by the composer on the scores indicate Mozart's friendliness towards him.

The music which Mozart wrote in Salzburg often was created in obedience to the Archbishop's regulations. The unfinished C minor Mass—a grandly expansive work—was written after his escape to Vienna, and the *Requiem*, also unfinished, was written at the end of his life for another patron. Almost all the other Masses were for Salzburg and its Archbishop, who commanded that High Mass, with a full musical setting for choir, soloists and orchestra, should not last for more than forty-five minutes: a less disciplined composer than Mozart might have found such a restriction totally inhibiting, but Mozart wrote a series of tautly economical and tightly organized works of great strength and considerable eloquence in which nothing sounds hurried or unnaturally laconic. The symphonies and violin concertos of his adolescence and early manhood, up to No. 33, are works for Salzburg, where Mozart was under obligation to present his ideas in the most symmetrical and polished style. Only a few works, like the 'Paris' Symphony, are not restricted in this way, and Mozart, faced in Paris with a large orchestra, was content like Haydn to enjoy the greater number of players and their greater richness of tone without altering the constituents of his orchestra except by relishing the special qualities of the clarinets in the Paris orchestra.

As in the piano concertos written later for his own use in Vienna, mostly for his own concerts, Mozart's orchestral music was designed to combine popular appeal with the most thorough and precise treatment of his themes and ideas; Mozart apparently felt that a work which failed to appeal both to the untutored audience which simply loved melody, rhythm and vitality and to what he called the 'connoisseurs' who were musically educated enough to appreciate the music's technical finesse, skill and knowledge, could be regarded as a failure.

Mozart had visited Mannheim on his way to Paris in 1778; he made a number of friends there and discovered the clarinet, which for the rest of his life remained one of his great loves. Though several of his later works were written for orchestras which did not include clarinets, the presence of clarinettists always stimulated him to create a richer orchestral texture, and his later friendship with Anton Stadler, the leading clarinet virtuoso of the period, led to the creation of two masterpieces, the Clarinet Quintet and the Clarinet Concerto; Stadler played an instrument which he had developed to maintain a special low register down to a fifth below that of the standard instrument, and it was for this instrument that the Concerto was written, so that it is chiefly known now in an arrangement for the normal orchestral clarinet which has, at times, to leap octaves to avoid Stadler's low notes. At the same time, the basset horn, an instrument with a longer pipe than a clarinet which has a range from the C an octave below middle C for a possible four octaves upwards and is plaintively hollow in its lower register, Mozart used in a number of orchestral works, notably the magnificent *Masonic Funeral Music*, but it never became a regular member of the orchestra; it gained a new lease of life in some of the works of Richard Strauss and other composers at the beginning of the twentieth century, but still remains primarily a voice associated with Mozart in moments of great solemnity. A sketch for the Clarinet Concerto shows the work, apparently, as having originally been designed for the basset horn.

Perhaps because of the early influence of Johann Christian Bach, and perhaps also because of the stimulus he gained from the Mannheim orchestra, Mozart was always inclined to use the woodwind with more freedom than his German and Austrian contemporaries. Clarinets at times replace the oboes, as they do in the E flat Symphony, No. 39. Flutes, oboes and clarinets often bear the brunt of the melodic argument, often over a relatively subdued accompaniment of sustained string tone and harmonies held softly by the horns. The result is often a freshness of colour and a delicacy of sound that can be completely enchanting, as in the first movement of the E flat Symphony, when flutes, clarinets and bassoon are left to discourse over throbbing harmonies from the double-bass sustained by the horns and a muted ascending figure in the cellos.

The third movement trio, with flute and first clarinet offering each other happy endearments, with the second clarinet bubbling away with an E flat arpeggio and the strings and bassoon murmuring a rhythmic accompaniment in almost static harmonies is, perhaps, the apotheosis on a Viennese street serenade on a warm summer night; Mozart writing to charm is always the supreme charmer amongst composers.

It was such passages in Mozart's work which stimulated Haydn to evolve the partnership of woodwind and strings which is the final development of his orchestration. At times they express not only a charm comparable to Mozart's but the elderly Haydn's own serenity and, in passages like that in the slow movement of the

'Clock' Symphony (No. 101) when the main theme and main key return after a somewhat disturbed episode in G minor, they sound almost as though they are ready to melt in the mouth. Widely separated flutes and bassoons keep up the tick-tock accompaniment, joined after a moment by oboes, while the violins play the melody.

The late-eighteenth-century orchestra, in the hands of its two supreme masters, achieves a beauty of texture which combines with absolute clarity and an unequalled grace of movement. At the same time, it achieves great strength and energy, but these qualities are always summoned up in obedience to the dictates of musical thought, never in order to create a merely factitious excitement for mere excitement's sake. Such movements as the finale of the 'Jupiter' Symphony (No. 41) exist as triumphantly exciting musical thought, as gripping and spell-binding as anything by later, more sensational composers; the form and the orchestration are not used simply to create a sense of overpowering emotion but contain the emotion because they seem to be created by the intensity of the composer's thought. They are subject to no external discipline because they create the discipline that controls them. The finale of the 'Jupiter' uses a handful of short, terse themes, and they become a world of varied incidents and varied personalities which begin to interact together polyphonically (Germans call the work "the symphony with the final fugue", for the name 'Jupiter' is given to the work only in England and America) in the most gloriously exciting combination of intellectual power and triumphant emotion that has, perhaps, ever been achieved in music. The universal order is imposed by a four-note theme E, F, G, A, in steady semibreves; when all the diversity has been slipped without violence into its proper place in the order of things, no listener has ever felt disappointed that the final statement of the commanding semibreves is not reinforced by the trumpets, which simply celebrate the victory in fanfare-like figures once it has been achieved; they do not create order by the brazen power of their voices, for the order is, ultimately, the natural order of musical sense and logic by a four-note theme which expresses nothing but a basic and undeniable musical truth often used by composers before Mozart as nothing but a cliché.

In the opera-house, Mozart made the orchestra into a character as indispensable as those on the stage; it is not, like Wagner's orchestra, a narrator-commentator, and it does not, as his orchestra does, describe events with great eloquence and beauty of language, but it is a musical equivalent of the chorus in a Greek drama. It sympathizes with characters, feeling the agitation of the page-boy, Cherubino, when adolescence begins to torment him as he introduces himself in his first aria, *Non so piu*, explaining that the presence of any woman or girl generates in him an incomprehensible excitement. It picks up phrases from the singers in *Don Giovanni*, the mock pity of the dissolute hero and the anguish of his discarded mistress, Donna Elvira, and turns it into its own sorrow, dwelling on the arrogance of the Count in *The Marriage of Figaro* and pointing out the deep but fundamentally silly pathos of the Countess. The characters themselves are too engrossed in emotion or action to dwell on these things; the orchestra is the onlooker who sees most of the game, and sometimes it sees the joke before they do. Early in the troubles of Figaro and his Susanna, as they are preparing the room that is to be theirs as soon as they are married, Figaro points out that it will be very convenient to have a room so near to those of their master and mistress, a touch on the bell in the bedroom of either, and Figaro or Susanna can be immediately at the service of either; the bell he thinks of is a tinkling treble sound from violins and flutes. Susanna, less prone to illusion, points out that it will be all too easy for the Count to send Figaro on a long errand, and as quickly as they can be at their employer's service, the Count, who is in angry pursuit of her, can be in her room. The bell that will send Figaro out of the way is a loud bray from the horns, and horns are worn by cuckolds. In *Don Giovanni*, the coming to life of the statue of the murdered Commander whom Don Giovanni has killed in an unequal duel brings trombones into the orchestra for the first time in Austrian opera, and the passages which introduces them remains, for all its simplicity, one of the most terrifying in all opera.

Mozart's opera orchestra is concerned with action, situation and personality much more than directly with atmosphere, and never with scene setting. When the disguised lovers of *Cosi fan Tutte* return to the two sisters whose constancy they are testing—they have gambled on their belief that if each, in disguise, lays siege to the fiancée of the other, the siege will fail—their music is a serenade as ravishing as any music ever created; it tells us at once that all this happens by the seaside on a perfect, languorous summer evening not because the composer imitates waves, scented Mediterranean breezes or anything else; we recognize the beauty of the evening, we feel, because the characters are all four almost rapturously aware of it.

For most of his work, Mozart was satisfied with the orchestra as a standard ensemble; occasionally he adds basset horns in moments of tragedy or deep solemnity. The operas call for occasional additions like the Statue's trombones; the Pasha's court band in *Die Entführung aus dem Serail* calls almost hilariously for what the eighteenth century called "Turkish music"—triangle, cymbals and bass drum; Don Giovanni takes a mandoline to accompany himself in a serenade. Trombones reappear for the solemnities of the Masonic Temple in *Die Zauberflöte*, where they are concerned with spiritual solemnity, not with terror. *Die Zauberflöte*, too, has the glockenspiel of the bird catcher, Papageno, an instrument which does not reappear in Mozart's work because, in the opera, he obviously regards it as not more than a charming special effect appropriate to a single character.

The eighteenth century saw the music of both Mozart and Haydn not as especially delicate and restrained; to their contemporaries, the two were often unpleasantly loud and forceful; and the Emperor Joseph II himself suggested to Mozart that *Die Entführung aus dem Serail* uses too many notes. Until he wrote the 'Paris' and 'London' Symphones, Haydn wrote for small audiences in small halls in his patron's palace, and less frequently for the larger spaces of a private opera-house. In the opera-house, Mozart could give free reign to the forcefulness of his style, for all his operas were written for court opera-houses to which the public was admitted and which therefore accommodated a greater power of sound. The orchestral works, concertos and symphonies he wrote both in Salzburg and as a freelance composer in Vienna were written for performance in small halls; only one or two of his piano concertos had their first performance at public concerts in the Vienna theatres with a professional orchestra. Most of these works were written for his own subscription concerts. The subscription lists for two series of these survive, and Mozart's delight at finding the hall filled and the prospect of a capacity audience of the aristocracy and the official class for his first series, in 1784, was expressed in letters to his anxious father; it contains less than two hundred names. The hall was small and would, like Prince Esterhazy's music room, be completely filled with sound by the typical small eighteenth-century orchestra playing *fortissimo*. In modern halls, seating thousands in response to economic necessity, the force and energy of Mozart's and Haydn's music is clear but their power tends to be lost if the orchestra is built to late eighteenth-century specifications. But its clarity and ease of movement is often sacrificed if the orchestra is allowed to use its complete modern string section, which would, incidentally, rob the two flutes, two oboes, two clarinets and two bassoons of their power to add their colour to the scoring.

FIVE

Beethoven

Beethoven was the grandson of a *Kapellmeister* at the Electoral court in Bonn, where his father was a tenor in the choir; he himself became deputy court organist and a viola player in the court orchestra as a boy who had already made a local reputation as a prodigy and begun to compose. In his late teens he was a prolific composer, and the death of the Emperor Joseph II in 1790 prompted him to compose a memorial cantata, powerfully emphatic, highly emotional music for soloists, choir and orchestra. Bonn was a very wealthy state, its neutrality bought by subsidies from France and its more powerful German neighbours, and the court music was on a grand scale, so that as a boy Beethoven played in the latest and most ambitious French and Italian operas as well as those of Mozart and the few notable German works by his contemporaries. In 1792 he left Bonn on extended leave to study with Haydn at his patron's expense; a year later the French overran the Elector's territories, and the *Kapelle* of which Beethoven was nominally a member ceased to exist. From that date until the end of his life, Beethoven lived as a freelance piano virtuoso and composer.

Mozart had lived as a freelance for the last nine years of his life, expecting always to find a court which would offer him an appointment worthy of his abilities, and died famous, popular but penniless. A freelance existence seemed to Beethoven, as it had seemed to Mozart, quite unnatural. As late as 1806, when his hearing had failed so disastrously that he could not longer play in public, he negotiated with Napoleon I's brother, the King of the new state of Westphalia, for the post of *Kapellmeister* of the new court and was still, apparently, ready to accept it had not his friends among the Austrian nobility offered him an income to keep him in Vienna.

Beethoven's way of life as a freelance is not irrelevant to the consideration of his orchestral music and the development of the orchestra. His symphonies and concertos were not written to fit into the normal pattern of court music, commissioned by a patron to be performed in a private music-room as part of the social routine of an established nobility. The first two piano concertos were written when he was the new sensational pianist who was the rage of Vienna, to play at concerts in the programmes of which he was invited to appear; the other three, and all his symphonies, were written only when he wanted to compose works of that kind, and were first heard at public concerts which he organized himself or which were organized for him by wealthy admirers. He did not compose to keep pace with an aristocratic patron's demands but completely at will. When he had a sufficiency of new works to make a concert worthwhile, he would organize the event and present, perhaps, two new symphonies and a new concerto to the public, and add to them anything else on which he had been working which would fit into a long evening of music with an orchestra. Such events he either financed out of his own pocket, expecting a reasonable profit as payment for his labours, or their expenses were paid by wealthy admirers. Such concerts were Beethoven's appeal to the general public. Beethoven was the first composer to make a regular and appreciable income from the publication of his works, and successful public concerts stimulated the sales of his piano works and chamber music.

In addition, public concerts were naturally given in one of the larger theatres or in such large halls as the *Redoutensaal* of the Emperor's court, where a new style of orchestration, more emphatic and more fully scored than that of Haydn or Mozart was necessary; circumstances demanded that he used a bigger orchestra than had been customary in the past, although the additional players that he needed would not always be available for the concerts of aristocrats who wished their own small orchestras to keep abreast with what was soon accepted as a new and immensely powerful style of composition.

Beyond this was the question of the new 'sound ideal' (to adopt a German phrase) of Beethoven's music. He wanted a different style of performance, different qualities of phrasing and emphasis, from those his immediate predecessors had demanded. Beethoven's addresses to the general concert-going public, which his reputation helped to create, is a music as close as music can be to categorical, conceptual statement. This is music in which themes and musical phrases become identifiably symbolic; in Beethoven's music. "Fate knocks at the door", heroism is a musical statement including a harmonic flaw—its fanfare-like theme immediately sinks out of tune, as it were. Two linked phrases are "The question it is hard to answer": the first is labelled "Must it be so?" and the second, "It must be." Beethoven's orchestra is called to make every point as forcefully as it can be made; in a sense, it is engaged in musical oratory, for it is the voice of a great composer who found it natural to see moral, ethical and religious statement in musical themes and phrases.

From the First Symphony onwards, Beethoven's music takes its substance from an exploration of key relationships wider than Haydn had found it necessary to attempt and carried out more openly than the explorations of Mozart. The *Eroica Symphony*, in 1803, is in E flat, but the fanfare theme which opens the work by stating its key sinks at once on to C sharp, a note as remote as can be from the main key of the movement, and the reconciliation of C sharp to the world of E flat is the business of the whole enormous movement, a piece far larger than any single movement in a symphony by Haydn or Mozart, just as the entire symphony is as long as almost any two symphonies by either of his great predecessors.

His point of departure was always, until late in his life, the tradition he had inherited. Insofar as he was Haydn's pupil and disciple, the Haydn he knew was the composer of the 'London' Symphonies, *The Creation* and *The Seasons*, the complete master, not the explorer and pioneer of the 1760s and 1770s. Before he wrote the First Symphony, completed in 1800 ready for the first concert which he himself organized in the following year, he had two piano concertos and the cantatas for the death of Joseph II and the accession of Joseph's successor, Leopold II, to his credit, as well as sets of dances for court balls, piano sonatas and chamber music. The dance music adds the piccolo to the orchestra, giving sharper definition to the melodic line, and the last of a set of twelve German Dances is dominated by a splendid post horn solo. Conceivably this dance ended a festive evening, and the use of a post horn hinted to the dancers that they had arrived at the time for travel. The German Dances are lively, enjoyable music in the tradition that a few years later was to lead to the waltz. They were, one feels, composed in the abstract and they laid out for orchestra in the most advantageous (and in a sense, quite conventional) way until the intrusion of the posthorn insists that the composer takes notice of its special qualities and tone colour, just as the early piano concertos seem to be not specially concerned with the special characteristics of any of the orchestral instruments while the solo part is designed to present the powers and personality of the piano itself. All Beethoven's concertos have this feature; the music for the orchestra is beautiful, and all the instruments speak idiomatically, according to their own natures, but subdue their personalities to that of the solo instrument; the solo music in the Violin Concerto arises, it seems, from the character of the violin, while the piano, violin and cello of the Triple Concerto adapt and develop the solo music, as they interchange, in response to their own musical natures.

Beethoven seems never to have been concerned, as later composers were, with orchestration as a specialist branch of composition or with the use of themes which seems to characterize this or
that instrument. He knew the capacities of the individual instruments and how the music could most effectively be presented by
orchestral instruments, avoiding the themes which lose their power
when transferred, say from violin to oboe or cello to bassoon. But
apart from this, the individuality of different instruments seems not
to have been so intense a preoccupation as the structure and evolution of the musical thought. Beauties of orchestral sound in his
music—and they are innumerable—are the result of his care for
the development of the musical ideas and not of a sense of the
instrument's personality as a thing in itself.

His First Symphony was the first work he presented directly to
the general public. Horns and trumpets play their traditional rôles
in sustaining the harmony, but they bring him for the first time to
a problem which arises from the actual nature of the old brass
instruments—their limitations as capable of playing only the notes
of the harmonic series in which they are tuned. Beethoven's harmony travels so far from his main key in which the combative,
ebullient style demands the power of trumpets which simply cannot,
because of their nature, join step by step in his argument. For
example, in the coda of the symphony's last movement, the strings
seem to be about to restart the movement in the key of D—a world
away from the movement's home in C major—after the music
seems to have come once to an end in C. While the woodwind
seem to be struggling to find their way back to C, the violins decide
to play the theme in G major; this passage is marked *crescendo*,
and in four and a half bars it leads from *piano* to *fortissimo* and
the whole orchestra puts an end to the wandering by roaring out
detached chords of C major and its related keys. Naturally, trumpets in C shout into the C major, G major and A major chords,
but the rest of the orchestra visits F major, where the trumpets
can contribute nothing of any importance; thus they are inter-
mittently silenced by the progress of the harmony until the music
settles finally into a jubilant C major. (*See* Appendix 2, No. 4.)

Such is the strength and penetration of trumpet tone that the
absence of the instruments from two important chords is heard as
a sudden weakening which, most musicians believe, cannot have
been the composer's intention, so that, at least since the days of
Wagner, the absent notes have been supplied by the use of valve
trumpets which are capable of reaching the missing notes and any
other notes within the trumpet's range. Naturally, Beethoven, whose
works were achieved through the most painstaking working out of
detailed sketches, must have been aware of the effect of silent

F

trumpets on the orchestral texture at such moments; the problem facing performers is to decide whether he approved of the withdrawals of power forced on him by the nature of the instruments he used, or would he welcome the ability of musicians now to close the instrumental gaps; most modern players and conductors supply the missing notes.

Additions and adjustments to Beethoven's orchestration to allow for the deficiencies of naturally tuned brass instruments can be found in most performances of all Beethoven's orchestral works; occasionally a conductor might play the works simply as they were written, but we tend to take for granted the idea that he would expect us to make good the weaknesses of the instruments he had to use. In the Finale of the Fifth Symphony, after the strange, dark transition from the terror of the Scherzo, Beethoven chooses to write for all the transposing instruments—clarinets, horns and trumpets in C so that the blaze of triumph is announced with all the force his orchestra can muster when trombones are added to the already powerful choir. Later in the movement, however, bassoons are set to carol away in their weak baritone register at a point where logic suggests that horns would be more satisfactory to give a new theme its full effect, but the register needed is too low to be available to the horns. Had they been capable of playing a new theme in this register, it seems reasonable to assume that he would have scored the theme for horns. But while the conductor is prepared to act on his conjectures about gaps in horn and trumpet parts during period of harmonic movement, the world naturally assumes that conjectures about the rescoring of any passage go beyond the freedom any interpreter can expect to be granted.

Beethoven seems to have avoided, as far as possible, making use of the 'closed' notes which the horn player can reach by the hand-in-bell technique. It may be that Beethoven distrusted the ability of the average player to find these notes and play them cleanly; he may more probably, however, have wished to avoid the sudden contrast in tone arrived at when the bold, round open notes of the horn are suddenly interrupted by the muffled sound of closed notes. The open notes of the horn he used to splendid effect in such passages as the Trio of the Scherzo in the *Eroica Symphony* or how the blissful sense of peace in the last movement of the *Pastoral*, which begins with the clarinet singing a *ranz des vaches*, a cowherd's tune with something of the style of a yodel in its wide intervals, is intensified when a horn ends the movement by singing it from a distance created by the use of a mute.

Though Beethoven could exploit the deficiencies of the horn, turning them into advantages in such passages as their hunting music in the *Eroica*, the trumpets seem always to have been a problem. Even in the Ninth Symphony he could find no way round their frustrations; the sublime slow movement hears them as a call to action, lower in their register than we usually hear them in Beethoven's work, but pays no attention to their summons, and as the movement dies away it is succeeded by an outburst of wild cacophony marked *fortissimo*, which to Beethoven means with maximum power; he never marked a passage *fff*, double *fortissimo*, so that *fortissimo* itself means the loudest sound the instruments will make. Trumpets in D lead the outcry—*fortissimo* and their pitch ensure that they will ride over the rest of the orchestra only to fall momentarily silent, with a second's loss of power, as the harmony passes out of their range. In this passage, the symphony's four horns are tuned two in D and two in B flat, and the maximum power they yield is that of either B flat or D instruments as the harmony moves out of reach of one pair or the other.

Strictly speaking, it would have been possible for Beethoven to solve these problems once and for all. The special qualities of clarino playing had died with the chaos of the French Revolution, which destroyed many of the smaller German courts in the orchestras of which it had been preserved so long as the trumpet guilds had been powerful enough to maintain their monopoly; the guilds had been powerful enough to prevent any wide cultivation of the instrument, so that there just were not any outsiders who had mastered their traditional techniques; in the same way, the technique of horn playing up to heights above the treble clef—really, it seems, a matter for the virtuoso horn players of Haydn's orchestra at Esterhaz and far too perilous for the general run of players (even Mozart's concertos for his friend Leutgeb did not ask their redoubtable player to scale any great heights)—was lost.

But Haydn's Trumpet Concerto, a delightful work written in 1796 (more than a quarter of a century before the Ninth Symphony), was composed for a keyed trumpet which had been invented in Vienna five years before; it had four brass keys, similar in nature and effect to the keys of woodwind instruments, which had the effect of virtually shortening the tube and thus converting it into other harmonic series, so that the skilled player, moving between the harmonic series available to him, could play a succession of complete octaves and thus act as a melodic instrument over a wide range. Despite Haydn's fine concerto, however, the keyed trumpet was not a success, but in 1815 valve trumpets of the modern type began to appear in Germany. The old trumpet tradition made their acceptance slow, and there is no evidence that Beethoven took any notice of them. Even in France, where old trumpet traditions did not apply so firmly, composers tended to import cornets into the orchestra to supply a brass treble part in the register where trumpets had no complete octave. The valve mechanism, which simply opened new lengths of tube as the pistons were depressed and thus lowered the instrument's harmonic series, was applied to the horn at about the same time, but was equally slow to gain acceptance; as late as 1865 Brahms declared that his Horn Trio was meant for a natural, and not a valved, horn.

Beethoven's addition of trombones to the brass of the orchestra in the Fifth, Sixth and Ninth Symphonies was primarily a means of avoiding fluctuations of dynamic intensity in passages where the harmony moves widely into distant keys when trumpets and horns are forced into silence. Like the strings and woodwind, trombones are capable of playing complete chromatic scales in every key, and while certain types of melody, notably the more intensely lyrical kind, are inappropriate to trombones, such exultantly ebullient tunes as that which open the finale of the Fifth Symphony and, incidentally, marks the début of the trombone in the symphony orchestra, are quite suited to its nature. But until the jubilation of the last movement of the Ninth Symphony is hushed into the solemnity of the vision of mankind united in the worship of a heavenly father, the trombone is used as the horns had been used before, to sustain and bind the harmony in passages where natural horns could not carry out this function.

Beethoven seems to have felt that some explanation of this new addition to the orchestra was necessary. In March, 1808, he wrote to Count Franz von Oppersdorff, to whom he sent copies of many of his works as they were completed and to whom for some time he intended to dedicate the Fifth Symphony (in the end it was the Fourth which carried the dedication) referring to what he must have realized could be regarded as a controversial feature of the score:

> The last movement of the symphony has three trombones and a piccolo—and, although, it is true, there are not three kettledrums, yet this combination of instruments will make more noise and, what is more, a more pleasing noise, than six kettledrums.*

"A more pleasing noise," however, is not a final and definitive description of the great addition of volume which Beethoven foresaw. "A more pleasing noise" in the theatre, where the work had its first performance, might well be a very displeasing in Count von Oppersdorff's music-room, but Beethoven does not seem to find it necessary to explain—if the rationalization ever occurred to him—that the evolution of his symphony's harmony, demanded the use of sustaining instruments which are not limited by the notes of a single harmonic series.

* *The Letters of Ludwig van Beethoven*, trans. Emily Anderson, Vol. 1, p. 189.

Actually, the innovation, while solving the harmonic problem, created its own extremely tricky problems of balance. To sustain string tone against the outburst of two trumpets, two horns and three trombones required far more instruments than could be found in most orchestras. Beethoven, mounting a public concert, arranged for the services of the orchestra of the Imperial Opera, of the Theater an der Wien or the Kärntnerthor Theater Orchestra; the Theater an der Wien had an orchestra of forty players in 1801, at the time of Beethoven's First Symphony, and the Kärntnerthor Theater kept about forty-six players. The first performance of the Fifth Symphony, with the Sixth, the Fourth Piano Concerto, the Choral Fantasia and several smaller pieces was given in the Theater an der Wien on 22nd December 1808, and for this event the orchestra could have been augmented, as was the orchestra assembled by Beethoven for the concert in the *Redoutensaal*, on 27th February 1814, for the first performance of the Seventh Symphony and *The Battle of Vittoria* together with another collection of smaller works.

According to Ludwig Spohr's *Autobiography*, all the musicians in Vienna who could "fiddle, blow or sing" were invited to take part in this later event, but Spohr does not mention the total of the forces assembled. With such an orchestra, it seems likely that a suitable number of string players was collected.

But the small court orchestras still existed in 1808 though the Napoleonic Wars were making their existence increasingly problematical, and though there seems to be no account of Count Oppersdorff's orchestra, the result of a performance by a court orchestra so typical that no one cared to draw attention to it meant a performance which must necessarily have been too unbalanced to be satisfactory. Beethoven's style of composition demanded, though it did not specify or always receive, strings in proportion to the weight of tone pitted against them in a *fortissimo tutti*; this, despite his deafness, was a fact he understood clearly. Beethoven himself explained in a letter to the Emperor's son the Archduke Rudolph, the most exalted of his patrons, pupils and friends, that the Seventh Symphony could not make its true effect with no more than four or five violins in each group.

The process of numerical expansion caused by Beethoven's additions to the orchestra gradually added to the number of strings, with the result that obedience to scores asking for only two flutes and two oboes meant that the voices of woodwind instruments were likely to be lost in all loud passages, but this, as double woodwind were components of the orchestra hallowed by tradition, was simply accepted until the 1860s or '70s, when composers began to ask for a strengthened woodwind section for the sake of more exact balance; in the 1890s, Mahler in Vienna brought down a storm of abuse on his head by announcing his 'retouching' of Beethoven's scores, by which he meant simply completing the brass parts left incomplete through the natural deficiencies of Beethoven's instruments, and multiplying the number of woodwind to maintain balance with the rest of the orchestra.

When Beethoven added a piccolo to the line of his woodwind band and a double bassoon to its bass, he seems to have felt these instruments to be quite capable of dealing, at least adequately, without assistance from other departments with passages at least as elaborate as those Mozart and himself had written for flutes, oboes and bassoons. The piccolo makes its entry in Twelve German Dances which he had composed for a court ball in 1795. It recurs in the finale of the Fifth Symphony, suggests the searing flashes of lightning of the 'Storm' of the *Pastoral Symphony*, in 1805 and 1808, and is heard in *Wellington's Sieg* or *The Battle of Vittoria*, a pot-boiling work from 1814 which also demands six trumpets. In 1810, it adds to the excitement of the triumph at the end of the *Egmont Overture* and from then on is a necessity in Beethoven's theatre music. The final version of *Fidelio*, however, omits the piccolo, perhaps because in revising the score in 1814, the insertion of an instrument which had not been used in the original version nine years before might demand too many changes in music which he considered satisfactory. The piccolo adds definition to Beethoven's top line, but it is possible to wonder whether he came to use it more frequently in the middle-period music because the deterioration in his hearing made it increasingly difficult for him to be aware of higher frequencies. It is only in the *Egmont Overture* and the *Pastoral Symphony* that it seems to be quite indispensable because it brings a new personality into the score.

The double bassoon, introduced in the Fifth Symphony and required in a number of later scores including that of the Ninth Symphony, simply added weight to the bass. Beethoven's bassoon parts, unlike those in the earlier works of Mozart and Haydn, do not simply play along with cellos and double basses in a general bass line; Beethoven uses it as the genuine bass of a woodwind choir which can, when necessary, carry the entire burden of his thought and, at other times can blend with the tones of strings and brass if a contrasting tone is not required of them.

Possibly the percussion gained as much as the brass from Beethoven. Berlioz, in his *Treatise on Modern Instrumentation*, published in Paris in 1842, draws attention quite frequently to Beethoven's use of timpani, especially when they are instructed to play quietly. A great *crescendo* at the end of the slow movement of the Fourth Symphony is followed by a *pianissimo* which throbs on two notes, C and G a fourth below, in the timpani, before two final *fortissimo* chords from the full orchestra conclude the movement. The long transition from the Scherzo to the Finale of the Fifth Symphony is accompanied by a steady, throbbing crotchet beat from the timpani, beating out a recurrent *pianissimo* until the violins, wandering lost above it, manage to struggle from C minor into the major and give the timpani a reason for a great *crescendo* as the light of a great C major chord comes flooding into the tunnel. From the beginning, Beethoven was inclined to extend the range of the violins. Haydn and Mozart seem to have been reluctant to ask them to climb more than an octave above the note of the open string on which they were playing, that is, to move above the fourth position, but even in the First Symphony, Beethoven sends them higher. Naturally, the Violin Concerto makes demands on its soloist that we can take for granted as being beyond the powers of the rank-and-file violinists in the orchestra, but in the Ninth Symphony not only does he confront violinists, as well as the rest of the orchestra, with difficult problems of co-ordination, balance and ensemble, but he also expected violinists to solve these problems while playing passages which were at heights most of his fiddlers cannot often have been asked to scale and at which the mere problem of remaining in tune may, in the 1820s, have seemed singularly hazardous.

Violas and cellos he treated on the whole with greater reserve. It is interesting to note how rarely either instrument is left to deliver any important theme or melody without support. As a youth in Bonn, Beethoven himself had been a viola player, but in his earlier orchestral works, any important entry finds them assisted either by second violins or by cellos. At the same time, they are expected to cope with very intricate passage work and to maintain good intonation and ensemble while they do so; whatever he had in mind, it was obviously not to make life easy for viola players. But when, for example, the gentle, meditative second theme of the Ninth Symphony's slow movement appears in the second violins, they are joined by violas; the first violins are left to play intricate variations on that theme without any assistance. Violas face a variety of demands: when the woodwind are set to vary the first theme in a passage of splendid richness, the first violins weave a beautiful filigree through the texture while the rest of the strings are left to play a *pizzicato* accompaniment which at one point briefly separates the violas into three parts; there are points at which the accompaniment where both second violins and violas each play independent parts while divided into two groups of each instrument. Not only are cellos and double-basses rarely separated, and then never for more than a few bars, but the cellos' period of exceptional prominence in the Fifth Symphony—its delivery of the melody of the slow movement over *pizzicato* double-basses—harnesses violas and cellos together.

These procedures may possibly have a greater influence on the actual tone colour of such passages in a modern performance than they had in Beethoven's own day; it may well be that violas rarely played independently, and that the cello melody of the Fifth Symphony's *Andante con moto* brings in the violas to double them because of the paucity of violas and cellos in the average orchestra to which Beethoven was accustomed. Many commentators ascribe the doubling in the Fifth Symphony to the composer's distrust of the cellists, but in many other matters where they are involved in difficult accompaniment figures, the composer leaves them alone to face their problems without help, and it is music which is melodically or thematically important which calls up other instruments to their assistance.

The recitative passages for unison cellos and double-basses at the beginning of the choral movement of the Ninth Symphony seemed not to have caused any special consternation among the cellists at the first performance, but later conductors found it impossible to entrust them to the double-basses, which left the cellists to tackle them without the support of the lower octave which adds to their power and authority. Wagner's historic performance of the work in Dresden in 1846 was apparently entirely faithful to the text (apart from the filling of gaps in the brass parts generally regarded as virtuous rather than selfish conductorial additions), naturally played the recitative passages as they were written, but twelve rehearsals for the double basses alone were necessary before Wagner was satisfied.

What in the 1820s was regarded as the near impossibility of these passages was rivalled by many others which pushed every instrument to the limit of its capacities. At the same time, the problems of balance, intonation and ensemble remained nearly insoluble until years after the composer's death. The compelling power and authority of Beethoven's music meant that it was frequently performed and that little by little orchestral players evolved a Beethoven style which at least saw them through in the days of minimal rehearsal. Franz Xaver Gebauer, choirmaster of the Augustinian Church in Vienna, instituted a weekly *Concert Spirituel* with the choir and orchestra of his church, and from 1819 onwards the concerts continued to draw audiences although they were nothing more than unrehearsed sight readings of the works in the programme, and Beethoven's symphonies were among the most popular works played although the performances must have been intolerably bad. It was in performances like Gebauer's that Beethoven's works began to dominate both orchestras and audiences although the composer's own attitude to them can be judged by his request to the publisher Siegmund Anton Steiner for a couple of "lavatory tickets" when he wanted to attend one of the *Concerts Spirituel*.

One thing about Beethoven's expansion of the orchestra should be noted; the addition of instruments simply to make 'effects' was not among his interests; what he demanded was more melodic and harmonic definition and power. In the music for *The Ruins of Athens*, and in the tenor solo of the Ninth Symphony's Finale, he asked for 'Turkish music'—the bass drum, cymbals and triangle which Mozart had used to provide a splash of local colour in the Jannissaries' Chorus of *Die Entführung aus dem Serail* and which Haydn, in London, had demanded in his *Military Symphony* (No. 100). In *The Ruins of Athens*, 'Turkish music' had been appropriate as local colour; in the Ninth Symphony it emphasizes the popular jollity appropriate to words which speak of humanity hurrying together down the road to joy. There is no question of such additions being called into action simply as musical effects.

Beethoven's orchestral innovations were apparently called into being in the interests of clarity of thought or weight of emphasis rather than for the sake of sonorous, sensuous beauty; the "better sound" of the Fifth Symphony's piccolo, trombones and double-bassoon does not seem to have been "better" because it was richer in colour. Nevertheless, Beethoven's orchestra produced music of great beauty, as in, for example, the slow movements of the Fifth Piano Concerto, the *Pastoral* and the Ninth Symphonies although Beethoven's orchestration invariably puts sound at the service of meaning.

SIX

Opera, Concerts and Composers

The orchestra as Beethoven left it was capable of following and sustaining the intricate harmonic processes which he followed. Though the melodic contributions of the brass were necessarily still limited, clarinets were no longer occasional instruments. The weakness of the bass line had led Beethoven to support it with the double-bassoon, but double-bassoons were not widely known outside Vienna. With bassoons doubling cellos in *forte* and *fortissimo* passages, and with double bassoon doubling double-bass, the foundation bass tone was more or less secure although there was no brass instrument in the double-bass register and whenever string tone was inappropriate or provided the wrong colour, the low orchestral double-bass became desirable.

It was for this reason that the orchestra of the Paris Opéra added an ophicleide to its forces. The ophicleide was not a particularly agile instrument and its tone tended to blare, but it provided a firm foundation for wind tone. Berlioz, in his book *A Treatise on Modern Instrumentation*, published in 1842, wrote of ophicleide solos (very popular in the mid-nineteenth century), that they sounded like a bull which has gone into a drawing-room to play games.

The ophicleide was not the first instrument to attempt to act as a brass double-bass. In eighteenth-century France and England, a bass serpent—an instrument of very wide bore, made of wood bound in leather and making its notes through finger holes—had been used quite extensively. The huge Handel festivals in England, which began in London in 1784 with an orchestra of 152 strings, fifty-nine woodwind, thirty brass, organ and drums, had fifteen double-basses and one double-bassoon; this meant a rescoring of Handel's music which, when all the 520 performers were storming in heaven in one of the great choruses—"Unto us a Child is born", "Hallelujah" or "Worthy is the Lamb"—left the double-bass line sounding undernourished until the ophicleide was imported into England in the late 1820s.

German composers of large-scale works therefore tried to avoid the necessity of any brass voice in the double-bass register, and Berlioz, the great orchestral expert, included the ophicleide only among the four separated brass groups in the *Dies Irae* of his *Requiem* and in the massed brass of his *Symphonie Funébre et Triomphale*. The ophicleide was ousted by the tuba, which established itself quite rapidly after its first appearance in 1845.

To some extent, the need for a brass double-bass equivalent was a matter of the size of an orchestra. Beethoven's later concerts were given with the largest orchestras he could muster, but there is no clear account of the balance prevailing within them. The Ninth Symphony asks for flutes, oboes, clarinets and bassoons, and as these divide into two parts, it is plain that he expected at least two of each. In the last movement, however, when they are playing *fortissimo* in their least penetrating middle register, with trombones marked *forte* and a choir marked *fortissimo*, it is plain that the dynamic level round the woodwind must be kept down if the handful of woodwind is going to affect the tone of the ensemble in any way. Similarly, we do not know how many strings Beethoven regarded as necessary, or whether he anticipated the use of quadruple woodwind.

The result is that after the Ninth Symphony the size of the orchestra could no longer be taken for granted. In 1781, the *Gewandhaus* Orchestra, in Leipzig, had four first and four second violins. In 1783 Haydn's orchestra, at Esterhaz, had six firsts and seven seconds while the Imperial Opera, in Vienna, had six of each. The orchestra which Salomon, in London, assembled for his subscription concerts with Haydn had from twelve to sixteen violins— six or eight to each part; each of these orchestras had double woodwind, two horns, two trumpets and drums. Exceptionally in Germany, the *Gewandhaus* Orchestra had three bassoons. In Vienna, there were four horns, and four horns were available in the Prague Opera. As the number of strings increased to match Beethoven's implicit demands, there was no move to add to the woodwind in order that the balance could be preserved in works by Haydn and Mozart. Wagner began to specify the number of strings (and incidentally of harps) which he regarded as necessary, regarding sixteen first and sixteen second violins as necessary both for tone and for balance with the rest of his orchestra, and the lower strings were built up in proportion to the violins, but the eighteenth-century principle that three or four first violins and three or four seconds could maintain a balance with double woodwinds seems to have been forgotten. No authority suggested that to balance thirty-two violins, it would be necessary to use treble or even quadruple woodwind.

The resulting confusion about proportions remains a problem. Until the end of the nineteenth century, neither conductors nor audiences were much concerned to establish the balance preferred by composers of the Classic age, which Beethoven and his predecessors took for granted, so that it seemed natural, as gramophone records from before the Second World War show, to hear the symphonies of Haydn and Mozart with double woodwind playing against a full post-Wagnerian complement of strings. Under these circumstances, not only was the music's athletic ease of movement in danger of being lost through the luxurious thickness of string tone but the crisper, brighter colours of the woodwind, with its added spriteliness or poignancy, tended to be smothered by the weight of the strings.

At the same time, the size of concert halls built to accommodate very large audiences makes it impossible for orchestras balanced according to late eighteenth-century principles to achieve the effects of strength, power and forcefulness which the contemporaries of Haydn and Mozart noted in their music. Even the Beethoven symphonies played by an orchestra with strings augmented to Wagner's requirements leaves the woodwind proportionately weak in passages marked *forte* and louder. Wagner, whose doctrines gained something like Papal authority over most musicians before the end of the nineteenth century, automatically used valve horns and valve trumpets to enable them to follow the harmony implied in those silences forced on Beethoven's natural brass. Other conductors followed in his footsteps, and still do so, taking it for granted that Beethoven could never have wished for the fluctuations of intensity and dynamics forced on him by the instruments he used. In 1900, conducting the Vienna Philharmonic Orchestra, Mahler's naïve honesty led him to write a programme note in which he explained how he had, so to speak, completed Beethoven's wind parts and augmented the woodwind to achieve the proportions which Beethoven would have expected. "In Beethoven's day," his note explained, "the entire orchestra was smaller than a modern string section. If we fail to bring the rest of the orchestra into a proper numerical relation with the strings, we cannot possibly get the right effect."

The building up of the string orchestra not only imperilled the traditional orchestral balance but increased the necessity for completing the brass choir with a genuine double-bass instrument. The predominance of reed tone in the woodwind—only flute and piccolo do not produce their sounds through a vibrating reed—created a sufficient homogeneity of tone to allow the woodwind to function more than adequately as a separate choir, but the brass—trumpets, horns and trombones—remain obstinately individual. Not only did the choir lack a true bass, but the individuality of the brass section tended to persuade composers to restrict the soprano of the brass choir, the trumpet, for moments of climax and for special effects. The addition of the ophicleide added to the diverse qualities of sound among the brass; it did not blend easily with the rest of the voices of the section.

Beethoven's orchestra, a powerfully rhetorical ensemble unrivalled when oratory is the composer's business, proved to be universally popular and universally significant, but it was not the sound which his immediate successors wished to produce or attempted to achieve. Schubert, who was twenty-seven years younger than Beethoven and survived him for only about eighteen months—he was born in 1797 and died in 1828—never aimed at Beethoven's violent intensity, composing passages no less powerful but aiming always at a smoother texture and an extended lyrical appeal.

From his schooldays in the choir of St Stephen's Cathedral in Vienna and at the Imperial Seminary, the most highly regarded secondary school in the capital, Schubert was familiar with the orchestra as a player and occasional conductor. His first six symphonies were played by the school orchestra or by an amateur ensemble which grew up round the Schubert family's private, domestic performances of chamber music. The Sixth Symphony, written when he was twenty, had apparently one performance in his lifetime—from his amateur orchestra. His operas and large-scale church music were written partly at least to establish himself in one of those areas of music where he could look for regular and profitable employment, and they all use the orchestra with great, usually unobtrusive skill. The Rossini mania which affected Vienna as it affected the rest of Europe in the years after the Napoleonic Wars, prompted the two Overtures in the Italian Style, works naturally gay, elegant and as athletic as anything by the composer who was their inspiration. Like the early symphonies, they are scored for an orchestra smaller than that of Beethoven's later symphonies.

Schubert's problem was to reconcile the powerful symphonic thought of such works as the 'Unfinished' Symphony and the 'Great' C major with a naturally and gloriously personal lyrical style. A Symphony in E minor and major, which is completely sketched but not completely orchestrated, was a step in this direction after early symphonies in which the beauty of the music does not attempt the marvellous organic growth and the sense of power which are overwhelming in the 'Unfinished' (Eighth) and 'Great' C major (Ninth) Symphonies. Schubert, whose symphonies involve not only the dominant and tonic as functional keys but often begin their recapitulations in the subdominant (so that a work in C major is based on C major, G major and F major) evolves rather than forces his way to new tonalities. He could recognize relationships, and demonstrate them in music with an undisturbed flow of music. The power of his music is cumulative, not explosive.

The 'Unfinished' Symphony makes us free of Schubert's own private world of lyrical expressiveness, with, for example, the oboes of the opening calling us into fantasy over a restless string accompaniment, and the clarinet of the slow movement singing of a poignant inner happiness. Instrument and theme, in the second movement, seem to belong together, as indissolubly married as mutually devoted lovers. The C major Ninth is not a means of entry to a marvellous private world. It is huge both in length and in its eventfulness. The horn call of its opening is really a call to action—not to marching in step with the world but to a pilgrim's slower, more meditative progress through a colourful and diverse world. For a long time orchestral players were puzzled by it, for if its trombones are thematically, and not harmonically, motivated, violinists were shocked to find that for long periods their function is to beat out dance-like rhythms in unchanging harmonies; but the work is the link between the classic symphony of Beethoven and the freer, expressively orientated symphony of the Romantic composers and the monumental symphonies which Bruckner was to write after 1860.

Mendelssohn brought the final glories of Schubert's expanded symphonies to the world's attention, already an experienced conductor before he was appointed conductor of the Leipzig *Gewandhaus* Orchestra in 1834, when he was only twenty-five. Mendelssohn was a very successful conductor, universally admired for the elegance, grace and control which he gave to the works he conducted, and for the shapeliness with which he endowed them. But shapeliness and elegance are only secondary qualities of great epic works like the symphonies of Beethoven and of Schubert's C major, of which he gave the first performance and which he conducted in London at a Philharmonic Concert, with a hostile orchestra which found the work boring and tuneless. As Mendelssohn, between about 1825 and 1840, could do no wrong in the eyes of audiences all over England and Germany, and as he was ready to find room in his programmes for any promising new works, his influence on audiences was profound. As a composer, he had neither the capacity nor the wish to write on an epic scale, and it is simply the course of musical history, the process of evolution which led from Beethoven to Wagner, and on to the symphonies of Bruckner and Mahler, that encourages us to undervalue his own orchestral music.

The great qualities of Mendelssohn's music are rhythmic vitality, ease and grace of movement, elegance both of style and of state-

ment. Approaching the orchestra from a standpoint quite remote
from that of Beethoven, once the magic of his personality had dis-
appeared from concert platforms, his music was increasingly pushed
aside while the consequences of Beethoven's music were worked
out by later composers.

Whatever Mendelssohn did was done beautifully, with scrupulous
effectiveness and polish. His use of the orchestra is utterly individual and appealing, and always in keeping with the purpose for
which it is employed. Lightness and grace, freedom and swiftness
of movement, are not the most prominent characteristics of the
music composed in Central Europe in the Beethoven-obsessed
nineteenth century, and these are the qualities always at his command, but exploited with such skill that it never seems that his
orchestra is kept under restraint; such movements as the Saltarello
finale of the 'Italian' Symphony sound, for all their limited dynamic
range—for Mendelssohn never scores a work to make an overwhelming noise—sound like explosions of pure energy. Even in the
oratorios, *St Paul* and *Elijah*, the *Lobgesang* (*Song of Praise*) which
follows the pattern of Beethoven's Choral Symphony by creating
three orchestral movements which lead to a choral finale with
religious words, or in the symphony written for the 300th anniversary of the religious settlement in Germany, the 'Reformation'
Symphony, Mendelssohn reaches a grandeur, serious and thoughtful
rather than spiritually exalted, of his own thorough, spare, athletic
orchestration which is never thick and never crowded in texture.
The early *Midsummer Night's Dream* overture, in its fantastic
lightness, is a composition rivalled for its speed, dexterity and use
of the orchestra to produce an unearthly orchestra only by Berlioz's
far more elaborate "Queen Mab" Scherzo in his *Romeo and Juliet*
Symphony. The originality of such movements as the slow movement of the 'Reformation' Symphony, with violins singing what
the eighteenth century would probably have called an arioso—
music too declamatory to be an aria, with an eloquent, pointed
but restrained accompaniment in which the woodwind provide the
essential colours—is again a use of the orchestra not only splendidly
skilful and precisely calculated but as moving as it is original.

It was during Mendelssohn's years as conductor that the *Gewandhaus* Orchestra became fully professional. It has always been in
the forefront of 'modern' music. From 1795 onwards it cultivated
Beethoven's music, playing each new work as soon as it was obtain-
able, and though Wagner, as an adolescent, had unhappy memories of some of these performances—the Choral Symphony, which
he heard in a muddled and ill-rehearsed performance when he was
eighteen, remained in his mind as an example of what should never
be allowed to happen—the most difficult and thoughtful music was

accepted by an audience which, to the surprise of William Sterndale Bennett, the best English composer of the early nineteenth century, included not only the well-to-do and the prosperous (as audiences in England did) but also the boots of the hotel at which he was staying on his first visit to Leipzig, in 1836. When Mendelssohn had become conductor, two years before, and until the player had finished his university course, the timpanist was a theology student. After that, the orchestra became completely professional.

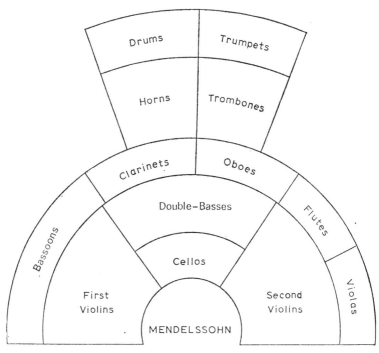

Mendelssohn: Leipzig *Gewandhaus*, 1835

Similar concert societies, most of them largely amateur, grew up in a large number of German towns, largely because of the great prestige given to symphony concerts by Beethoven's works, which joined those of Haydn and Mozart in providing a repertoire for orchestras all over Europe, but the development of professional orchestras was much slower. Regular concerts by the court orchestra, the descendants of the great Mannheim Orchestra, had been given in Munich since 1811. The Elector had inherited the Bavarian throne and taken most of his orchestra to Munich with him in 1779, but outside the court there was little musical activity; amateur orchestral societies arose and withered away, because, to a large extent, of the accessibility of the court music. The professional concerts of the *Musikalische Akademie*, as the court orchestra called itself when it gave public concerts, was the idea of the senior members of the Court Orchestra itself, under the inspiration of their *Kapellmeister*, Joseph Winter. They gained the permission of the King, Maximilian I, to give subscription concerts in the *Redoutensaal* of the court on up to twelve evenings in the year when they were not required for other duties. The profits of the concerts were to be divided among the players who took part in them—an inducement to underpaid musicians to make a success of this new venture, which they did to such an extent that in 1825, after the concerts had left the *Redoutensaal* for the theatre, the Bavarian Government decided to build a concert hall, the Odeon, especially for the 'Academy' concerts. For a long time, none of the other centres of opera in Germany bothered to copy Munich's example.

Vienna, of course, had frequent concerts but, until 1818, no regular concert organization and no regular concerts by a professional orchestra until the middle of the century. Composers like Mozart and Beethoven could rent a theatre, with its orchestra, for concerts at which they brought their new works to the widest possible public. Similar concerts were organized for the benefit of singers and instrumentalists, but a regular concert series was not given until 1782, when Phillip Martin, at first with the collaboration of Mozart, began to give concerts in the Pavilion of the Augarten, a royal park, which the Emperor permitted them to use. Mozart financed subscription concerts of his own, but it seems to be impossible to gain any real information about the orchestra which played either for Mozart or for Martin; probably both were mainly amateur ensembles with professional 'stiffening' to play the less popular instruments—trumpets, drums, bassoons and possibly horns. The presence of a pool of freelance professional musicians in Vienna made such an arrangement possible.

The *Tonkünstlersocietät*, an organization of professional musicians who elected their own new members from musicians who seem to have reached sufficient eminence, gave two or three concerts each year, usually for charity. The society itself chose the soloists, and an invitation to take part in any programme was regarded as a high honour. Such spasmodic events, however notable they were in themselves, did not amount to the regular diet of music provided by any lesser but accomplished orchestra in which a conspectus of available work can be presented, but in 1813 the *Gesellschaft der Musikfreunde* began its activities; 'Philharmonic Society' would be an acceptable translation of the name, which

G

literally means "Society of the Friends of Music". The *Gesellschaft* consisted of members some of whom were notable professional musicians but most of whom were eminent amateurs from the upper classes or the well-to-do business men and bureaucrats. Men like Beethoven's patron and friend Prince Lobkowsky became members because, for one reason or other—most often the difficulty of maintaining their own orchestras because of the rise in prices and inflation at the end of the Napoleonic Wars—they found it easier to support a widely based body than to maintain musicians of their own. The *Gesellschaft der Musikfreunde* gave regular concerts with an orchestra made up of amateur and professional musicians, directed by members of its organizing committee, and it became responsible for important performances and commissions, and for the foundation in 1817 of the Vienna Conservatoire.

Regular professional concerts did not become a feature of Viennese musical life until 1842, when members of the Opera Orchestra decided that the popularity of their regular Pension Fund Concert (their only appearance in the year outside the theatre's orchestra pit), warranted an attempt to give regular concerts at times when they were not occupied in the theatre. Concerts were given spasmodically but more frequently until 1860, when the orchestra gained permission to give regular concerts on Sunday mornings as the Vienna Philharmonic Orchestra. In this guise it was a self-governing body of musicians which elected its own conductor and undertook all the organization of its concerts, including publicity and the sale of tickets.

Up till this time, the concert orchestras with the highest reputation were those of the Philharmonic Society in London, founded in 1813, and the orchestra of the *Société des Concerts du Conservatoire*, in Paris, founded in 1828. Both were at least partly the result of the enormous international prestige of Beethoven's music. In London, regular concerts by professional orchestras lapsed after the two series of concerts promoted by Johann Peter Salomon, who had invited Haydn to London as composer and director of two series of concerts (1791–3 and 1793–5). Salomon gave concerts in 1796 with the collaboration of notable singers, and was responsible for a performance of Haydn's *The Creation* in 1800. The success of his collaboration with Haydn had wiped out a slightly older organization, the Professional Concerts, with which he had originally been associated and which had been organized by a group of professional musicians, so that for some years London, where concert music was already an old tradition, had found only occasional concerts available and no professional orchestra in regular existence to play them.

The absence of any such orchestra led to the formation of the

Philharmonic Society (which became the "Royal Philharmonic Society" when it reached its centenary). This was the creation of thirty professional musicians working in London. As well as English musicians—the composer Henry Bishop, William Horsely, most notable for his part-songs and glees, William Shield, who wrote enjoyable ballad operas and theatre music, and the younger Samuel Webbe, another composer of effective glees, Sir George Smart, organist and church music composer who had known Beethoven in Vienna, as had the pianist Charles Neate, who claimed to be Beethoven's only English pupil—there were a number of foreign musicians working in England—Salomon, Clementi the pianist-composer who had been set to play in a pianist duel with Mozart, J. B. Cramer and one of the Moralt family, who had been notable musicians since the great days of the Mannheim Orchestra. The society began its life with a great enthusiasm for Beethoven's music, which had a prominent place in its programmes from the start.

Though they depended on the subscriptions of wealthy patrons, its own committee of musicians was responsible for the entire organization. Its orchestra was that of the Opera, so that Philharmonic Concerts were originally given on Monday evenings, which were traditionally opera-free. The conductors were the leader of the orchestra and a committee member sitting with the score at a redundant piano; these duties were shared by the various members of the committee in turn. Choral and orchestral music was played, but no solo work was heard until 1819, when a Beethoven piano concerto was played; vocal solos were not admitted until later, when failing finances made it convenient to accept the services of the great heroes and heroines of the opera, to fill the hall. Apart from the music of Beethoven, whose Ninth Symphony the Society commissioned and which the composer dedicated both to it and to the King of Prussia, it formed friendly relations with Spohr, from whom it commissioned the Second, Sixth and Eighth Symphonies, joined in the general idolization of Mendelssohn and commissioned his Trumpet Overture as well as giving the first performance in England of the C minor and *Italian* Symphonies, the *Melusine* and *Calm Sea and Prosperous Voyage* overtures.

Originally the Society was financially as well as artistically successful, so that it could afford to commission works from international celebrities, Spohr as well as Mendelssohn and Cherubini, and to encourage English music; new works submitted to the Society were tried out in the hearing of the committee with a view to their public performance, but unfortunately none of those received was judged worthy of inclusion in any of the Society's programmes. By 1842, however, the Society found itself short of money and had to abandon the policy of commissioning new works and trying out uncommissioned ones. To try to rebuild its fortunes, in 1845 for the first time it appointed a permanent conductor, Sir Henry Bishop, who resigned almost immediately because of ill-health and was succeeded by the Italian-born conductor of the opera, Michael Costa, who conducted the Society's concerts for eight years.

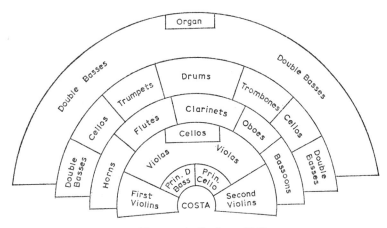

Philharmonic Society, 1846

The standard of performance in these years was not high. In 1825, the first performance in London of Beethoven's Ninth Symphony, conducted by a reluctant George Smart, seems to have been disastrous. Costa, a strict disciplinarian though a limited interpreter of orchestral music, was the first musician to preside with real authority over the orchestra since the visits of Spohr and Mendelssohn. The orchestra was not only inefficiently led; it was, too, at the mercy of the 'deputy system'. The engagement of the musicians was not for a season at a time but simply for each individual concert, so that membership of the orchestra meant work for little financial reward; players faced with a clash of engagements therefore chose the more profitable of them and merely sent a deputy to the other; the deputy might attend only the concert after the original player had been present at rehearsals. The deputy system continued to bedevil London music until 1904.

The orchestra of the *Société des Concerts du Conservatoire*, created in Paris in 1928, had the advantage of the hall of the Conservatoire for its concerts, was partially supported by the government through its association with the Conservatoire, and had a thorough, determined conductor, François Habeneck, who was more than anyone else the creator of the orchestra. Habeneck was determined to give performances of the Beethoven symphonies which would be worthy of the music and refused to put works into his programmes until the orchestra had grown to understand them through extended rehearsals. Wagner, living in poverty in Paris from 1839 to 1842, was overwhelmed by the Beethoven performances which he heard from Habeneck and the Conservatoire Orchestra, as was Berlioz, who knew Habeneck personally and regarded the great conductor as one of his persecutors in the Parisian musical establishment.

The speciality of the Conservatoire Orchestra was the time it found for really exhaustive rehearsal which enabled every player to undertake his part with complete familiarity with the music and a clear sense of how to overcome the problems it presented. Few of the German orchestras, even those of the great theatres and musical centres, had learned to approach the scores with equal scrupulousness or could afford the time in which to apply it. After the death of Beethoven, there was no immediate continuation of the supply of great orchestral works except those of Mendelssohn and Schubert. Few continental organizations were ready to commission works in the style and on the scale of the London Philharmonic Society's commissions to Spohr and Mendelssohn, and later in the century to Dvořák, though the major German festivals attempted to find new large-scale choral and orchestral works to be their centrepiece. Thus, a composer devoting several months to the composition of an orchestral work—and the size of the post-Beethoven orchestra means that the mere task of writing out an orchestral score absorbs a long time—could hardly expect to earn any money from it even if he were lucky enough to secure a performance of it; a commission secures the composer some money to live on; publication secured him some return for his efforts, but few countries admitted the composer's right to a fee for performances until the end of the century. On the other hand, the composer of an opera which won the attention of a theatre management (and operas were in much greater demand though not all succeeded) could expect a reasonable fee from any major opera house, and in Paris a continuing royalty on performances; the continuing royalty was an idea gradually applied throughout Europe; the composer could then bargain for performances in other theatres so long as he kept the essential material—the score which set out the work and its musical organization for the conductor, and the orchestral parts—in his own hands to be hired by any theatre which contemplated a production of his work.

For these reasons, rather than for any presumed lack of inspiration or ambition, the most ambitious work was still composed for the opera house. A composer like Weber, who was born in 1786 and depended for his earnings on concert tours as a virtuoso pianist until 1813, travelled, as virtuosi naturally did, with a stock of concert works which he would play, usually unrehearsed, with the orchestras, amateur or professional, of the towns on whatever route he had planned. A concert musician naturally travelled with his stock-in-trade, and established his reputation as a composer by doing so. Weber's stock-in-trade naturally included not only the *Konzertstück* for piano and orchestra but also the Clarinet Concertos and Concertino written for his friend the clarinettist Heinrich Bärmann, who shared several tours with him. As soon as he had won a resident position—*Kapellmeister* of the Prague Opera in 1813—Weber set out to fulfil his destiny as composer of German operas in his new revolutionary nationalist style.

The most successful composer of the period which coincided with the last decade of Beethoven's life was Rossini. Wherever concerts were available, Beethoven's music triumphed over performances which, more often than not, must have been little better than travesties of his intentions. Perhaps because of the long miseries of the Revolutionary and Napoleonic Wars, and perhaps because, after 1815, a rigid censorship in German-speaking Europe discouraged any approach to serious composition which might reflect unenthusiastically on the society of the day was discouraged, Rossini's operas, brilliantly written for fine singers and usually far from any current controversy in their subject matter, captured all the world's important opera houses. His music, and his personality, made a deep impression wherever he went, particularly in Vienna, London and Paris, where Italian music, unwelcome at the Paris Opéra, had its own home in the Théâtre Italien, and where he was commissioned to write in the French style for the Opéra, officially the Académie Royale de Musique, tailoring his powers to suit idiosyncratic French taste.

Rossini's greatest gifts were an almost infallible sense of theatrical effect and an unfailing gift for expressive, elegant vocal melody with a reserve of power rarely called into action but released at times in grandly impressive choral writing. To his Italian contemporaries he was a genius seduced and corrupted by the temptations of the orchestra; even the French novelist Stendhal, a great admirer eager not to admit a single critical word into his biography of the great composer, felt that from *Tancredi*, first produced in 1813, onwards, Rossini had paid too much attention to the orchestra. Beautiful melodies, which could have been given to singers, were squandered on instruments, and orchestral accompaniments became too full of independent invention, and too detailed, to allow the audience to concentrate exclusively on the vocal line. Schubert, growing up in Vienna during the period of Rossini mania, wrote his two Overtures in the Italian style in 1817 under the intoxicating influence of the Italian master.

There seems to have been little in the Roman, Milanese, and Venetian orchestras for which the early operas were written to inspire Rossini. But *Elisabetta, Regina d'Ingilterra,* written in 1815 for the first-rate orchestra of the San Carlo Opera, in Naples he abandoned the custom of setting most of the recitative in the *secco* style, for voice and harpsichord only; recitatives with orchestral accompaniment were determined to point every stroke of drama with appropriate colour. The new importance of the orchestra was only one of Rossini's unorthodoxies which collectively scandalized the conservatives in their Italian audience, who tolerated his unorthodoxies because the operas still gave superb melodies to superbly trained singers and took control of the stage with indefatigable vitality. Revising two Italian works, *Maometto II* (1820) and *Mose in Egitto* (1818) for the Paris Opéra, where they became *Le Siége de Corinthe* and *Moise,* he added to the power of their choruses and elaborated their orchestration because the orchestra of the Opéra was better equipped and better in style than any orchestra with which he had previously worked. The opening of the Overture of *William Tell* (which for many years was one of the most popular and inescapable of operatic overtures) presents, even apart from the suave beauty of its opening for four-part divided cellos, a remarkable combination of eloquence, fluent lightness, proportion, grace and atmospheric appropriateness. Rossini's effects are never disproportionate to the fluency and energy of his music. They never become more than incidental to the music's real expressive purpose.

To look at a Rossini score, with its light accompaniment and effective simplicity of orchestration, is to find the criticism of his over-elaborate orchestration almost ridiculous; what irritated Italian contemporaries among his critics was probably the colour brought into his accompaniments by his obvious pleasure in woodwind tone. When Rossini and Wagner met in Paris in 1860, the long-retired Rossini, who had composed no major work since *William Tell* in 1829, said that he had learned more from studying the scores of Haydn and Mozart than from all the lessons he had ever received. One of the most valuable lessons that the masters taught him was how to use the orchestra, particularly the distinctive colours of the woodwind, to contribute to the effect of music designed for voices without dispossessing the voices of their supremacy, applying the lessons of Mozart and Haydn to *bel canto* opera. Among the composers of Rossini's lifetime, only Schubert never claimed to despise, or spent time in despising, or affecting to deplore, the easy effectiveness of his music; but even Weber, who could see nothing in Rossini's music but a cynical exploitation of easy effects, found himself placing and accompanying important woodwind passages in the style Rossini had developed. Weber's orchestra, however, like Weber's melodies, still sounds original and entirely characteristic. Weber, although he was a fine concert pianist, was also fascinated by the timbres of the woodwind instruments, writing concertos for clarinet and for bassoon, two Clarinet Concertinos, and Variations for Bassoon and Orchestra as well as a Concertino for Horn. Possibly the maturity of the clarinet in Weber's youth, together with his meeting with Heinrich Bärmann, who used an improved instrument more flexible than earlier clarinets, influenced his writing for the instrument.

But it is the opera which most effectively roused Weber's imagination. There is always an eager, ardent enthusiasm about his orchestral works. Accompanying figures have an impetuosity of their own, and his overtures always reach their climax in a fine violin melody of great energy and excitement. He was a master of atmosphere, and *Der Freischütz*, an opera which grows out of German folk tales and the vivid imaginative qualities of the new German Romanticism of the early nineteenth century, exists in an atmosphere of forests, mountains and rocky chasms in which the forces of a somewhat pantomime-style good and evil exist. These are things which permeate the German Romantic imagination. But Weber was conscious, too, of nature and its sounds, as an immediate delight rather than as a symbol; breezes and the rustling of leaves, forest noises picked up by quiet brass and woodwind as well as the eerie demons and black magic of the Wolf's Glen, where the hero trades with the devil for magic bullets, still sound as new as they did at the first performance in 1821, and if behind the originality is a certain lovable naïvety, the naïvety was there as a branch of the originality—the result of taking folk tales with artistic seriousness—in 1821.

Weber had a fine ear for unusual sonorities; the opening phrases of Agatha's song *Leise, leise, fromme weise* in *Der Freischütz* are accompanied by violins in four parts with a viola providing the bass. A clarinet in A provides the bass to a lyrical cello melody in the *Oberon* overture; the clarinet part lies very low in the instrument's register, and between it and the melody are the violas, doubling the melody a third below; this inversion of the orchestra makes use of the melancholy of the clarinet's low register while exploiting the plangency of the cellos and providing an accompaniment with the same tonal qualities as the melody. The storm in the forest suggested in the *Der Freischütz* overture is conveyed largely by trombone chords in the bass, *tremolando* strings and long lyrical phrases for the clarinets, with the dynamics of each part separately marked for clarity of effect: a long-held E flat on the bass trombone lies beneath an E flat chord distributed through the string *tremolando*; the trombone remains quiet while the strings play a *crescendo* which reaches a *forte* marking a mere semiquaver after a *fortissimo* entry by the horns, which immediately lose the power to play *forte* as the strings move from their restrained to a climax and a solo clarinet enters *fortissimo* and remains at that level while the strings continue at not much more than a whisper. It is not only Weber's precisely graded dynamics, of course, that are novel. The dynamic levels had to be differentiated in this way because there is nothing in earlier music which could stand as a precedent for a conductor working on this passage, and such directions are the only possible guidance to the composer's effect as he aims to find a means of transforming natural sound into music. He is not trying to evoke natural sound by musical means, or to represent it in some traditional musical way. He is, so to speak, trying to achieve the effect of trees and wind if they played musical instruments, to take his music direct from them.

Weber died in 1826, a year before Beethoven, having found not only new subject matter and a new style for opera but also having brought nature into music while other composers had only dealt with human responses to nature. Seven years after his death his friend Giacomo Meyerbeer, a composer who had been a youthful associate of Weber's at Darmstadt and whose career had up to that time been a series of promising starts, as an orchestral composer, and as an adoring disciple of Rossini, produced his opera *Robert le Diable* in Paris. He had previously produced the most successful of his Rossinian works, *Il Crociato in Egitto*, at the Théâtre Italien, but *Robert le Diable* was in French style and produced at the Opéra itself.

French opera, the idiosyncratic form which stemmed from Lully, Rameau and the operas by which Gluck reformed and gave dramatic vitality to the Italian opera of the late eighteenth century, had grown into a monumentally impressive style through the work of Spontini, an Italian composer born in 1774 who, after an initial success in his homeland, had arrived in Paris in 1803 and composed for the Théâtre Italien. He became a favourite of the Empress Josephine and composed a cantata to celebrate her husband's victory at Austerlitz in 1806, by which time, his masterpiece *La Vestale* was in rehearsal for the Opéra, where, despite opposition on both musical and unmusical, political and nationalistic grounds, it was a success. It subordinated personal emotions to a drama of social causes, demanded the maximum of impressiveness from a great chorus and large orchestra but still provided singers with music which would display their vocal qualities. In 1810, *La*

Vestale provided Paris audiences with the loudest music they had so far heard, so that Parisian wits told the story of the patient whose doctor had advised him to attend *La Vestale* to see what effect it might have upon his sadly impaired hearing. Doctor and patient went together to the performance and at the end of the first act the rapturous patient applauded vociferously. "It's wonderful, Doctor," he said to his companion, "I heard every note!" "What's that? What's that?" asked the doctor. "I can't hear a word you say—I've gone deaf."

Spontini continued to compose in Paris for the Théâtre Italien and for the Opéra until, in 1819, he accepted the appointment of conductor at the Berlin Opera, and most of the remainder of his life—he died in 1851—was spent in Germany as composer and conductor, developing the style of *La Vestale*, the work which gave France its nineteenth-century operatic model for what became known as 'Grand Opera'.

Meyerbeer learnt the grand style from Spontini, and *Robert le Diable* follows in the footsteps of *Le Vestale*, Rossini's *William Tell* and Auber's *La Muette de Portici* (which Victorian England knew as *Masaniello*). These were operas in which public causes were dramatized and personal relationships were subsumed in them. Such works were designed to appeal to the new Paris audience drawn from the successful bourgeoisie, a post-revolutionary generation who demanded elaborate spectacle, pageantry and processions, coronations, royal weddings and natural or man-made catastrophes on the largest scale. Their tastes were catered for by commercial managements to whom the Opéra was leased by the government and who ran it for their own profit. The most elaborate stage designs and décor, a fine orchestra, a huge and well-trained choir and an attractive *corps-de-ballet* were all essential; the Dumb Girl of Portici brings the final curtain of Auber's work down by leaping into Vesuvius whilst the volcano erupts, and whoever followed that work had, if possible, to find something at least equally remarkable in event and stage picture to rival that conclusion. The composer had also to remember that the ballet should be part of Act II, so that balletomanes and the fashionable young men could watch the dancing or the girls after dinner, without having to endure an unballetic Act I.

Meyerbeer, as soon as *Robert le Diable* was seen, dominated French opera and found himself the leader of modern operatic taste. His rise was due to several things; for a start, he could compose what the public wanted with complete sincerity; his taste corresponded with that of his audience, and he was a skilful musician who, if his invention was limited, could always find convincing music for the great show pieces which the audience required. He was influenced, too, by the Opéra itself, and by the facilities it put into his hands. Its orchestra contained about eighty players (there were seventy-eight in 1803 and eighty-five in 1847), among whom were players of instruments not normally found in other orchestras such as the ophicleide and the cornet (the modern brass instrument, not the Renaissance cornett); the percussion section invariably contained bass drum, triangle and cymbals; it maintained four horns, three trombones and four bassoons; the number of violas was proportionate to the size of the violin and cello sections. Since the days of Lully, French taste had demanded woodwind tone more penetrating, and more aggressive, than had pleased other countries, and the extra bassoons were needed to balance the stronger treble woodwinds, and it made it possible for composers to write for bassoons in two or more parts. Valve trumpets were only slowly accepted into French orchestras, so that the cornet was imported because it was a fully melodic instrument for more than an octave below the pitch at which the trumpet was capable of completely melodic playing without any gaps in its harmonic series. With the upper-register brass so strengthened, the necessity of co-opting the ophicleide from the military band became obvious.

Meyerbeer was consciously an orchestrator in a way that no earlier composer had been. His music dealt in sensationalism and therefore in sensational effects; it matches the startling events on the stage, and communicates the atmosphere of the plot even when it does not so vividly create character. Everything he does in *Robert le Diable* and the operas which follow it is designed to create excitement, so that an event like the Massacre of St Bartholomew's Eve, the final excitement of *Les Huguenots*, becomes something close in nature to a Hollywood historical epic, a brilliant surface which excludes the fanaticism and psychological violence which makes it possible, and excludes, too, the compassion which it should arouse in any composer and an audience; it is music calculated to shock and amaze.

Meyerbeer's mastery of effect in the orchestra as well as on the stage had a lasting effect throughout the nineteenth century; the great cymbal clashes off the beat of each bar in the 'triumph' scene of Verdi's *Aida*, produced fifty years after Meyerbeer had left Paris audiences intoxicated with excitement, are an old Meyerbeerian effect which Verdi might have borrowed from any of Meyerbeer's French opera. Meyerbeer invented the effect of interpolating *fortissimo* brass dissonances into quiet, lyrical textures without preparing the dissonances so that they evolve naturally from the course of the music.

Meyerbeer was as fascinated by the bassoon as Weber had been by the clarinet. In *Robert le Diable*, the ghosts of debauched nuns provide a ballet for which the word 'spooky' is perhaps more appropriate than 'eerie' would be, and they rise from their tombs to a broken, halting triplet rhythm played by bassoons in two parts. In *Le Prophète*, Meyerbeer's last opera for Paris, three Anabaptist ministers (the libretto deals with the persecution of the Anabaptists) preach in unison, their voices doubled by the bassoon. He was as completely a master of orchestral effect, so that Berlioz's *Treatise of Modern Instrumentation*, notes with enthusiasm his employment of what can be called musical effects; Berlioz explained the effectiveness of the use of a single bell, tuned to F in the bass clef, its tone extended as it loses power by holding its single crochet through complete triple-time beats, while the brass—horns, three trombones and ophicleide—play unison Cs three octaves deep. Meyerbeer, too, realized the effectiveness of *pianissimo* gong strokes under dissonant brass chord marked *pianissimo* or triple *piano*. Meyerbeer is one of Berlioz's most frequently quoted authorities for remarkable dramatic effects in the orchestra.

His mastery, however, is not simply a matter of finding sound effects to heighten moments of tension and add *frissons* to sinister or spooky action. When tunes of broad, pompous dignity are needed in a register where trumpets are not at their most effective, he employs cornets in a manner that never tempts them to sound vulgar. In the love duet in the second act of *Les Huguenots*, he extracts all the possible poignancy from the situation by setting cor anglais and clarinets to whisper broken phrases to each other, the clarinets divided beneath the lower-pitched instrument so that the cor anglais becomes the more penetrating voice. The ill-fated lover, Raoul, who is to be slaughtered in the massacre, sings a beautiful Romance in Act I, accompanied by the archaic, seven-stringed viola d'amour; its tone quality immediately shows us that Raoul is a man apart, an idealist and lover with a mind and character above the common run of people.

The style and the effects that Meyerbeer developed, the huge sensational scenes of ritual, procession and calamity, remained to be used by almost every nineteenth-century composer of opera. To call him a specialist orchestrator is to point out what Berlioz meant when, to point out the areas of their compass in which instruments are at the most effective, and to show what effects they can make in other areas, he found himself frequently citing the example of Meyerbeer.

SEVEN

The Art of Orchestration

Berlioz was born in 1803, the year of Beethoven's *Eroica* Symphony. His home was the small town of La Côte St André, not far from Grenoble. From his father, a doctor, he learnt Latin and developed a passion for classical literature. Dr Berlioz noticed his son's instinctive passion for music, arranged for the boy to have piano lessons—he hardly profited from them—and provided him with a flute and a guitar, which young Hector managed more effectively. Harmony he learned from old text books, and by the time he was fifteen he had begun to compose; apart from a few songs with piano accompaniment he wrote chamber music, usually for flute and instruments with assorted tone colours. Sent to Paris to study medicine, he spent all the money and time he could afford at the Opéra or at concerts, neglecting his medical studies for the study of scores, notably those of Gluck, whose operas fascinated him by their combination of intense emotion and classical restraint. Gluck's orchestra, its eloquent, unhysterical woodwind and its almost statuesque poise, moved him intensely. Forced by circumstances to earn money as a music critic, Berlioz wrote reviews and essays in superb prose, intense in expression, witty, sardonic, imaginative, emotional but brilliantly lucid and economical; more than any other writer he expressed the mind of the Romantic musician. Music must be an expression of passionate emotions in all their immediacy; traditional rules and conventions must never be allowed to prevent the composer from expressing the truth of his own feelings; if the rules came into conflict with the demands of expression, it was the rules which must be abandoned.

For all the limitations of his skill as a performer, Berlioz became the first, and perhaps the supreme, master of the orchestra as a body capable of the widest imaginable range of tone colours and of a dynamic range which from the barest whisper to the almost unbearably powerful. In a group of ceremonial works—the *Requiem*, the *Symphonie Funébre et Triomphale* and the *Te Deum*, he made unprecedented demands for performers, but these were works designed for special occasions in special auditoria, the

Requiem for the chapel of Les Invalides, the *Symphonie Funébre et Triomphale* for open-air performance in the Place de la Republique and the *Te Deum* for the church of St Eustace. In such works, the composer could give himself freedom to explore the acoustic qualities of huge, resonant buildings in works which demanded magnificence of utterance because of the occasions for which they were written; there are passages in the two church works in which Berlioz explores the limits of sonority, but there are also passages of austere restraint and quietness. Most of his music makes no unusual call for instruments not to be found in the standard French orchestra of his day, with an ophicleide in the brass double-bass register until the tuba became a more satisfactory voice from the deeps, with four bassoons, and cornets in the brass section adopted because of the slowness with which the French accepted the valve trumpet. He regarded two harps as essentials in any powerful ensemble if they were to make any notable effect. The drier voiced side and snare drums, and the bass drum, which are far less resonant than timpani and sound only at the moment of impact, with no power to prolong their note, came into his orchestra, as did both the standard size cymbals and small, "tinkling" (according to 1 Corinthians 13) antique cymbals.

These grandiose ceremonial works make demands for almost unlimited power. The text of the *Dies Irae* in the *Requiem* is a Latin hymn about death and the Last Judgement, imagining the terrors of the end of the world. Writing music to be heard in a large, lofty cruciform church, Berlioz set out to saturate the building in sound. Taking the heavy brass away from the body of the orchestra and the horns, he demanded four separate groups of trumpets, trombones and ophicleide to be placed one on each side —to north, south, east and west—of the orchestra, so that the Last Trumpet becomes a huge fanfare, the four brass groups answering each other until the entire building vibrates with their power; the world ends in great, rolling timpani chords over which the voices shout in consternation. The effect of brass fanfares echoing and re-echoing from all corners of the universe, and of great alternating timpani chords was first attempted by Berlioz in the *Resurrexit* he composed in 1824 and 1825, and which he twice revised for concert performance. He was, apparently, not interested in the rest of the Mass which surrounded this single movement. The *Requiem*, in 1837, made more of the same idea and the *Resurrexit* seems then to have dropped out of his consciousness.

There are passages of overwhelming dynamic power in the *Requiem*, but Berlioz was able to keep a sense of vigorous, athletic movement even when using the heaviest orchestral weight. The great sensational pages are restricted to the setting of the *Dies Irae*,

after which the heavy brass is discarded except for a strange
punctuating effect in the choral recitatives in the *Hostias* of the
Offertorium and later; trombones low in their register hold a note
which grows from *piano* to *forte* and back to *piano* while three
flutes fill out the harmony of which the trombone plays the keynote,
attempting to suggest the effect that comes, for example, from playing an extended note low on a piano keyboard when the damper
pedal is pressed and higher strings are free to vibrate in sympathy
with the note played. The effect is usually doubtful because of the
difficulty in sustaining a very low note without inviting ugliness of
tone and an almost rattling *vibrato*. (*See* Appendix 2, No. 6.)

The orchestration of the rest of the *Requiem* is no less original
than that of these huge purple patches, but it is far less sensational.
In the *Offertorium*, the choir chants on two adjacent semitones
while the orchestra has the melody, a reversal of rôles which virtually turns the choir into the accompanist. The effect was one
which pleased the composer, who used it elsewhere, notably in the
funeral cortège of Juliet in his *Romeo and Juliet* Symphony. In the
Te Deum, which opens with great rolling chords from the orchestra at the east end of the church answered by similar but unrelated
chords from the organ in the choir gallery at the west end, Berlioz
writes for high pitched antique cymbals as well as for multiple
cymbals of the ordinary kind, played quietly together as "Cheru-
bim and Seraphim continually do cry"; the quiet clashing suggests
the sound of censers swinging before God's throne. The work was
designed for a military occasion, with massed side drums in a
rarely-played march for the Presentation of the Colours.

The *Symphonie Funébre et Triomphale* was commissioned by
the government to celebrate the tenth anniversary of the revolution
of 1830. The work was intended for a ceremony in the Place de la
Republique; the first movement, a magnificent symphonic march,
was meant to be played on the march to the ceremony and conducted by Berlioz in bandmaster style, wearing the uniform of an
officer of the Legion of Honour. It was scored, originally, for brass
and woodwind, a huge military-band; 200 instrumentalists played,
losing co-ordination as they moved through the streets; the sound
made an impression when the procession moved through tree-lined
boulevards but was lost where nothing was available to reflect the
sound.

The second movement is a funeral oration, a long slow movement for trombone and orchestra; it was ruined by the massed
side drums of the Garde Republicaine as they stood down as their
share of the ceremony ended. The last movement, called 'Apotheosis' is another march, not a funeral march like that of the first
movement but a triumphal march with a jolly, popular tune and

the whole is summed up in a chorus which uses the cheerful march tune. The work, despite the comic disasters of its first performance, was a great success and Berlioz made it available for concert performance by adding strings and adjusting the original orchestration to accommodate them.

Ceremonial music in France was traditionally on an extremely grandiose scale, designed from the days of Lully to achieve great magniloquence of utterance, and Berlioz, in his three great ceremonial works, was totally a master of this style, but his ceremonial works stand at the farthest imaginable extreme from the charm and gentleness of another masterpiece, *The Childhood of Christ*, which is delicate and restrained. The music has a tenderness and a grace of melody; its orchestration is full of colour and originality not by the building of colossal edifices in sound but by virtue of his precise understanding of the capacities of every instrument he needs. It was in this that Berlioz was the first composer who could be called an orchestral specialist.

The *Fantastic* Symphony, for example, was composed only three years after Beethoven's death. It uses clarinets in B flat, A and E flat. The B flat clarinets are richest in tone and tend to be melancholy in their lower register while cheerfully perky towards the top of their range, and Berlioz always uses them in the register which serves his expressive purposes. Clarinets in A tend to be rougher in tone but more consistent in mood throughout their register. Clarinets in E flat are stridently shrill and impudent at the top of their range, and Berlioz chooses them to introduce the distorted, parodied version of the symphony's *idée fixe*, its main theme in which the artist hero of the work imagines his Beloved ruling the roost over a witches' Sabbath. The rough-toned clarinets in A provide grotesque counterpoints to the grim, lurching March to the Scaffold.

Berlioz always uses instruments in the register in which they are most eloquent and most characteristic. When they are given a melody it is always placed in the portion of their register where it gains the type of tone which is appropriate to it in that stage of its existence—rich sonority of a violin's lowest, G, string and the piercing beauty of its highest, E, string, as well as the more neutral quality of its A and D strings, for example, are used always by design, just as clarinettists can take three instruments so that they are able to give the composer precisely the quality of sound he requires. The mood of almost frenzied excitement in which a great deal of Berlioz's music was conceived—"The text of the *Requiem* was a quarry that I had long coveted. Now at last it was mine, and I fell upon it with a kind of fury. My brain felt as though it would explode with the pressure of ideas," he wrote in his *Memoirs*—did not prevent him from calculating the details of a work with cold precision. If nothing like the heavy tread of the double-basses divided to play four parts at the beginning of the March to the Scaffold in the *Fantastic* Symphony had ever been heard before, the effect has a growling ferocity completely in the mood of that grotesque, fierce music. (*See* Appendix 2, No. 5.)

No earlier composer had made so exhaustive a study of the actual voices of instruments, the areas in which their voices are rich and eloquent, and those in which they sounded thin and colourless. His *Treatise on Modern Instrumentation* is detailed to the point at which even trills and *tremolando* effects on unusual instruments are possible are written out. The title of the book itself indicated in nature: to Berlioz, "instrumentation" was the study of individual instruments and their qualities; the art of combining them in an effective score he calls "orchestration".

Furthermore, he had heard, and marvelled at, Paganini's violin technique and saw how it could be applied to other instruments. Paganini had so expanded the violinist's technique that, during his lifetime, no other violinist was capable of attempting to play his compositions; he invented styles of bowing like *spiccato*, with the bow leaping from the strings between detached notes, and *martellato*, the bow striking the strings to give an almost percussive effect; he detached notes from each other within a single bow stroke. He would not only play *pizzicato*, with the strings plucked instead of bowed, but developed a left-hand *pizzicato*, the unoccupied fingers of his left hand plucking an accompaniment to notes fingered in the normal manner and bowed at the same time.

Many of these tricks, for all their cleverness, were of little practical use to the orchestral composer, for any orchestra could make the same effects simply by dividing the violins; to Paganini, their value was that they suggested that he was doing the impossible and they worked his audience into frenzies of almost superstitious adulation and helped to create the legends about him that had a vast commercial value to a virtuoso passionately fond of money: his shambling walk was the result of years in prison wearing gyves between his ankles; the G string of his violin was made not from catgut but from the intestines of his wife or mistress—whichever it was—for whose murder he had been imprisoned; he owed his almost supernatural skill to a Faustian bargain with the devil, whom some people seem to have seen on the platform with him, guiding his bowing arm as he played.

To Berlioz, Paganini suggested the possibility of a great expansion of technique not only among the strings but throughout the entire orchestra, and was able, from his precise knowledge of instrumental possibilities, to make demands which no previous composer had considered to be either practicable or necessary while expecting his players to be capable of entering accurately on some minute subdivision of the beat. Especially from Paganini he discovered the possibility of string harmonics, the almost whistling notes an octave above their natural pitch which string players can obtain by touching the string lightly instead of pressing it firmly down. The existence of harmonics had been known since the seventeenth century, but earlier musicians had never systematized them as Paganini did, and had regarded them as cheaply sensational effects. The 'Queen Mab' Scherzo, in the *Romeo and Juliet* Symphony (music that is a rapid, light-textured study in delicate sonorities) has a magical passage in which flute and cor anglais introduce a new theme against a high trilled note and a slowly changing series of chords in high harmonics on the violins which Berlioz has divided into four parts. (*See* Appendix 2, No. 7.)

To Berlioz, the viola was an instrument with a distinct personality of its own, not a mere component of the bass in a string orchestra. It personifies the Romantic poet and his longing in *Harold in Italy*, and is a suitable vehicle for melancholy thought. Berlioz never gives it any of the brilliance he devotes to the violins but reserves it for melancholy reflection; apart from Mozart in the Sinfonia Concertante for viola and violin, no earlier composer had found the necessity for granting it independence or found the type of expression which suited its character.

New instrumental combinations appear on almost any page of Berlioz's work, together with new effects. Violins and flutes in unison, sharing a melody create a sound he seems to have enjoyed. The combination of flutes and violins doubling a melody in octaves, with the flute lying uppermost, was a combination which, in Haydn's hands, sounds delicious and light, but in the *Fantastic* Symphony the urgent plangency of the violin and the breathy innocence of the flute in unison create a new sound for the *idée fixe* of the *Fantastic* Symphony as the beautiful, asymmetrical melody begins to evolve. Berlioz leaves the new sonority almost naked, with an accompaniment which cannot distract the attention.

Like other French composers of his period, French reluctance to use the valved trumpet left him to exploit the cornet, which carries the waltz melody of the Ball in the *Fantastic* Symphony in a register where the trumpets are condemned to the wide gaps of their harmonic series, and Berlioz uses them to make the romantic dream of the symphony something real and actual; the cornet by nature speaks in a more commonplace voice than the trumpet, and Berlioz's Ball becomes a mere social occasion while it is playing though the music avoids the vulgarity of utterance to which the instrument is sadly prone. In the March to the Scaffold, however, it becomes part of the military band which leads the condemned hero to his death, with woodwind, horns, trumpets and an ophicleide to make the music horribly jaunty and vulgar to offset the lurching march of the victim and the disgusting excitement of the onlookers. The lurching, ungainly progress begins in cellos and double-basses, with bizarre counter-melody from the bassoon. When the band has bassed, the trombones take over the lurching theme.

The percussion section of the orchestra owes more to Berlioz, perhaps, than to any other composer. The *Fantastic* Symphony ends its lonely, beautiful *Scéne au Champs*—oboe and cor anglais calling and answering each other, it suggests, from vast distances—with a subdued muttering of distant thunder; two sets of timpani playing chords create this effect. The cymbals, used by most composers to create great, climactic *fortissimi*, have a much wider range in his work; they can be stroked gently together, clashed quietly or struck gently with drumsticks, as the moment demands. The side drum, with its dry rattle, comes whenever its voice is appropriate, but Berlioz uses the side drum only when there is a military context for it; Berlioz's side drum has no important civilian duties. Before Berlioz, drumsticks were wooden-headed, allowing no variation of tone; the timpani as Berlioz knew them were shallower than modern timpani, so that few conductors today would consider that the sixteen demanded for the *Requiem* are all necessary with our deeper-shaped instruments. In addition, he prescribed the use, both for timpani and for the other percussion, of a variety of sticks—traditionally wooden-headed, leather-headed and sponge-headed.

Any instrument in Berlioz's orchestra can sing when song is required from it. Romeo, in Berlioz's symphony, is naturally melancholy and poetic. His melody opens the first movement after the choral introduction; it is one of those melodies which the composer develops by a process of evolution; it grows into qualifications and after-thoughts and leads directly into the music of the 'great festivities at the Capulets', a ball scene that grows increasingly noisy and excited; before the end, the melody of Romeo alone, beautiful and melancholy, is heard over the excitement, sung (the word seems more appropriate than 'played') by a trombone.

Orchestration, to Berlioz, was not simply the disposition of notes conceived in the abstract among the instruments of the orchestra and the skill required to dispose them in the most effective way. Many things in Berlioz's scores seem to be created by the instrument which plays them, expressing its personality in a way which would destroy their point and effectiveness if they were played by some other instrument; the colours and sonorities of his scores have an importance in his works hardly less than the importance

of harmony and balance, so that if Romeo has to meditate with
the voice of a trombone, the trombonist's duty is to find a *legato*,
meditative tone of voice in his instrument. The point is that Romeo
is thinking at a noisy, successful party. The lurching progress of
the condemned hero's progress to the scaffold and the brassy vulgarity of the military band in attendance at his death, in the
Fantastic Symphony, are there because they are true to the situation, just as the bizarre glee of the bassoons are right because they
are in the crowd relishing the repulsive spectacle. In the great
ceremonial works, Berlioz seeks the maximum of power and dignity
that can be combined with his naturally athletic movement and an
intensely nervous style; he himself wrote that anyone playing his
music had to remember its nervous energy, its elegance and its
melancholy. Outside the ceremonial works, much of his music is
extremely restrained, for his originality was not restricted to finding
new ways of writing louder music than had been heard before. In
Lelio, the strange addition to the *Fantastic* Symphony for speaker,
soloists, chorus and orchestra which Berlioz used as a hold-all for
a variety of small works which he did not know what to do with
as separate entities, is a movement called 'The Aeolian Harp', the
classical instrument which the ancient Greeks hung up so that its
strings could vibrate in the wind. Berlioz's evocation of this un-
thematic music of nature is breathtakingly quiet, gentle, almost
intangible and, after more than a century and a half, dazzling in its
originality.

To what extent Berlioz was aware of the consequences of his care
for colour we do not know: Berlioz the prose writer was prepared
to rhapsodize about the poetical effects at which he aimed and to
point out with pleased factuality how exactly he brought them off.
Their consequence, an unusual clarity of line, does not enter into
his discussions although his care to see that instruments are used
in their most eloquent register and that however difficult the music
they are asked to play, they are never asked to do anything which
belies their own nature; the instruction to the violins to play *col
legno*, with the wood of their bows, in the last movement of the
Fantastic Symphony is very rare in Berlioz's work. Berlioz's
orchestration is, strictly speaking, purely functional because the
colour is an essential function of expression and clarifies the work's
thought-processes as well as its presentation.

The idea of orchestration as a specialized branch of the composer's work, needing study apart from the other elements of his
work, or in addition to them, grew from his compositions and
from the study of instrumental possibilities and practicalities in the
Treatise on Modern Instrumentation. Schumann's symphonies, composed between 1851 and 1861, are the work of a composer who

admired Berlioz and, as a critic, wrote eloquently about such of Berlioz's compositions as came his way; the quality of their themes is striking, their harmony impressive and their aim nobly ambitious. They are much superior to many works which have won far greater popularity. They remain problematical works because their orchestral presentation is less than expert and they need special sympathy from the conductor, so that when Mahler performed them he re-orchestrated them, or rather amended their orchestration widely enough to have his versions regarded as re-orchestrations. Schumann's inexperience of the orchestra leads him to thicken the scoring, to indulge in doublings which cease to add emphasis and can make his music, in under-rehearsed or unsympathetic performances, sound sadly stodgy and heavy in movement. The orchestra had become too complicated an instrument for those who had not mastered its special technique, and Schumann's flawed but impressive symphonies come from a composer who could neither resist nor properly digest the orchestra's new richness; Schumann was for a time a conductor in Dusseldorf, but too late in his career to utilize his experience of the orchestra in practice in his music; he was, too, it seems, an unsuccessful conductor.

Most of Berlioz's music was heard for the first time at concerts which he himself mounted. In Paris he hired the hall or theatre, organized the best *ad hoc* choir and orchestra he could find, had the orchestral parts copied at his own expense, arranged the publicity and the box-office staff; he rehearsed his forces exhaustively. Usually his concerts were played to capacity audiences and great enthusiasm, but the expenses were so great that his earnings from these great efforts were usually pitifully small.

That is why his growing fame as a composer and his skill as a conductor took him to London in 1848 as conductor of the opera promoted by his eccentric compatriot Louis-Antoine Jullien, the conductor of successful Promenade Concerts. In 1852, having spent a year as conductor of the New Philharmonic Society, challenging the conservative policies and social exclusiveness of the original Philharmonic Society, he was later offered the conductorship of the Philharmonic Society itself. Concert tours, with programmes of his own music and chiefly, that of Beethoven, took him to all the major German music centres, to Vienna and to Russia. The accounts of his travels, written as open letters to his friends and printed in the *Journal des Débats* (the newspaper of which he was music critic) were included eventually in his *Memoirs*.

They provide, amongst other things, a vivid picture of orchestral conditions in Central Europe between 1840 and 1850. At Stuttgart he found an orchestra with the instruments necessary for what he called "Modern operas", including a harpist—a rarity, he discovered, in mid-nineteenth-century Germany, but at Hechingen, a small town nearby, he rearranged movements from the *Fantastic Symphony*, *Harold in Italy* and the *King Lear* overture for a tiny orchestra of only fifteen strings and with only one trombone. His report of his visit to Mannheim begins with a hilarious account of a typical rehearsal at which the trumpeters were equipped with trumpets playing in the wrong key and timpanists who knew no other sticks but those with wooden heads; he had, however, taken an assortment of sponge-headed sticks with him. After three or four hours of getting things straight, the musicians showed themselves to be enthusiastic, disciplined and eager to rehearse until they knew the music well enough to be sure of giving a good performance. Mannheim provided him with a harpist, but the cor anglais was played badly by a good oboist; as there was no ophicleide, a valve trombone was given a special extension to enable it to cope with ophicleide notes outside its range. At Weimar, Liszt had pressed all the string players in the neighbourhood into service to provide the visitor with twenty-two violins, seven violas, seven cellos and seven double-basses.

Mendelssohn, who thought Berlioz a musical barbarian (Berlioz himself had a great admiration for Mendelssohn's music), had done all he could to prepare for Berlioz's visit. The orchestra had been augmented to include twenty-four violins; there was a cor anglais, but it was so bad that all its solos had to be given to a clarinet; and there was neither harp nor ophicleide. At Dresden, where Wagner had recently been appointed *Kapellmeister*, apart from a double-bass player so old that he could hardly support the weight of his instrument, he found everything he wanted though the oboist could not be cured of the habit of adding decorations to his part. Brunswick could not provide an ophicleide or a cor anglais; the harp was an old-fashioned instrument without the nineteenth-century system of pedals which enabled it to play in every key, and the harpist was a fine musician but only a novice as a harpist. But the orchestra took to Berlioz's music and played it with fiery enthusiasm. Hamburg provided an ophicleide but no cor anglais, but Berlin was a musician's paradise; orchestra and military bands were matched by a choir large enough to do justice to the monumental music of the *Requiem*. Hanover offered him an orchestra of good musicians but only twenty-four strings; there was no ophicleide, so Berlioz used a tuba from the military band as a substitute. The orchestra at Darmstadt was bigger and had a good ophicleide.

In Vienna, Berlioz found the court orchestra as good as the best orchestras he had encountered anywhere in Europe, and Nicolai was one of the few conductors he singled out for praise. He noted that programmes in Vienna normally consisted of old music. The concerts he heard, unlike the one he conducted, were played by amateur orchestras which he admired for their enthusiasm and the fact that they came to rehearsal with their parts already studied. What he did not seem to analyse was that these orchestras, and the professional Court Orchestra, had grown up with Beethoven's music but had seen no reason to try to expand their style to cope with any music later than Beethoven's; like the Philharmonic Society in London, and the *Société des Concerts du Conservatoire*, they existed in the past and had no interest in the way the orchestra was expanding to meet new expressive needs. That is why Berlioz spent two years of his life and a vast amount of energy attempting to create a concert society and orchestra capable of understanding and performing contemporary works, like the New Philharmonic Society in London, the first season of which, in 1852, Berlioz conducted.

Like every other composer who, by the 1850s, composed music which did not remain decorously within the limits set for them by Beethoven's admirers, Berlioz was described as a disciple of Wagner though the music of the two is temperamentally and technically poles apart and despite the fact that the *Fantastic* Symphony was written when Wagner was still in his teens and the *Requiem* when he was only in his early twenties. From 1839 to 1842, Wagner was living in abject poverty in Paris and undertaking every musical chore which could earn him a little money. He had begun his climb up the German musical ladder with conductorships at increasingly respectable theatres; however his inability to keep his expenses within a sensible relationship to his income had made it necessary for him to run away to Paris in the hope of getting rich quickly through the composition of an opera which would sweep the authorities of the Paris Opéra off their feet. He had little money with which to patronize the Opéra or the Paris concerts, but he heard Berlioz's four symphonies. To his mind they had great faults of construction and a lack of artistic restraint which worried him, but their imagination, their passion and their unprecedented orchestral colours and textures made him feel, he wrote later, like a mere schoolboy. The two leaders of the modern revolution met, as they did in Dresden in 1842, but they never became friends. Berlioz wrote warmly of such of Wagner's music as came his way and seems to have had little difficulty in coming to terms with the German master's style though he wrote adversely of Wagner's too frequent recourse to strings *tremolos*, a device which he regarded as lazy and unimaginative. Wagner later wrote harshly of some of Berlioz's works before he could possibly have heard them, but Wagner, during his stay in Paris, was a completely obscure German musical hack who had, so far, created nothing to indicate his genius, so that Berlioz's sympathetic handling of his early works indicates the French composer's insight. Wagner was ten years younger than Berlioz. His first professional engagement had been as chorusmaster in the tiny opera at Würzburg in 1832, when he was nineteen; his task was to drive a choir of fifteen through elaborate new operas, like Meyerbeer's *Robert le Diable*, which demanded massive choral and orchestral forces. In 1834 he moved on to a conductorship at the slightly less undernourished opera-house at Magdeburg—a promising post for a musician not yet twenty-two years old. In 1837 he became conductor of the reasonably well organized opera in Riga, but two years later, overwhelmed by the accumulation of debts that had followed him from Würzburg and Magdeburg, he took to flight and made his way to Paris to compose an unsolicited work for the Opéra and thus make his fortune and an unassailable reputation.

At this time, Wagner was still a promising but entirely immature composer looking for a style. He had, however, trained himself to become an extremely efficient conductor, looking for performances in which he could achieve the subtleties of interpretation which few of his contemporaries could understand but knowing how to conduct in a manner which could achieve them.

Although he knew that his real future lay in the opera-house, where he planned to regenerate (that was his word) German life and German art through music and poetry and through the mythology of his people, he realized that the orchestral and chamber music of Beethoven, and to a lesser extent the symphonies of Haydn and Mozart, pointed out the direction in which music must travel; opera was to make use of the techniques developed in the symphony. An orchestra which had not got the symphonies of Beethoven into its blood stream, he believed, was an orchestra denied the real fruits of its training.

Therefore he set to work in Riga to establish regular concerts by the theatre orchestra. He gained the permission of the theatre management to organize subscription concerts with the twenty-four musicians who comprised his band; when he appealed to them in an open letter to support his plan, the orchestra joined him to a man, perhaps because of the idea that any profits—and he admitted that at first profits would be slow to come—would be shared among the players. But the concerts never began, and Wagner lost his post six months later.

In Dresden, where he was appointed *Kapellmeister* at the Royal Opera in 1842 after the production of his first really effective opera, *Rienzi*, concerts had been given by various short-lived amateur orchestras and, from 1844 to 1847, by Ferdinand Hiller, a composer, conductor and pianist, and a disciple of Mendelssohn in the 1830s. Hiller's reputation at that time stood higher outside Saxony than Wagner's. His orchestra consisted of professional musicians not attached to the court establishment, and though Wagner had no respect for Hiller as either conductor or composer, Hiller moulded his team into a workable orchestra.

The court musicians, employed in the opera and the royal chapel, gave one concert each year, on Palm Sunday, for its own pension fund, and both the court authorities and the players themselves objected to the idea of regular concerts as likely to diminish the appeal of the all-important yearly event. In 1846, Wagner used the pension-fund concert for a performance of Beethoven's Ninth Symphony, still regarded in Dresden as an incoherent, difficult work which could not win a capacity audience. In the event, the performance was so great a success that the Ninth Symphony became standard fare at later pension-fund concerts and aided Wagner in his campaign to establish regular concerts by his orchestra. And though both Hiller's and Wagner's ventures failed, regular concerts in Dresden continued under the direction of two freelance musicians, who took over Hiller's ensemble and made it successful by playing their programmes in the open air, for one of Dresden's deficiencies was the absence of any suitable concert hall.

Wagner's determination to make concert as well as operatic music part of his province was in tune with the ideas of many other musicians of the time. Spohr, for example, not a revolutionary figure either in political beliefs or in musical doctrine, had secured permission to give regular public concerts with the court orchestra in Cassel, popular and effective subscription concert series were well established in Halle, Frankfurt and many other German towns which were following the example of Leipzig, so that the traditional division between opera as the art of the aristocracy and the concert as a middle-class amateur substitute was coming to an end.

When, in 1848, Wagner left Dresden as an exiled revolutionary with a price on his head, he ceased to be a regular professional conductor. In Zürich, where he made his home, he worked for a time with the Music Society and the Opera, but for the most part he was free to concentrate on composition; his experience as conductor of the Philharmonic Society concerts in London in 1855 was dispiriting enough to lead him to abandon any idea he might have had of earning his living in the one musical sphere where he was an acknowledged master. After London, Wagner conducted little except thoroughly rehearsed, model performances of his own works, and those were few because he refused to permit productions which might prove through the deficiencies of a theatre's equipment or personnel to be unworthy; like Berlioz, he found that performances by other conductors discouraged rather than did service to his cause.

By this time *Rienzi*, grand opera on Meyerbeer's scale, *The Flying Dutchman* (the first truly Wagnerian work), *Tannhäuser* and *Lohengrin* were going the rounds of the German opera-houses with great success, though Wagner knew that many of the productions showed little understanding of what he was actually trying to do. He was at work on the opera of *The Nibelung's Ring*, though many years were to pass and his style was to develop much farther before he completed the cycle of operas with *Siegfried* in 1869 and *Die Götterdämmerung* in 1874.

As a master of the orchestra, Wagner was Berlioz's equal, but their aims and their styles were entirely different. The brilliance and colour of Berlioz's orchestration goes along with elegance and fluidity of movement; his power is achieved not so much by weight and mass as by energy and muscular strength. Wagner's 'soundideal' (to anglicize a useful German term) was richness of sound through blended colour out of which, from time to time, important themes flash with great brilliancy of colour; at the same time, it is sound designed to saturate any auditorium. In the *Rheingold*, when Valhalla has been built for the gods and their shady business transactions are momentarily forgotten by all except their leader, Wotan, they make their way over the rainbow bridge to their new fortress. Wotan picks up the sword which he is to pass on to his human descendants, though Wotan does not yet realize this, to be created to redeem the world from his own sharp practice. The music at that point is a sonorous and splendid processional march as the gods enter their new abode, and the motif which is to represent the sword and be developed as the sword plays its part in destiny flashes with superb power and clarity from the trumpets.

Both Wagner and Berlioz, when writing to achieve maximum power, wrote louder music than any of their predecessors, but there is, of course, a vast distinction to be drawn between loudness and noisiness; in his early works, as in *Rienzi*, the opera to which he owed his initial success, Wagner's orchestral technique leads to noisiness from uncertainty of texture. He had not, at that time, learned how to organize his orchestra so that it assimilated great outcries from the brass, and at times the brass stands out with strident ferocity. As his use of the orchestra developed and as his musical ideals became more subtle, Wagner's orchestral textures contain and assimilate the hugest orchestral *fortissimi* which are designed and scored with such roundness and deliberation that they remain beautifully mellow and rich. The climax of Siegfried's Funeral March, in *Götterdämmerung*, when the brass rises to its grandest climax in praise of the murdered hero, or when, as the opera ends, the old world of the gods collapses in flames, the Rhine overflows and an ancient wrong is finally righted, what seems to be unleashed is not unbearable volume but mighty, irresistible power.

It is Wagner's search for orchestral textures capable of sustaining the power of his vision and achieving the gorgeously sensuous climaxes in which dramatic tension explodes into intense emotion, as at the end of Act I of *Die Walküre*, which forces his orchestral style to reach unparalleled richness and beauties, as in the perfect, unbroken arch of the *Lohengrin* prelude, a meditation on a single theme (that which characterizes the Holy Grail, whose servant Lohengrin was). Four solo violins, with the rest of the violins divided into four parts, with three flutes and two oboes, all high above the stave soaring in ethereal heights, expound no more than a chord of A major. This is echoed by the flutes and oboes, and it swells from *pianissimo* to *piano* while the woodwind carry it back to *pianissimo* again. As it dies away, the four solo violins take it up an octave higher, in harmonics, and into this atmosphere of effortless gentleness, the 'Grail' theme, on which the prelude meditates, appears first in the highest violin register; first woodwind and then brass enter, climb to a mighty *fortissimo* which dies away, in the distant heights of the opening; Wagner himself said that he had thought as he wrote of the Holy Grail descending from heaven in a vision, revealing itself to mankind and then ascending until it was lost to sight.

The subdivided violins, imposing themselves on the hearer's attention at a register which exploits their most piercing sweetness, have a beauty which is not disembodied but which is almost swooningly sensuous, and the whole effect of the prelude is to exploit an orchestra in which there seem to be no real contrasts; Wagner wrote, very often, and perhaps nowhere more gorgeously than in this prelude, to achieve an entirely homogeneous orchestration. Ultimately, it seems, he wished for an orchestra which contained all the possible contrasts of tone and colour as enrichments and not as differences.

It was unity of texture rather than ever-increasing power which led Wagner to attempt to complete the brass choir, in which divergencies of tone rather than deficiencies in the register seemed to worry him most; he set out to give it not only as wide and complete a range as the strings but also a similar unity of tone. For the orchestra of *The Ring*, he invented the instruments which we know as 'Wagner tubas'; their primary purpose was to fill the gaps between trombones and horns, and they were to be played by a second quartet of horn players; their tone is closer to that of the horns than any of the other brass, and the word 'tuba' in their name seems to be a misunderstanding of the German word *Tuben,* which simply means 'tubes'. Wagner used them in a group of four: two in the tenor register, tuned in B flat, and two in the bass register, tuned in F; they are played through horn mouthpieces; they have four valves to improve the intonation of their lower notes.

Even as late as 1862, when he prepared the score of *Tristan und Isolde* for publication, Wagner was still not content with the brass section of the orchestra. Because the valve horn, apparently necessary for such complex harmony as that of *Tristan* did not play with the mellow richness of tone which had been the great beauty of the old natural horn, and because the difference of tone between open and hand-stopped notes on the natural horn disturbed him, Wagner prefaced the score with notes about the orchestration. In these he more or less specifies the use of natural horns, instructing the players to equip themselves with all possible crooks so that as much as possible of the score can be played in open notes, and to resort to hand-stopping only for those notes which could not possibly be reached by any other means; at the same time, he looked forward to the time when the tone of valve horns was sufficiently improved to make it not only convenient but correct to use them.

Wagner's search for richness and homogeneity of time was eventually satisfied in the Festival Theatre at Bayreuth, which, if not exactly designed by him, was built to his requirements. We are accustomed to Wagner singers struggling often both unmusically and unsuccessfully through the sound of his orchestra in traditionally designed opera-houses, and this was one element in performance he planned to avoid. The orchestra pit in the Bayreuth Theatre is closed in, invisible to the audience, as is the conductor, behind an acoustic shell which directs the sound towards the stage, so that by the time it reaches the audience it is completely blended and damped sufficiently to carry with, but not to overwhelm, the voices of singers on the stage. But the greatest glory of the Bayreuth Festival Theatre is its resonance and richness, the extent to which sounds heard in the theatre are alive in their own right. Shortage of money when the theatre was built determined that both its interior and exterior walls were built of wood as a purely temporary measure. Stone, concrete or brick—and the theatre was meant to be built of brick—covered in plaster or curtained, either reflect or absorb sound, but in the Bayreuth Festival Theatre, the only sound-absorbing material is the canvas 'ceiling' (another temporary measure), while the wooden body and the decorative 'pillars' of wood, which were empty and simply acted as sound boxes; the whole theatre is itself a vast resonating box, vibrating in sympathy with the music played within it. The resulting sound was so glorious that, while the outer walls of the theatre were rebuilt according to the original plan, the wooden interior was left unaltered and has been carefully preserved, any replacements provided by the types of wood originally used in the 'temporary' construction. As the theatre was built with little regard for expense until its original framework was completed, and as there was no effort to compromise Wagner's 'sound ideal', music heard in the Festival Theatre is Wagner's music heard precisely as Wagner wished it to be heard; these are not, of course, the ideal conditions for all kinds of music. Wagner engaged 115 players for his first Bayreuth Festival, and the acoustical conditions he had designed were not meant to emasculate them, so that the tone was rich, sumptuous and permitted singers to sing beautifully without forcing the orchestra into unnatural restraint.

Within the terms of his ideal, Wagner's orchestra is capable of great varieties of expression. As much as Mozart's opera audience it is involved in the drama which provides it with its own point of departure. The storm which beats against Siegmund as he makes his way to shelter in Hunding's house at the beginning of *Die Walküre* is, at first, an elemental natural force directed against him; it becomes the situation in which he is trapped, it encapsulates the fate that awaits him and which nothing can avoid. The flash of light from the hilt of the sword which his father Wotan had driven into the roof tree of Hunding's house, the brilliance of the moonlight as, magic sword in hand, he runs with Sieglinde from his enemy's home, the magic of the forest in which Siegfried kills the dragon and learns the language of birds: these are sound pictures as vivid as any in music, but they are also expressions of the inner nature of the action in which the *dramatis personae* are involved; the music demands the scene it creates, for the music is always the meaning and purpose of the drama it helps to enact, and Wagner's richness of colour and magnificence of utterance springs always from the inner nature of the scene which interprets the essential drama in the music. If, for much of the time, Wagner's instruments sink their individuality to the music, but without sacrificing it, they do so to become part of a superb and beautiful wash and blend of colour. The magic of Hans Sach's midsummer eve in *Die Meistersinger* is, as much of the greatest of Wagner's music always is, musical intoxication, but the intoxication is created by the characters and their situation, for it is out of these that the gorgeousness of the music rises.

A Wagnerian music-drama (to use the term that the composer preferred to opera) is an application to opera of the style and technique of symphonic composition. But whilst the symphony sets its own limits on the number of themes a composer handles and the harmonic range of his development, any passage by Wagner can involve not the development of a theme but the development of a number of themes involved in an interplay motivated by characters and situation. Even so spectacular a purple patch as 'The Ride of the Valkyries', which opens the last act of *Die Walküre*, deploys and develops three themes all in one way or another expressing aspects of the Valkyrie personality, their habit of riding through the air and the horses on which they do so. A whole process of thought and the ideas related to it, is bound up in the 'Magic Fire Music' with which *Die Walküre* ends; it combines themes associated with the magic fire which defends the sleeping Brünnhilde, the divine spell that puts her to sleep, with her loss of divinity, with Wotan's sorrow at the punishment of the favourite daughter who has disobeyed him. The music has a great, rich, sensuous beauty, but the beauty is the fruit of an intense, symphonically organized development of themes and the splendour of his orchestral style of glowing, blended, splendidly coloured sound. The orchestral intoxication is not a way of treating the music, applied to it by a brilliantly skilful craftsman; it is simply the audible manifestation of the music because it is the way, perhaps the only possible way in which Wagner's proliferating thematic material and its development can be made lucid and comprehensible; in this sense, its beauty is a by-product.

The love music of *Tristan und Isolde* is the expression of a love too demanding and too passionate to reach satisfaction in human life; its fullest expression comes in the huge love duet in several movements which occupies a great deal of the opera's second act. This itself is a development of a number of distinct but related themes, most of them mere short phrases, which express, or manifest, or which are associated in the composer's mind with (there is no really acceptable way of putting into words the relationship between Wagner's motifs and the thought which they embody), the fate which made the love of Tristan and Isolde inescapable, of the impossibility of its fulfilment, of the guilt it involves by demanding the betrayal of a friend, of love as the only reality in a world of unrealities, of day as illusion and of night as the time of reality because it is the time of love, and finally, of irresistible sexual excitement. Whatever the metaphysical value of Wagner's poetic expression of these ideas in Wagner's obscure, metaphysical text, the music is at least as explicit as *Lady Chatterley's Lover*. Commentators on the opera find some forty *leit-motiv* (or essential themes) out of which the music grows, all given added significance by the various dramatic situations through which they develop and gain new implications, and they are developed in a wonderfully seamless polyphonic style. The music of inevitable frustration, of an endless longing to be satisfied only in death, opens the prelude, and from it, a whole complex of related themes germinate, each manifesting a new aspect of the love of Tristan and Isolde. Any few bars of the Prelude show how themes only a phrase long develop from each other and intertwine. (*See* Appendix 2, No. 8.)

Wagner's polyphony is not only or always the subtle development of small motifs by combination and transformation. At the other end of the world from *Tristan und Isolde* is *Die Meistersinger*, the subject of which, behind its happy plot of a song contest and a love affair, is the strength of musical tradition and the power of tradition to assimilate new and apparently revolutionary musical expression; the revolutionary learns the true worth of tradition, the traditionalist the power of originality; it is the love music, of course, which is revolutionary and has to find the way to reconcile itself with the tradition. The Mastersingers have a fine, proud, processional theme; their tradition is a shorter theme, almost a march and closed in on itself; once it has spoken, it can do little but repeat itself while the Mastersingers' theme is open-ended and can move along in sequences which make possible exciting harmonic changes and movement; the new note of revolution is sounded by the love song with which the young hero-artist wins the contest; at the end of the overture, the three combine masterfully to make the reconciliation of revolution and tradition entirely explicit.

To Berlioz, the art of modern instrumentation was, in a sense, to use the various instruments and themes in a way which showed them to belong to each other, to set the instruments of the orchestra free to express their own personalities and to add the power of their personalities to the essential purposes of the music. To Wagner, on the other hand, the orchestra was really a multiple instrument of vast power, with a vast range of expression and colour; his orchestration was the art of choosing the instrument or combination of instruments which could most perfectly convey his thought and emotion. One needs only the final chord of *Tristan und Isolde*—a resolution of dissonances, harmonic problems and therefore emotional, intellectual and spiritual problems for which the ear has longed since the opening of the work—to see in its spacing through the orchestra, its various colours blending as the colours of a rainbow blend, to recognize the composer's consummate mastery. If nothing else by Wagner survived, the final life-enhancing pages of the overture to *Die Meistersinger* and the closing bars of *Tristan und Isolde*, though they would tell us only a little about Wagner the musical thinker and almost nothing about Wagner the dramatist, would show us that he was one of the supreme masters of the orchestra.

EIGHT

The Conductor

The enlarged orchestra, with its additional brass and percussion balanced by increasing number of strings and playing more and more frequently in large halls for the general public, created a variety of new problems. It played the symphonies of Beethoven and his successors, who had so expanded classical style that there were problems of formal co-ordination to be answered if the players were to follow a clear sense of direction from beginning to end of a movement. In addition, the enlarged orchestra was not easy to balance without some sort of overall, bar-by-bar control. Who was to decide the relationship of quicker and slower passages within the overall *tempo* of any movement; if the composer had marked *accelerando* or *ritardando*, to what speed was the music to gain or lose pace? If dynamic levels were to be altered by a *crescendo* or a *diminuendo*, what was the degree of loudness or softness at which the composer intended them to remain; are all passages marked *pp* or *fff* to achieve the same degree of quietness or noise, or is one to mark the actual climax? If so, who is to decide which passage it is and how much force, in the terms of the movement, is needed? Ideally, perhaps, matters like these can be settled in discussion by the members of an orchestra, who are all highly skilled musicians with perfectly valid views about musical form and structure and about the intentions of any composer. But large scale discussion of this type is a time-exhausting business even if it never becomes acrimonious. If an orchestra can rehearse almost endlessly, without a time limit, it would be possible to achieve beautifully organized performances without the permanent gesticulations of a conductor. But rehearsal is an expensive business, which is why, in the early nineteenth century, rehearsals were neither extensive nor, it seems, particularly thorough before Berlioz and Wagner arrived to agitate orchestral players with their unappeasable perfectionism. The conductorless orchestra which functioned for some time experimentally in the U.S.S.R. came to an end despite its success in playing with no less sense of form and structure than an orchestra obedient to the dictates of a conductor.

Jullien conducting a Promenade Concert in Covent Garden Theatre in 1846

Berlioz conducting in 1847. A caricature by Grandville

Richard Wagner
conducting

Brahms as conductor;
drawings by Willi von
Beckerath

Mahler conducting; silhouettes by Otto Böhler

Beecham in action; drawn in 1936 by E. Fairhurst

Richard Strauss conducting

Stravinsky rehearsing

Stokowski rehearsing

Leonard Bernstein
rehearsing

In addition to such considerations, players in an orchestra are positioned over too large an area to achieve complete unanimity of attack throughout a work, and can never hear everything that is happening in an orchestra with as much clarity as the audience and be able to control momentary defects of balance or control simply by listening to what is going on all round them; for most of the time they hear their neighbours and any specially penetrating voice raising itself over the mass of players. Thus the orchestral conductor came into being because the balance and co-ordination of any music on a large scale was impossible without his assistance.

Techniques of time-beating had been familiar since the Middle Ages for any music in which a large number of musicians had been involved, or in which, during the Baroque period, divided forces had performed in different quarters of a cathedral or large church; it is impossible to envisage the performance of elaborate Venetian choral works, for example, without some overall direction and control. It was, perhaps, possible for Handel to direct performances of his operas and oratorios from the keyboard of a harpsichord, with occasional gestures to guide the performers through tricky passages, but it seems from early eighteenth-century references and pictures that Lutheran cantata performances, with the players relatively close together and few in numbers in a church organ-gallery were often conducted by a time-beater who controlled them by his gestures. In the eighteenth century, apart from the composer-conductor directing a performance from the harpsichord (as Haydn is shown to be doing in a picture of an opera performance at Esterhaza) the 'leader' or *Konzertmeister* could conduct a small orchestra as he played his own part; for the sake of unanimity of approach, many pianists and violinists in modern times have proved that the method is perfectly satisfactory.

French conductors, in the opera-house or church, were often literally time-beaters in performances of large works with a multitude of performers; they beat out the music with a ruler or short-stick on a desk, quite audibly or, like Lully, with a heavy staff on the floor in front of them, a method which must have been extremely irritating to the listeners. They had their revenge, however, when Lully, beating time in his accustomed way with his long, heavy staff, struck and hurt his foot instead of the floor; the wound developed blood poisoning and was responsible for the composer's death.

Mozart, or any pianist playing a concerto, would beat time for the orchestra before his entry and during passages in which his instrument was silent; if problems of ensemble arose whilst his hands were occupied, or at the beginning of a slow movement

I

where both soloist and orchestra were often engaged from the opening bars together, he could conduct with his head. In a purely orchestral work, the task of ensuring a unanimous attack and maintaining co-ordination was that of the leader.

Beethoven, born into this system, seems to have abandoned it before 1805, when he played his fourth Piano Concerto for the first time with a conductor taking charge of the orchestra while he himself played the solo, and he continued to direct performances of his music long after increasing deafness had made it impossible for him to do so adequately. But what he understood by 'conducting' it is almost impossible for us to say. The great violinist Ludwig Spohr, who was born in 1784 and became a renowned composer and conductor, was appointed leader of the orchestra at the Theater und der Wien in 1813, so that when Beethoven's friends arranged a concert for him in the *Redoutensaal* on February 27, 1814, Spohr and his orchestra were invited to play in an orchestra which, Spohr mentioned in his *Autobiography*, involved every Viennese musician who could "blow, scrape or sing". The great attraction of the programme was the first performance of Beethoven's Seventh Symphony, and Beethoven himself conducted it; apparently the sponsors of the concert thought it unwise to keep the hero of the occasion in the background. Spohr, a gifted but conventional musician and strait-laced personality, had already developed doubts about what he regarded as the violence and emotional extravagance of Beethoven's music, and was bewildered and pained by the composer's idea of conducting.

"Beethoven," he wrote, "had accustomed himself to give the signs of expression to his orchestra by all manner of extraordinary motions of his body. So as often as a *sforzando* occurred, he tore his arms, which he had previously crossed upon his breast, with great vehemence asunder. At a *piano*, he bent himself down, and the lower the softer he wished to have it. Then when a *crescendo* came, he raised himself by degrees, and upon the commencement of the *forte*, sprang bolt upright. To increase the *forte* yet more, he would sometimes, also, join in with a shout to the orchestra without being aware of it." As early as 1805, at the first performance of the fourth Concerto, with a conductor sharing the responsibility of the performance, Beethoven had not been able to remember, as he played the opening of the Concerto from the score, with two boys from the choir holding candles to give him light, that it was not his responsibility to bring in the orchestra and did with a wide sweep of his right arm, hitting the boy who stood by the keyboard at that side of the piano in the mouth and causing him to drop his candle; all this delighted the audience and infuriated Beethoven. Obviously what Beethoven understood by the idea

of conducting was not involved with maintaining a steady beat and
had little to do with what is nowadays regarded as a conductor's
principal duty.

In January, 1809, with his first six symphonies and all his concertos already composed and performed, three weeks after the
concert at which he had conducted the Fifth and Sixth Symphonies
in spite of his deafness, Beethoven wrote a letter to the publishers
Breitkopf and Härtel in which he complained about the musical
situation in Vienna: "We have *Kapellmeisters* who not only do not
know how to conduct," he wrote, "but can hardly read a score."
But what sort of technique Beethoven believed the conductors of
his day to be deficient in, it cannot have been the careful precise
beating of time; Spohr pictures him standing with his "arms across
his breast".

Some sort of technique seems to have evolved, by this time, for
the conductor of large scale choral and orchestral music in church
and for the conductor in the opera-house, but such techniques
seem to have been entirely rudimentary, and Beethoven himself
was known to get ahead of his orchestra, which apparently kept its
head, refusing to be thrown into confusion by demands for effects
the players had not yet reached, and remained as much together
as they had been at the beginning. Spohr's account suggests that
Beethoven, as a conductor, left the orchestra alone to maintain the
tempo and was concerned only with vividness of expression.

The conductor in the opera-house took a position with his desk
immediately in front of, and facing, the stage, with the orchestra
behind him, so that he concentrated entirely upon the singers while
the orchestra did its best to follow his beat. This was a method
generally adopted in theatres and it persisted in, for example, the
Imperial Opera in Vienna until Mahler became conductor there
in 1897; it was Mahler who moved the podium and desk to the
back of the orchestra pit so that he had everyone, orchestra, chorus
and singers, under his direct control; his predecessors, who included
Wagner's greatest disciple and musical heir, Hans Richter, had
been content to work from the middle of the orchestra pit with
their eyes towards the stage. Portraits of Weber show him conducting at Covent Garden with a roll of paper but do not place him
in any relationship to the stage and the orchestra. In Germany,
however, Weber used a baton when he was appointed *Kapellmeister* of the German Opera in Dresden in 1817, as did Spohr,
who became director of the Frankfurt Opera in the same year.

As there was no accepted technique of conducting, and therefore no method of training for the would-be conductor; whoever
had the task of controlling and directing the performance worked
out his own method for himself. Spohr, visiting London for the

first time in 1820 to play at a Philharmonic Society Concert and to 'lead' the orchestra, claims to have been the first musician to conduct a Philharmonic concert in the modern way and rather proudly tells the story of how he did so in his *Autobiography*. He had played two concertos at his first concert, and been allowed to leave the rest of the performance to the regular leader and pianist, the latter being one of the directors of the Society who sat at the keyboard with the score, filled in for any missing instrumentalist and joined in with the piano to correct anything that had gone wrong. At his second concert, where he was not involved as a soloist but as 'leader', Spohr decided to change things.

My turn came [he writes], to direct at one of the Philharmonic Concerts, and I created no less a sensation than with my solo playing. It was still at that time the custom that when symphonies and overtures were performed, the pianist had the score before him, not exactly to conduct from, but only to read after and play in with the orchestra at pleasure, which, when it was heard, had a very bad effect. The real conductor was the first violin, who gave the *tempi* and now and then, when the orchestra began to falter, gave the beat with the bow of his violin. So numerous an orchestra, standing so far apart from each other as that of the Philharmonic, could not possibly go together, and, despite the excellence of the individual members, the ensemble was much worse than we are accustomed to in Germany. I had therefore resolved, when my turn came, direct, to make an attempt to remedy this defective system. Fortunately at the morning rehearsal on the day on which I was to conduct, Mr Ries took the place at the piano, and he easily assented to give up the score to me and to remain wholly excluded from all participation in the performance. I then took my stand with the score at a separate music desk in front of the orchestra, drew my conducting stick from my pocket and gave the signal to begin. Quite alarmed at such a novel procedure, some of the directors would have protested against it; but when I besought them to grant me at least one trial, they became pacified. The symphonies and overtures that were to be rehearsed were well known to me, and in Germany I had already directed at their performance. I could therefore not only give the *tempi* in a very decisive manner, but also indicated to the wind instruments and horns all their entries, which ensured to them a confidence such as hitherto they had not known there. I also took the liberty, when the execution did not satisfy me, to stop, and in a very polite but earnest manner to remark upon the manner of execution, which remarks Mr Ries at my request interpreted to the orchestra. Incited thereby to more than usual attention, and conducted with certainty by the visible means of giving the time, they played with a spirit and correctness such as till then they had never been heard to play with. Surprised and inspired by this result the orchestra immediately after the first part of the symphony, expressed aloud its collective assent to the new mode of conducting, and thereby over-ruled all further opposition on the part of the directors.

From then onwards the Philharmonic Society concerts invariably announced a "conductor", but the title seems to have meant many things. When Mendelssohn came to London in 1829 and conducted his C minor Symphony at a Philharmonic Concert, he did so from the piano and, in a letter to his sister Fanny, explained how he was escorted to the keyboard "like a young lady".

Beethoven's condemnation of Viennese conductors who could hardly read a score should not be dismissed as the censoriousness of a composer who found it impossible to believe that anyone else could do justice to his work. Conducting was a new technique, and the qualities necessary to success as a conductor were not clearly understood. The Orchestra of the Société des Concerts du Conservatoire in Paris was conducted for more than the first twenty years of its life by François-Antoine Habeneck, who conducted the orchestra at the Opéra. Wagner, during his first miserable stay in Paris between 1839 and 1842, and whose failure to make any impression on Parisian music rapidly taught him to detest all things French, was forced to admit that he had never heard performances of the Beethoven symphonies to equal those given by the Conservatoire Orchestra under Habeneck. Wagner's first hearing of Beethoven's Ninth Symphony, in Leipzig in 1830, had caused him to doubt not only his high estimate of the work, which he had studied and of which he had made a pianoforte transcription, but also the value of the music, its coherence and logic. The first three movements had been conducted by the leader from his desk at the head of the violins, and it had been incoherently played and badly co-ordinated. After the slow movement a conductor, August Pohlenz, arrived to conduct the choral finale, because at the *Gewandhaus* it was the custom to employ a new-style conductor only for choral works; but even Pohlenz's efforts did not succeed in giving a coherent, eloquent account of the music; the orchestra struggled through the score as best it could. Pohlenz had set a pitifully slow *tempo* for the movement to give the players a chance to play the notes at all. Habeneck's conducting of the work, the result of long, detailed and thorough rehearsal, came like a revelation to young Wagner.

But Habeneck used neither score nor baton. He conducted with a violin bow from the first violin part; we do not know whether or not he had cued into it the important events in the rest of the orchestra, but after the amount of rehearsal the orchestra had undertaken, the first violin part was probably enough to activate his memory. Habeneck set the *tempo* and, when the music was running satisfactorily, would cease to conduct until his efforts were again necessary to vary the *tempo,* to control a *crescendo* or *diminuendo* or to pull the orchestra together if the performance seemed to be growing ragged. Thus it is easy to believe the story Berlioz told of the first performance of his *Requiem,* in 1837. The *Requiem* was composed for a state occasion, which meant that Habeneck was *ex officio* its conductor. In the second movement, the *Dies Irae,* the Latin hymn for the dead, Berlioz scored the verse dealing with the last trumpet for the four separate brass groups he had placed away from the orchestra and choir to their north, south, east and west, with sixteen timpani rolling out great chords. The third verse which describes the sound of the last trumpet is begun by a long fanfare for the four brass groups, entering one after the other and filling the church of Les Invalides (where the work was first performed) with a great harmonious tumult; the movement is designed so that the huge, resonant building would seem to come alive with sound.

Habeneck, at the first performance, noting that the first two verses were going well and that he could relax his control for a moment, put down his violin bow and took out his snuff box for a little refreshment just at the moment where the tempo broadens out expansively for the fanfare: disaster threatened. It was, however, averted by the composer himself. The history of the *Requiem* before its first performance had been anything but happy, and Berlioz saw in Habeneck's decision to take snuff a deliberate attempt to reduce one of his grandest passages to chaos; he leapt to his feet and gave the beat, guiding the orchestra and choir through the transition, and saved the day. Though this story, as Berlioz tells it in his *Memoirs,* has been dismissed as a romantic fabrication invented by a disappointed failure to show that the world was against him; Carl Halle, the pianist who settled in Manchester and became a blessing to English music, was at the performance, however, and in his *Autobiography* he too mentioned Habeneck's lapse and Berlioz's swift seizing of control.

Had there been a full score on Habeneck's desk, it is unlikely that he would have failed to notice the approach of the crisis for which he had to prepare his huge forces. As the situation was, when Berlioz wrote his *Treatise on Modern Instrumentation* he added to it a chaper on conducting in which he still found it necessary to point out that a conductor should be able to read a full score. Berlioz concentrated in his chapter not on problems of interpretation but on the essential techniques which effective conductors should acquire. Berlioz's *Memoirs,* and most of his critical writings, are witty, colourful, often grotesque and fantastic, openly emotional; the *Treatise on Instrumentation* and the short study of conducting technique it contains are, apart from occasional lyrical remarks on effects he considers especially beautiful, severely practical in text-book style. They are meant to convey to the reader the methods by which the conductor could communicate with his orchestra through clear and decisive gestures however complex the rhythm of the music and however often the beat might be subdivided. He did not discuss the necessity of giving dramatic visual clues to the players at moments of special excitement, or mention the value of indicating instrumental entries as they arise in the score; apparently Berlioz trusted the instrumentalists to count their own rests. Berlioz was, according to reports, a superb conductor who relied on clarity of beat and not on extravagance of gesture; his habits of unrelenting rehearsal and his total response to the emotion of any music which seem to have been what he relied on ensure not only accurate and well-balanced performances but also a totally excited, responsive attitude in the orchestra. Berlioz was favourite figure for the French cartoonists of his day, but their accounts of his conducting suggest a calm imperiousness of demeanour rather than any frenzied attempt at expressing the music through movement.

Berlioz never held a long tenure of office with any orchestra, as Mendelssohn did with the *Gewandhaus* Orchestra. Mendelssohn's ideal as a conductor was natural fluency, neatness and elegance. Mendelssohn became conductor of the *Gewandhaus* in 1835, only five years after the players had shocked Wagner by their inept performance of Beethoven's Choral Symphony. Duties in Berlin and appearances as a guest conductor kept Mendelssohn from the platform of the *Gewandhaus* during the later years of his life, but he remained the orchestra's musical director until his death, and his various assistants were his ardent and devoted disciples. Mendelssohn seems to have preferred *tempi* on the fast side—both Berlioz and Wagner suggested that this was to drive the orchestra at speed through passages which, taken at a more measured pace, might have led them to disaster, and that he relied upon speed to get through passages which seemed dangerous, but he himself explained that he believed the *tempi* he adopted necessary to give a sense of determined forward movement to any music he conducted. His work in Leipzig not only developed the orchestra's sense of style; because he was interested in the music of the past he made the players more versatile and brought a broader musical appreciation to the audience. The *Gewandhaus*, and the city of Leipzig, gained musical authority from the fact that the most influential German musician of the age directed its musical life and virtually created the Leipzig Conservatoire. Mendelssohn was a conductor who avoided fuss; like Habeneck, when all was going smoothly and modifications of *tempo* and dynamics were not needed, when the balance remained satisfactory, he would cease to conduct and simply listen until his efforts again became important. Until the Dresden revolution of 1849, Wagner followed the conventional German path to eminence. Ten years younger than Berlioz, four years younger than Mendelssohn, he had climbed quickly up the musicians' ladder in spite of the weaknesses of his character which courted disaster in every post he held. From chorus master at the fiftieth-rate opera in Würzburg before he was twenty to the conductorship of the slightly less poor opera at Magdeburg in 1835, to a brief stay in a similar post in Königsburg a year later and then to the conductorship of the reasonably satisfactory opera in Riga in 1837, Wagner was obviously a man destined for an important post, which came with his appointment as *Kapellmeister* of the Royal Opera House in Dresden in 1842 after three years spent in utter failure in Paris. In Dresden, as in Riga, he endeavoured to involve the orchestra in the performance of regular concerts, but with only limited success; Berlioz had to collect an orchestra and instil into it a sense of style for almost every concert he gave; Wagner, endeavouring to change the musical establishment in a famous capital city, had an even harder task.

The Dresden Orchestra was overworked in the opera-house, with all its players demanded for every performance even if there was no part for their instruments; there were no musicians available to deputize for any instrumentalist who had fallen ill. They held their positions for life, so that there was no reason for them to attempt to conquer their boredom when playing uninteresting music and could not be retired even when they had grown too old to work efficiently; Berlioz, visiting Dresden to conduct a concert of his own music in 1842, wrote compassionately of the double-bass player who had grown too old to hold his instrument but who still took his place in the orchestra. Empty places, when they occurred, were filled by players chosen from a list of applicants according to the date of their application irrespective of their abilities; posts were not advertised and thus made open to the best available players. In addition, they were grotesquely underpaid.

Wagner, whose interests as a conductor comprehended all these things as well as the awkward seating arrangements in the orchestra pit and the bulky, inconvenient music desks in use there, drew up rational and practical schemes for enlarging the orchestra, allotting increased leisure through a more sensible schedule of work and the promotion of regular concerts which would augment the derisory salaries paid to the musicians (in all these respects, Wagner's plan could have been adopted to the benefit of music as well as of musicians in any German theatre of the day). The rejection of his schemes for reform, more than any of the political theories he investigated when he found that his plans were not to succeed, drove Wagner into revolutionary politics and brought about his exile from Germany.

Settled in Zürich, Wagner conducted from time to time at the concerts of the Zürich Musical Society, which had a semi-professional orchestra with which he gave some memorable performances and a short festival of excerpts from his own operas, as *Tannhäuser* and to a lesser extent *Lohengrin* had been taken up by German management and were proving enormously successful. But true to his character, Wagner saw the deficiencies of music in Zürich and set out, unasked, to reform them; part of his scheme was the amalgamation of the orchestra of the Musical Society with that of the Zürich Opera, and the failure of his plan, which cut across personal loyalties and made nothing of personal status among the authorities either of the Musical Society or of the theatre was due not to any impracticability but to Wagner's conviction that music was more important than personalities and their pride. The amateurs who augmented the orchestra of the Music Society supported Wagner's plan for a livelier musical life in Zürich only to the extent of playing for those concerts which he himself conducted. As Wagner was constitutionally incapable of accepting a compromise, the scheme came to nothing and the conductor Wagner—who is inseparable from Wagner the orchestral and musical organizer—took less and less of a part in Zürich music-making.

Though the Zürich musicians were ready to add to their musical commitments to play under Wagner, London musicians found him difficult to play for and personally less pleasant than they expected a conductor to be. In the first half of 1855 Wagner conducted the concerts of the Philharmonic Society; he barely knew but bitterly disliked London, where his early works, by that time successful in Germany—were still unknown and his reputation was simply that of a musical and political revolutionary of the most dangerous sort. The Philharmonic Orchestra was reasonably good, he said, but it seemed to know nothing about any dynamic shadings beyond *mezzo-piano* and *mezzo-forte*, and was incapable of any subtlety. Many of the critics were impressed by the excerpts from his own operas which he put into his programmes, each of which included a Beethoven symphony. The critics said that he played slow movements too slowly and the fast movements too quickly. The musicians themselves found his beat uncertain and were baffled by the rhythmic flexibility at which he aimed, relaxing the *tempo*, for example, for Beethoven's lyrical second subjects in the symphonies, drawing out *rallentandos* and whipping up *accelerandos.* Wagner conducted with a sense of rhythmic give and take, of *tempo rubato,* which was new to English players, and his interpretations were always extremely personal.

Fourteen years later, in 1869, Wagner published his essay *On Conducting.* Unlike Berlioz, he was not concerned with the ABC of technique, the way to beat time and to subdivide the beat, or the necessity of score reading and a capacity for tireless physical effort, all of which are topics to which Berlioz devoted attention. His concern was interpretation; if the conductor found the right *tempo*—a matter of basic musical sensitivity and a sense of musical clarity—everything else would, he said, fall into place even if variations of *tempo* were needed; Wagner seems to have felt music dramatically and emotionally, rather than structurally, but he took care to suggest the means by which his dramatic instincts, or any other conductor's, would be controlled by a sense of form and structure. Berlioz's essay is a text book for beginners, but Wagner's is a treatise for advanced students.

The two between them make clear that there are two different types of conductor among those who have really studied the art and thought out their interpretative position. Musicians who studied the methods of Berlioz noted the strictness of his beat, his fidelity to the letter of the composer's law and the intense excitement he achieved simply by ensuring that everything was played and heard as the score set it out. The conductor Felix Weingartner, when he wrote his book on conducting in 1895, quoted a musician who had played in the Dresden Opera Orchestra under Wagner as saying that when Wagner conducted, the players had no sense of being driven or led but felt themselves free to play naturally; this is to suggest that Wagner had found the *tempo* at which each work moved naturally and therefore in a way totally satisfying to the instrumentalists. While Berlioz saw no need for any interpretative licence to be granted to the conductor and accepted the composer's text as the law it was his duty to observe, Wagner had a Romantic musician's belief in the necessity of such licence because there must always be a great deal in any work which cannot be written down and because even the simplest musical directions need to be understood in their context; they are not objective directions but only indications which must necessarily remain vague. It seems to be obvious to anyone sitting, say, at the piano, that 'allegro' at the head of a score by Mendelssohn means something different from 'allegro' on a score by Brahms or Bruckner.

This division of conductors into two types of which Berlioz and Wagner were the prototypes can be heard and probably seen, at least among 'great' conductors at any time. Gramophone records of the two most admired Beethoven conductors of the 1930s (though both continued their work beyond that decade), Toscanini and Furtwängler, show that Toscanini's *tempi* never relented except when the score demanded relaxation or increase of speed, while Furtwängler, accepting a degree of interpretative freedom, sensed relaxations and intensifications not marked in the score and perhaps too slight to be annotated without exaggerating their effect. Many of Wagner's fluctuations of *tempo*, and many of those of Mahler at the turn of the nineteenth century, seem to have been of this kind. Such freedom is, of course, disastrous unless it is controlled by a sense of the music's essential form; Furtwängler never dwelt on expressive details at the expense of the music's forward movement, and neither, so far as we can tell, did Wagner, whose beat might not have baffled London musicians trained by Michael Costa if his fluctuations and variations had been larger and more pronounced.

Costa, perhaps partly from his Italian inheritance and training, was inclined to find faster *tempi* than many of his hearers could justify, so that the composer Sterndale Bennett hoped that Costa was not going to conduct a performance of one of his overtures as a Philharmonic concert. The only advantage of Costa, Bennett suggested, was that before he retired he would have learned how to play all Beethoven's symphonies in one evening and still leave the audience time to have dinner.

Tempo, as Wagner realized (and many others must have realized before him) can never be an absolute. A composer can, for example, mark *tempi* exactly by giving them a metronome figure to guide the conductor, but Wagner himself pointed out that a conductor can beat time exactly to the dictation of a metronome and still get the *tempo* wrong; any auditorium, for example, can modify the effect of a *tempo*, for 'allegro' in St Paul's Cathedral is necessarily slower than 'allegro' in a less resonant building; the conductor who forgets this turns the music heard in St Paul's into an incoherent scramble.

In other words, a conductor has more than the mathematics of *tempo* to consider. The record collector can, for example, study the recordings of the great though sometimes undisciplined Sir Thomas Beecham: in Beecham's performance, the slow movement of Haydn's Symphony No. 101 ('The Clock'), marked *andante*, is extremely slow when timed by a stop watch, but no listener notices the slowness as a defect and is probably unaware of it until he compares Beecham's with another performance. In the same way, some of his enchanting performances of Wagner's *Die Meistersinger* were accused of excessive speed until Beecham demolished the charge by pointing out that official stop watch timing of his performances act by act showed that he had actually conducted a performance rather more leisurely than that of most Wagner conductors. The extreme slowness of Beecham's performances was justified, and the sense of speed in *Die Meistersinger* was caused by vitality of rhythm and phrasing, which made the performances seem more eventful, and therefore more hasty, than those of most other conductors. Actual *tempo*, even measured by a stop watch, is not an objective musical reality, for any sense of speed is affected by rhythmic eventfulness, vitality of phrasing and clarity of delivery; a performance in which events in rhythm, harmony and orchestration are given proportion, clarity and balanced emphasis seems quicker than a performance played at the same *tempo* but without these other virtues simply because it offers more to be listened to.

It was these considerations which Wagner studied in his essay and apparently conveyed by his conducting. To him, such a direction as 'allegro' was not an objective command to be answered by the application of some ascertainable rule because, he pointed out, 'allegro' at the top of a score by Mozart means a different sense of speed and different qualities both of rhythm and sound to the word 'allegro' at the top of a score by Beethoven. *Tempo* is governed by a wide variety of musical factors—the phrasing of the melodic line, the clarity and continuity of rhythm and the treatment of incidental events in the course of a work or movement, and the slowness or speed of one movement in relation to the others. To take a very familiar example, the stampede of cellos and double-basses in the Scherzo of Beethoven's Fifth Symphony, played as a really quick 'allegro' (Beethoven's instruction for that passage), gives less sense of speed if the conductor's *tempo* reduces the double-basses to an indiscriminate scurry than it does at a speed which allows every note to be heard clearly but not dwelt upon. That was what Mahler meant when he told his wife (who reported his dictum in her *Gustav Mahler: Memories and Letters*) that the correct speed for a 'prestissimo' (which can be translated as "as fast as possible") is simply the greatest speed at which every note can be clearly heard.

The conductors of the Mendelssohn–Berlioz–Wagner generation were, like traditional *Kapellmeisters*, composers exercising the composer's secondary function of directing performances. Later conductors, from Nicolai in Vienna, Lindpainter in Vienna and London, Mahler in Vienna, Richard Strauss in Munich, Vienna and Berlin, and even Costa in London, were composers whose creative abilities were the qualification as conductor. Mahler came to regard conducting as a purgatory through which his poverty compelled him to travel, forcing him to put all his creative work into his summer holidays and compelling him to accept debasing com-

promises whenever he felt himself to be responsible for performances which failed to come up to his standards of perfection.
Berlioz and Wagner, more than anyone else, established conducting
not only as a technique but as a musical specialization. Berlioz
accepted his career as an international star conductor without
repining; to Wagner as to Mahler, it became a detestable distraction
from the real task of composition. In his later life, Richard Strauss,
like Elgar and others, restricted his conducting to his own works
although gramophone records exist which show Strauss to have
been a splendid conductor of the 'standard repertoire', especially
of music by Mozart.

With Berlioz and Wagner, however, the old *Kapellmeister* tradition really came to an end and the specialist conductor emerged.
Hans Richter and Hermann Levy, who conducted Wagner's operas
in his theatre at Bayreuth, worked at first under his supervision;
they were professional conductors, not composers with a useful
secondary skill. Charles Hallé, who became a conductor in Manchester in 1848, founded an orchestra there and continued to conduct until his death in 1895 at the age of seventy-six, was a concert
pianist with a wide international reputation. Like Hans von Bülow,
who conducted the first performances of Wagner's *Tristan und
Isolde* (probably the most daunting first performance any conductor
has ever undertaken) and *Die Meistersinger*, Hallé continued his
career as a pianist in double harness with his work as a conductor.
The technique of conducting differs from that of any instrument
because, while any player is obviously, perhaps disastrously, ham-
pered by uncertain technique, any conductor who can bring an
orchestra effectively into action on a down beat can substitute
whatever musical understanding he has for baton technique. Many
conductors who have been accepted as masters have begun by
evolving a technique of their own. As a young man, Mahler began
his career as a conductor with no training of any sort, and won
remarkable results, as did Richard Strauss, almost exactly Mahler's
contemporary, through almost wildly extravagant gestures. Mahler,
a year before his death, conducted his Eighth Symphony, controlling nearly a thousand players and singers, standing almost motion-
less and with hardly any use of his left hand for nuance and
emphasis. Strauss followed a similar path, and later photographs of
him in action as a conductor in the 1920s and 1930s show the stillness and calmness with which he achieved control of vivid performances by largely expanded orchestras. In *Notes for Conductors*,
Strauss advised the conductor "to put his left thumb in the armpit
of his waistcoat and follow the orchestra with his right hand". "It
is the audience who should sweat," he declared, "not the conductor."

The great development of conducting technique came, in the 1880s, with the work of Artur Nikisch, who in his early teens showed brilliant promise as a violinist and in 1874, at the age of nineteen, became a member of the Vienna Court Orchestra. Three years later he became coach of the chorus at the Leipzig Opera, and in 1879 conductor of the orchestra there. He almost immediately found himself in demand as a concert conductor and rapidly became famous for his revival of important works which had not really been accepted into the standard repertoire, like the symphonies of Schumann.

Nikisch was a conductor who allowed the baton to do the work and to make all the necessary effort; its bulb grip rested against the palm of his hand and its shaft balanced between thumb and forefinger; conducting from his wrist, not from elbow or shoulder, Nikisch used the baton, especially its point, to convey beat, phrasing and everything that gesture could convey; he used his left arm sparingly and moved so little that any movement of the baton which originated above his wrist could prompt a 'fortissimo' almost cataclysmic in its ferocity. He never distracted either players or audience by elaborate gestures designed to stimulate the players' emotion or excitement. Conducting of this sort did not preclude performances of great power and emotional tension, as modern listeners in Britain know from the conducting of Sir Adrian Boult, a disciple of Nikisch in matters of technique. Among Nikisch's disciples there have been some who seem to have taken delight in conducting with the minimum of gesture and creating performances of extraordinary power by doing so. Fritz Reiner, the Hungarian conductor who was born in 1888, conducted in minor German theatres at Bucharest and Dresden, and then moved to America, where he conducted the orchestra of Cincinnati and Pittsburg before reaching New York. Reiner combined the minimum of physical effort with intense concentration and clarity. He was by temperament tyrannical at rehearsals and never on easy terms with any orchestra, so that one day his deliberately tiny beat led a doublebass player to attend a rehearsal with a telescope, which, he told the *maestro*, he was using in order to see the beat.

Sobriety of action, as practised by such masters as Felix Weingartner, Sir Henry Wood and Sir Adrian Boult has never inhibited orchestras from playing that is brilliant, powerful and intensely responsive, while others, whose technique seems at best eccentric have often given to the music they have played no less intensity, power and clarity. Thomas Beecham, whose records as well as his legend indicate his enormous range of interest and accomplishment, can hardly have been said to have had a technique at all; his baton and his left hand did whatever the music, and the state of the

performance prompted him to do. The critic Neville Cardus claimed
to see him once get his baton mixed up with the tails of his jacket
and players declare that, as he conducted from memory, his
memory sometimes failed and the failure could be noted from the
wide circles in which his right arm swept until he heard a definite
landmark which enabled him to find his way again. Beecham
apparently disdained to beat anything less complex than phrase
lengths; this he did with total precision and great eloquence; one
musician, however, watching him guide the London Philharmonic
Orchestra in its magnificent early days through a rhythmically
complex passage suggested that while his baton was phrasing the
melody and his left hand marking accentuations he was at the same
time beating time by opening and closing the fingers of his left
hand.

Wilhelm Furtwängler, a conductor at the antipodes from any
literal and inelastic treatment of a score, who conducted like
Wagner or Mahler to achieve unwritable but convincing fluctuations of *tempo*, seemed incapable of giving precise instructions
with his baton. As an interpretative artist, he seemed incapable of
giving a routine performance, as though he were thinking out the
most familiar work for the first time whenever he conducted it. At
times Furtwängler seemed to experience appalling difficulties in
beginning a work and would stand, right hand and baton raised
but fluttering indecisively, and though, at the fifty-ninth minute of
the eleventh hour, he was making a last determined effort to secure
the final, definitive performance of music he had conducted all his
life; the indecisiveness seemed to have little effect on any orchestra
familiar with his methods, and a member of the Berlin Philharmonic
Orchestra, expert in all Furtwängler's idiosyncrasies, when asked
how the orchestra could decide and play to the conductor's first
beat, said: "We don't; we simply come in on the ninth preliminary
wiggle." But however odd and unconvincing Furtwängler's beat
could be, his performances of great music by Beethoven, Mozart,
Wagner and Bruckner seemed always to rise to the height on which
the work itself existed.

Furtwängler and Beecham always left an audience feeling that
much of the performance they had heard had been almost extem-
porized, fresh and moving and apparently spontaneous. They conducted the sounds the orchestra made and not a performance
worked out in every detail at rehearsal. Everything in their performances seems to have been thought out afresh, with new excitement, as the music came to life. Otto Klemperer, on the other
hand, seemed to be reading from scores carved in stone somewhere
on the upper slopes of Mount Sinai, and to raise personal prefer-
ences in such matters into matters of doctrine is, perhaps, foolishly

narrow-minded. Klemperer brought a complete and long predetermined conception of a work to life, but neither Beecham nor Furtwängler seemed to have a Klempererian final conception of any great work, as though, perhaps, the work was too great to allow them any final decision.

Asked how he achieved such magnificent results, Beecham is said to have replied, "I simply find the best musicians and then leave them to play", and musicians who played for him bear witness to the amount of freedom he gave to instrumentalists to play their own parts as they themselves felt them; it was these often beautiful personal approaches to a work which he could mould together into a complete whole and from which he achieved not only delightful performances of the light music—his "lollipops" as he liked to call them—which provided him with encores, or simply of works by Mozart and Haydn who brought out the best in his often wayward genius, but also by Beethoven and by Wagner, whose music he often professed to dislike. Wagner, to Beecham, was a composer whose music has not only power and colour but also grace and ease of movement and, above all, an irresistible lyrical appeal.

The quality of conducting does not therefore depend upon technical finesse. When Spohr, in 1820, took his baton from his pocket to confront the orchestra of the London Philharmonic Society with modern conducting, the baton seemed completely essential as a means of securing the utmost precision and unanimity. Its point was the focus of the orchestra's attention, and even if the players did not follow its travels through every beat of every bar (a dedication greater than is really necessary) at least they remained in sufficient contact with the conductor's gestures to produce the performance they had rehearsed. Conductors in the tradition which Nikisch brought to its culmination over seventy years ago, expressing everything they wish from the orchestra with the baton alone, are not the only conductors who can claim both complete absorption in the music and the power of communicating its grandeur and excitement.

In 1912, Leopold Stokowski (despite his name a London-born organist with a Polish father and an Irish mother) who had settled in the United States four years before, was appointed conductor of the Philadelphia Orchestra. He had previously conducted the Cincinnati Symphony Orchestra since 1909. In 1912, Stokowski was thirty years old, tall, fair-haired, slim and handsome, with the quality of personality which the late twentieth century has decided to call 'charisma'; he made the Philadelphia Orchestra into one of the world's great virtuoso ensembles. He also made it one of the world's best known, taking it into film studios and giving with it the first concert to be seen on television in the United States. His programmes were remarkably adventurous, and he was prepared to tell adoring audiences that it was their duty to listen to difficult modern music and to insist that they did so. At the same time, he was a specialist in orchestral sonorities and balance, experimenting for a long time with varied methods of seating the orchestra and even, for a time, putting the woodwind into the front of the orchestra and placing the strings behind them. His actual conducting technique was, to say the least, flamboyant, and he used his natural flamboyance as he used his remarkable sensitivity of ear to serve the orchestra and the music it played.

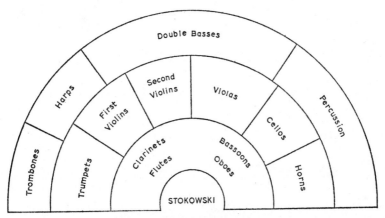

Philadelphia Orchestra, 1939–40

Stokowski was one of the first conductors to grow disillusioned with the baton; he decided that more precise and flexible indications of what was needed than a rigid baton could supply. Stokowski's hands, beautifully shapely and extremely expressive, moulded phrases with great subtlety and stylishness, and it was typical of his panache that his next decision was that audiences would concentrate more thoroughly on the music if the lights were lowered; naturally, for the sake of the orchestra spotlights had to follow his hands as they worked.

Batonless conducting has become an accustomed method which a large number of extremely skilful musicians have used, among them the highly theoretical Hermann Scherchen and Pierre Boulez, whose reputation as a conductor has come to stand as high as his renown as a difficult, uncompromising composer. To what extent results would be different if batonless conductors used a baton it is hard to say; the quest, in the case of some of their number, is not for a greater flexibility and elasticity of musical style that can

K

be achieved with a baton; Boulez, whose repertoire contains much highly complex and hugely scored music, like Schoenberg's *Gurre-lieder* and Mahler's Sixth and Eighth Symphonies, conducts work like this from the shoulder, so to speak, with a right arm which rarely bends and takes little notice of subtleties of nuance. Like all other aspects of the peculiar art of the conductor, the use or abandonment of the baton seems to be of less importance than the personality of the conductor, his musical responsiveness and sensitivity and his attitude to the players who sit in front of him.

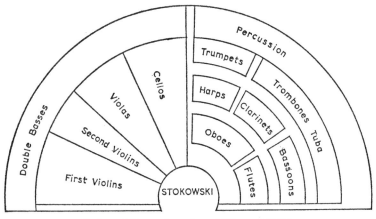

Stokowski's seating plan, 1960s and 1970s

Any mention of Stokowski, of course, leads to reflections about the showman-conductor. A conductor, unless he chooses to work behind a curtain, is naturally the focus of the audience's attention and his gestures indicate their approach to the music as much as they dictate the orchestra's. Boult, the least showy of conductors, imposes a quality of concentration on listeners as on the orchestra; Reiner's immobility and Beecham's almost gymnastic, balletic movements ("The performance was good," said a member of one of his audiences at the conclusion of a concert, "and the choreography was superb") both impress, and perhaps are ways of impressing, the audience; a retiring introvert conductor may not be a contradiction in terms but is at least a paradox.

So far as portraits can be trusted, Berlioz conducted with a sort of imperial, Napoleonic calm, and without any choreography; musicians who played in his orchestras spoke of his calmness, his clarity and decisiveness and his courtesy to them. Wagner, too, was not a very demonstrative conductor; his search for rhythmic subtleties seems to have been entrusted entirely to his baton. His disciples, Hans von Bülow and Hans Richter, do not seem to have set out to give the audience an interesting display.

The first showman conductor to endear himself to Britain and America seems to have been Louise-Antoine Jullien, who conducted Promenade Concerts (originally concerts given in a theatre, not a concert-hall, in informal circumstances and containing a fair amount of light music) in London. Jullien obviously had great musical abilities; his orchestras were finely rehearsed and extremely disciplined. His concerts themselves, when he made London the centre of his activities after 1840, when he was twenty-eight, included quadrilles of his own composition or compilation, often involving the addition of military bands to the orchestra. Portraits suggest that whatever was happening, from a quadrille or a cornet solo to a symphony, his style remained dignified and authoritative. But behind his desk was a deep and throne-like armchair into which he sank in exhaustion after the climax of a piece in which he would add to the orchestral sonority by seizing a piccolo or a violin and joining in the final 'fortissimo'. Jullien was a serious musician as well as a showman, and it is quite probable that his performances of the Beethoven symphonies (which he persuaded his audiences to enjoy) were better played than those of the Philharmonic Society during this period. But to demonstrate that Beethoven's music is specially great, he conducted it wearing clean white kid gloves, brought to him on a silver salver, and with a jewelled baton. Whatever else he was—and we have no way of knowing the real quality of his interpretative abilities—Jullien was a fine orchestral trainer and a splendid popularizer of music; his audiences would have never listened to symphonies if he had not conducted them.

Jullien seems to have been more responsible than anybody else for the legend of the conductor as a sort of Svengali, hypnotizing orchestras into slavish obedience to his commands; at least, he knew that it was he who would draw the eyes of the audience, and what he seems to have wanted them to see was a calmly impassioned, authoritative commander-in-chief. Audiences still like visible proof that the conductor is in control and dictating his terms to the orchestra although orchestras can normally be trusted to grow hilarious over exaggerated conductorial antics and are usually ready to deflate the pretensions of any conductor. There was one who insisted on repeating a phrase over and over again in rehearsal, using it as a text for lectures in metaphysics but not, to the players' minds, making his wishes sufficiently clear. At last, as they ached with boredom, he seemed satisfied. "That's it," he said. "Let's just do it once again and see what it sounds like." "No," said the players, "you do it again and we'll see what you sound like."

Nevertheless, an orchestra delights in the work of a conductor who, whatever his way of working, achieves exciting, consistent results. Orchestras as well as audiences are among the admirers of the emotionally extravagant Bernstein, and orchestras usually loved (with intervals for hatred) the exigent, humorous, witty, impish but often possessed Beecham. The great conductors' qualities—insight, communication and musicianship—are immediately recognizable though they defy analysis.

Their relationships with orchestras are equally mysterious. Toscanini, Mahler and Georg Szell (who rapidly turned the Cleveland Orchestra from a respectable provincial ensemble into an instrument of immense precision and polish) were remorseless tyrants. Barbirolli, a slave of music, expected his orchestra to share his slavery and usually found it willing to do so. Beecham, an eccentric wit in public, provided the orchestras he rehearsed with a dazzling display of wit, eccentricity and 'temperament' in the most romantic sense of that word. Bruno Walter seemed, in his later years, to regard any orchestra as a favourite collection of nephews and nieces. There is, perhaps, a style and an approach for every conductor. There are those who regard the essential skills as those concerned with handling men, but there are those who are convinced that anybody who knows how he wants to conduct a work, however simple or however complex, and how to demonstrate the effects he wants to achieve without too much talk or waste of time, will find any orchestra eager, co-operative and enthusiastic.

NINE

Consolidation and Expansion

It was hardly necessary, by the time Wagner's works were written, to think of expanding the orchestra any further, except perhaps for the sake of dramatic effect in the opera-house, though such expansions would provide inevitable additions to the vocabulary of the concert hall. The power, range and mass of orchestral tone had reached, it seemed, the point at which additions were not needed. Even Wagner tubas, which gave the brass section the homogeneity of tone which composers had desired for a century, did not become a permanent feature of the orchestra. The composer's colour palette had achieved almost its complete range without Wagner's invention, and as composers began to be concerned with blending and contrasting their colour rather than with massiveness and weight of tone, they seemed to be hardly necessary.

Massive as Bruckner's music is, from his First Symphony composed in 1865 and 1866 to his Ninth, left unfinished at his death in 1896, its massiveness comes from its time-scale and its harmonic processes rather than from an expanded orchestra. Despite Bruckner's adoration of Wagner, only the slow movement of the Seventh Symphony, written as an elegy to Wagner after the news of the composer's death had reached Austria, uses Wagner tubas. Though Bruckner's orchestral style owes more to Wagner's than to any other composer's, as does his harmonic scale and time-scheme, and, although well-meaning friends insisted that Bruckner should revise his music to make its orchestration still more Wagnerian, Bruckner was content with Beethoven's instruments balanced as Wagner wanted them balanced in performance, with the tuba, which had become obligatory in the 1860s. The climax of the Seventh Symphony is a single cymbal clash, the only cymbal clash in Bruckner's work, and this was an addition suggested by friends who did not realize the true nature of Bruckner's work or recognize that he was too independent in outlook to need additional Wagnerisms.

In many respects, Bruckner abandoned a great deal of Wagnerian colour. His oboes or trumpets, for example, will send a line of glowing colour across an almost neutrally tinted score, but the climax of a movement is usually a matter of stark black and white, the entire orchestra thundering an affirmation in a unison four or even five octaves deep, the allurements of orchestral colour abandoned.

For reasons like these, the saxophones, invented by the Belgian Adolphe Saxe and patented in 1846, never became regular members of the orchestra but found a place, like Wagner tubas, in the 'additional brass' which could be called upon when needed. Saxophones provide a family of fourteen instruments, from sopranino, in the piccolo range, to double-bass. They are brass instruments played through a reed, which puts them into a class of their own, and they have a complete homogeneity of tone throughout their register; this might have been an asset to composers who had been searching throughout the nineteenth century for such homogeneity. The saxophones, however, refuse to blend or merge with other orchestral instruments, and their obstinate individuality has meant that composers have reserved them for moments when their characteristic tone, ingratiating but rather oily, is appropriate to some special purpose.

Ten years after the invention of the instrument, the Alsatian composer Georg Kastner used them in his opera *Le dernier Roi de Juda*. Berlioz arranged his *Chant Sacre* for an ensemble of six saxophones; both Meyerbeer and Bizet (in *L'Arlesienne*) wrote for saxophones, but in solo passages where their inability to blend into the ensemble would not be a disadvantage. Vincent D'Indy, the French composer who died in 1931 at the age of eighty, found that a quartet of saxophones could be invaluable in supporting voices in unaccompanied music because, played quietly, their tone could hide behind that of the voices and ensure accuracy of vocal intonation without obtruding themselves. In 1902 Richard Strauss asked for a quartet of saxophones in his *Sinfonia Domestica*, using them in the monster orchestra he demanded for his works at the turn of the century simply to add their tone to the harmonies in the middle of the orchestral register.

By the end of the First World War, saxophones had begun to appear in American jazz groups and by the 1930s four saxophones had become, with drums, the essential instruments in the dance music of the period; their players exploited the instrument's special qualities of tone and gave it an agility earlier composers had not attempted to explore or develop. It was, perhaps, its combination of glib virtuosity with assertive oiliness of tone which persuaded Vaughan Williams, in 1930, to add an E flat saxophone to his orchestra in *Job* to depict Job's 'comforters', who are seen in the work as hypocrites. The saxophone reappears to make a similar effect in Vaughan Williams's Sixth Symphony, where it has a solo passage to play in the Scherzo.

While the saxophone failed to establish itself in the orchestra, the bass clarinet became indispensable. The bass clarinet began its life with a complete chromatic range, and its individual tone, tending to be hollow and sinister, even with the suggestion of a rattle in its lowest register, not only strengthened but added a new quality to the bass of the orchestra. In the *Casse Noisette* ballet by Tchaikovsky, the Sugar Plum Fairy's dance is scored for celeste and bass clarinet, the fairy tinkling of the celeste offset by the hollow, sinister sound of the bass clarinet plunging into its deepest register.

Most other nineteenth-century additions to the orchestra were really effects available to the composer when he needed them. Those who, like Brahms as well as Bruckner, were content with a balanced orchestra of the instruments which satisfied Beethoven, took no notice of them. Brahms never needed more power or more colour than Beethoven had bequeathed to his followers, so that many listeners think of Brahms as a composer whose interest in the orchestra was restricted to the physical capacities of its instruments and the most straightforward way of disposing of his music among the available instruments. While Brahms never set out to colour his music as though colour could be an important element in any work, his use of the orchestra in pastel shades and for the sake of mellow, glowing effects rather than brilliance is always entirely individual. The first entry of the violins, for example, in the Second Symphony—high in the leger lines above the treble clef after the horns and cellos have crooned their lullaby, is not an effect which blazes vividly—but it lifts the heart with a sense of ease and utter naturalness; had he brought it in with harmonies of thirds and sixths, it would be more colourful and far more sentimental, but its simplicity alone is a thrilling quality.

The Song of Destiny, perhaps the most grimly outspoken declaration of pessimism that Brahms ever made, contrasts the happiness of a world of blessed spirits with the stresses and miseries of human life; the orchestra opens the work in a mood of absolute bliss that ends with a solo flute alone above the orchestra dying away almost as though it was pronouncing a benediction. Brahms's handling of the orchestra for his own purposes was masterly.

To him, the orchestra was a single, many-voiced instrument, rich and varied in tone but essentially homogeneous. The slow movement of the Second Symphony opens with a descending melody from the cellos; it is accompanied by an ascending melody from the bassoons, which, though it becomes almost as important as the cello theme in the growth of the movement, appears almost as though it is only an accompaniment to the cellos' song, and most conductors take the composer's aim to be a blend of tone which minimizes the differences between the instrument's colour. But though such effects are common even in the most relaxed and ingratiating of his symphonies, Beecham and a few other conductors have shown that the work loses nothing of its quality and integrity of thought if such passages are played with a real but unexaggerated sense of colour. If colour as an end in itself was not one of his concerns, it seems entirely unnecessary to treat his music, as many conductors do, as though it is all polished and well-cared-for mahogany.

The appearance of the nineteenth-century nationalist composers in Czechoslovakia and Russia did not noticeably expand the orchestra though it developed new varieties of colour through the mere fact of nationalism. The music of Smetana and Dvořák, for example, often provides vivid new colours simply by writing for customary instruments in a national way; the Bohemian delight in strong, pungent woodwind tone, less refined than that of players from Germany, Austria or France, is a Czech national style which delighted all Europe. The Russians, too, for all the novelty of their music, found new colours in the familiar palette. Balakirev's symphonies—and Balakirev was the teacher and theorist of the splendid first generation, the 'mighty handful', the 'Five', of Russian composers—wrote melodies never far from folk song and suggested vistas of hugely extending landscape and vast distances with a traditional orchestra. Mussorgsky's *Boris Godunov,* arguably the supreme if awkward, imperfectly organized masterpiece of Russian nationalist music, makes its effect by the spacing of the instruments of the normal orchestra; the great cathedral bells of the coronation scene are a magnificent effect, but Mussorgsky recognized that they belong only to that single scene.

Tchaikovsky, a great non-nationalist conventionally trained and distrustful of the school of Balakirev (which rejected any conventional, systematic training and regarded Tchaikovsky as a composer handicapped by his conservatoire training at St Petersburg) created an entirely original, individual orchestral style not by adding new and exotic instruments but by exploiting the conventional orchestra's capacity for emotional expression and vivid colour; Tchaikovsky's exultations, miseries, glooms and depressions are all gigantic, and the music of his ballets, disciplined and controlled by stage action, is vivid and colourful enough to set the scene almost without décor and designs. The *Pathetic Symphony,* composed in 1893, adds only one flute, one clarinet and a tuba, with bass drum, cymbals and gong to the orchestra which satisfied Brahms in his First Symphony, almost twenty years before, and

Beethoven, in the first movement of his Ninth, seventy years before; furthermore, Tchaikovsky uses his extra percussion only sparingly. The bass drum and cymbals make their presence felt in the wild march of the Scherzo, but the great crash which dispels the lyrical dream of the second subject in the first movement comes from timpani and orchestra, not from the potentially deafening percussion, and there is a single gong stroke, marked 'piano', in the finale; it is the signal for the tragic passage for brass which romantically minded commentators have compared to a descent into the grave and the final lament of the *Coda*.

The master of exotic orchestration among the Russians was Rimsky-Korsakov, who grew to be doubtful about Balakirev's anti-academic prejudices and undertook a strict academic training of his own devising. Rimsky-Korsakov's more professional attitude led to his individual, and remarkably brilliant, orchestral style. Like Tchaikovsky, he understood the areas in which each instrument is specially effective or lamentably dull, and he wrote for instruments in the range which he needed for colour and brilliance and not simply for pitch. He was more enterprising than Tchaikovsky in his use of percussion, but the brilliant surface of his music owes more to his habit of displaying solo instruments against a background strongly coloured in its own right, and by deliberately diversifying the orchestra by setting important themes in vivid instrumental ranges while maintaining bright colours in the subsidiary parts. In addition, harps, percussion and the instruments which exist for effects are used to splash colour brightly across his scores. His delight in quasi-oriental melody in *Scheherazade*, *Sadko* and *Le Coq d'Or* gives Rimsky-Korsakov's orchestra a brilliance all its own. His professionalism and his sympathy with the other members of the Balakirev group made him their conscience, ready to orchestrate and organize music which they left incomplete or disorganized, and though his complexion and orchestration of Mussorgsky's *Boris Godunov* and *Khovantschina* is now frowned upon as too exotic and too brilliant for the subject matter, it made possible the triumph of these works in the world's opera-houses. The more recent treatment of these works by Shostakovitch, another superb master of the orchestra, is more sober, perhaps more genuinely Russian, but it does not remove the world's debt of gratitude for Rimsky-Korsakov, who treated them as he treated his own music, in a way designed to exploit the contrasts of tone possible in the orchestra.

Such expansion as there was in the orchestra was an expansion of the percussion section. Tchaikovsky's use of the celeste in *Casse Noisette* is one of the earliest examples of the use of melodic percussion; the celeste, unlike the side drum and bass drum, cannot be dismissed simply as an effect. Like Tchaikovsky, other composers found the celeste's purity of tone, clarity and delicacy, invaluable. Mahler in his Sixth Symphony found a means of suggesting that the instrument has reserves of strength not discovered by Tchaikovsky, but in the closing passage of *Das Lied von der Erde* he, as did Delius at the end of *Sea Drift*, made a wonderful effect through its serene tinkling above an atmosphere of pain and loss.

The xylophone, with its hard, penetrating, unresonant tone has a slightly longer history: Saint-Saëns used it in the less than passionately serious *Danse Macabre* in 1874 and twelve years later in the tongue-in-cheek humour of the *Carnaval des Animaux*. The xylophone was of course available to Mahler, who had a use for every instrument with a tone and personality of its own.

Apart from the tuned percussion instruments, a number of new 'effects' instruments were taken into the percussion section. The gong found a place not only in Tchaikovsky's *Pathetic Symphony*, where it is marked 'ad libitum' and is heard only for a single stroke. The gong became the natural instrument for creating an atmosphere of foreboding, for expressing the sinister and fearful by means of strokes rarely marked as stronger than 'piano'; the free reverberation of a beaten gong keeps the sound of a 'piano' stroke alive for a considerable time; a gong struck 'fortissimo' would obliterate the sound of the rest of the orchestra.

Side-drums and the deeper tenor drums, hardly used in the orchestra since Handel had employed a side drum in the last movement of the Fireworks Music in 1749 became more frequently employed, and tambourines occasionally joined them. With the tuned percussion, antique cymbals often tuned to a definite pitch, the glockenspiel, forgotten since Mozart had scored it into *The Magic Flute* and, occasionally, tubular bells, the percussion section grew more in the nineteenth century than any other section of the orchestra.

Wagner died in 1883, at the age of seventy. Within ten years of his death, his heirs Gustav Mahler (born in 1860) and Richard Strauss (born in 1864), had made their presence felt. Mahler grew up in poverty in Bohemia, but in a Jewish enclave where music and culture in general were German. Strauss, the son of a fine horn player in the Munich Court Orchestra, was born into opera and concert music while Mahler's first musical experiences were of folk songs and the military music of the nearby barracks. As a child, the young Mahler was an unusually gifted pianist and he was admitted into the Vienna Conservatoire at the age of fifteen; he composed his first large-scale work, *Das Klagende Lied*, when he was twenty; this, he later said, was the first work in which he had found his own voice and style. Strauss, who had first had enrolled behind Brahms in the ranks of the anti-Wagnerians—his father had disliked Wagner and Wagner's music and proved to be a thorn in the flesh of Wagner's conductor disciples—composed his orchestral fantasy *Aus Italien* in 1886 and *Don Juan*, the first of this symphonic poems two years later in 1888, the year in which Mahler completed his First Symphony. By this time, Strauss was as dedicated a Wagnerian as Mahler had always been, and liked to think of himself, as 'Richard the Second', the spiritual heir of the great Richard Wagner.

For many years, critics and would-be historians have liked to couple the name of Mahler with that of Bruckner, a composer whom he knew and liked but with whom he had little in common. However, to himself and to the world at large Strauss was a man apart. Strauss thought of himself as the great revolutionary, carrying on the work of Richard the First, but Brahms, who had first become aware of Mahler as an unusually gifted young conductor, when shown one of Mahler's scores, said that Mahler was the true revolutionary; whether he said this in admiration or in horror was not reported. In 1888, the two young men seemed to occupy an almost identical position, both brilliant conductors, both devoted to the music and the musical doctrines of Wagner, both fascinated by the power and weight, the colour and brilliance, of the orchestra at its hugest. Strauss, as a brilliant young conductor, did more than Mahler himself to draw attention to and to perform Mahler's music, for Mahler exercised his terrifying perfectionism as a conductor chiefly on the works of others; as Director of the Imperial Opera in Vienna, Mahler offered to resign because the court authorities refused to allow a performance of Strauss's *Salome*.

Strauss's orchestra began as large: by the time he reached *Ein Heldenleben*, in 1898, the *Sinfonia Domestica*, completed in 1903 and the *Alpensinfonie* in 1916, it had become gargantuan. It builds on a large and luscious body of string tone, which provides almost all his music with a luxurious basic texture. Even in the Hero's battle against his 'Adversaries' (one of the most unflattering portrayals of music critics; the whole battle is easier to accept as high spirits than as the struggle of a daring adventurer against hidebound reactionaries who hinder his work) he never really discards the rich, cushioning sound of his strings, not even for the sake of adding acerbity to the out-of-tune fanfares and the spiky woodwind figures to which the forlorn hope of advancing critics marches into battle and a vastly noisy but easily achieved defeat.

No composer knew the orchestra better than Strauss. His ideal was a more than Wagnerian richness, so that he demanded not only unusual instruments—the archaic oboe d'amore, for example, in the *Sinfonia Domestica*—but also more and more of the standard instruments on which tone and colour really depend. Quadruple or even quintuple woodwind are joined by eight horns and six or eight trumpets. Strauss handles his orchestra superbly, but the audience, when Strauss's orchestra was hard at work, cannot and is not expected to hear everything; details are lost in a marvellous sweep and wash of orchestral sound; melodies are often played in mixed colour by several different instruments; almost everything, especially melodies and important accompanimental figures, is doubled at the octave, or for two or three octaves; richness is all, and Strauss's orchestra is usually as rich as the best available fruit cake. These superb mixed colours are deployed in elaborate polyphony with all their doublings and the cushioning strings to support them, and the effect is that of a solid, iridescent, yielding block of sound, always sensuously beautiful, always involved in expressive melody but capable, with an inefficient or unsympathetic conductor of suggesting the efforts of a boneless creature to stand erect and walk purposefully. In properly sympathetic hands, Strauss's music, even when its themes and melodies are not the most impressive he invented, is sumptuous and moving. The love music of *Ein Heldenleben* and the *Sinfonia Domestica*, is overwhelming in its emotional power; men and women, we feel, are rarely so happy, so ecstatic as this, but they should be. And if the baby Strauss's bath, in the *Sinfonia Domestica*, suggests that its splashings are huger than tidal waves and its tantrums more destructive than cyclones, it is only the listener who cannot accept the idea of the mock heroic who grumbles. Others surrender happily to the rich, controlled sentimentalism which his crowded orchestration expresses at such moments.

The symphonic poems, which came to their mighty conclusion with the *Sinfonia Domestica*, led him to opera. *Salome* and *Elektra*, his first successful and mature operas, find time to indulge his passion for a rich soprano voice delivering great lyrical, ringing phrases, but escape the influence of his almost equal passion for luxurious string tone. Both operas are fierce, combining in a unique way a sense of decadence with a terrifying energy. Salome's Dance of the Seven Veils and her final, singularly horrific scene with the severed head of John the Baptist yield to the composer's passion (Viennese, though Strauss came from Munich), for a waltz in which strings, much divided, with first violins high in their register, dance with a passionate nostalgia; but the expression in these terms of Salome's perverted eroticism is dramatically compelling. Elektra's madness, a sort of obsessive blood lust, has no such appalling raptures and permits lyrical expressiveness only when Elektra, the down-trodden daughter of the murdered King Agamemnon, recognizes her brother, come in disguise to avenge their father's death by killing their mother and her guilty lover, and in the jubilant dance of triumph with which she greets her brother's success.

Both operas are built from short themes and *motifs* in a way that suggests that the orchestra is making music by grinding themes harshly together. Neither is moderate in its demands for instruments, but the remorseless vigour with which Strauss uses the instruments precludes any of the rapturous sensuality which takes possession of the audience's mind during performances of his orchestral works and later operas. The energy of the music, which suggests that the instruments themselves are grinding the music into shape from the most basic raw materials gives the works an almost shocking mastery.

The *Salome* and *Elektra* style was brought into existence for only two works; *Der Rosenkavalier*, Strauss's gorgeous, sentimental social comedy produces the accustomed sumptuousness and the Straussian surrender to gorgeous string tone and the soprano voice. What might be called a love theme in *Der Rosenkavalier* is a tinkling chain of chords associated with the silver rose, the engagement token presented by the ardent, romantic adolescent hero to the adorably sweet, silly heroine on behalf of the husband her father has chosen for her, a gross, elderly, lecherous minor aristocrat. This love theme is not lyrical, but it appears always with great distinctness simply from its scoring for celeste, harp, high woodwind; it is obtrusive rather than amorous, perhaps because it remembers that the opera's two lovers are adolescents. But everything in *Der Rosenkavalier*—social observation, comedy, sentiment and boisterous farce—exists in the perspective created by a richly expressive string orchestra which, in addition to its moments of domination, supports the horns for which Strauss always wrote beautifully, the very active brass and the woodwind; the oboes too, are given a multitude of passages which must delight a player's heart, but everything in the score, and every instrument, is in place and treated with something like favouritism.

Strauss delighted, as his multiple doublings suggest, in complexity. Bruckner's huge unison climaxes, which are simply octave doublings by the entire orchestra over four or five octaves, are deliberate simplifications of complex textures; Strauss's doublings simply add to a richness which robs them of individuality. His virtuosity, in addition, makes him capable of trickeries which have led puritanical musicians to question his taste. Rossini once claimed that he could set any text, even a mere laundry list, to music. Strauss might equally well have claimed that he could imitate anything, turning any sort of sound into acceptable music and finding the musical equivalent of any action. The orchestra carries love scenes, in *Don Juan* and the introduction of *Der Rosenkavalier*, to their unmistakable physical climax. The moments of the death of *Don Juan*, in a duel and of Don Quixote after his return to normality, are unmistakable. The orchestra of *Don Quixote* includes a wind machine for the scene in which the hero and his comic squire ride through the air, and muted horns imitate the sheep whom he mistakes for wizards; the windmill which he sees as a giant is not imitated but composed into a figure which suggests the ponderous movement of its sweeps. Only a sadly over-refined taste could fail to share the composer's pleasure in his ingenuity.

As an old man, Strauss simplified his style. His gargantuan orchestra slimmed itself, in his final works, almost to the proportions of a chamber orchestra in music as splendidly composed, as inventive in orchestration, as any of his earlier works but far more natural and neatly proportioned. The lovely *Four Last Songs* for soprano and orchestra, incredible as the work of a composer over eighty years old, echoes the true Straussian rapture and sensuality in simple terms but with no loss of emotional richness.

Post-Wagnerian composers were either consolidators or enlargers. The orchestra of Edward Elgar, a composer three years older than Mahler and seven years older than Strauss, is an orchestra of almost Straussian dimensions, though Elgar never demanded the massed brass of Strauss at his most grandiloquent; it is an orchestra created for richness as gorgeous as Strauss's, and often used as sumptuously. The amazing achievement it represents, even apart from the greatness of Elgar's power and originality, is that none of his English predecessors had a similar command of the modern orchestra, so that the skill of the *Enigma Variations* of 1899, its orchestral layout, its feeling for instrumental colour and its sureness in handling the orchestra had no precedent in recent English music; Elgar had, too, the tactical skill to deploy his forces in the most effective way.

The difference between Elgar's orchestra and Strauss's, however, is not simply the difference between Strauss's relationship to a great tradition and Elgar's English idiosyncrasy; the nerves of Elgar's music are nearer the skin. Even in his most sumptuous music there is a great nervous energy. Strauss's music relapses into delight at the rich sound in which it clothes itself, but even Elgar's most ebullient moments never rests; when it delights, it delights in its power of movement.

Often, at its most inventive, Elgar's music seems to express a troubled spirit. In *The Dream of Gerontius*, the dying man describes the approach of death as "this emptying out of each constituent and natural force by which I come to be", and the orchestra, in a short sequence of harmonies, empties itself of all colour and animation. It is, of course, the spacing of harmonies and the coalescing of instruments into a chord topped by an open octave which achieves this totally deadening effect and its sense of complete dereliction. The sense of 'emptying out', achieved by similar means, often 'empties out' the sense of joy in action, so that the passage in *The Dream of Gerontius* is almost a key-passage to the understanding of Elgar's emotions. Elgar's colours glow rather than shine or burn, and in some accustomed techniques seem to be over-used—very many climaxes grow out of rapid chromatic ascents from the trombones, an effect so natural to the composer that he uses it, transferred to cellos and double-basses, in the splendid *Introduction and Allegro for Strings*—his power survives them.

But Elgar's understanding of the orchestra is always complete; potentially awkward instruments, like the bass clarinet, are always given time to warm up unobtrusively, so that when their voice has to take the lead they can speak confidently and securely. In the great hymn of the angels, which Gerontius hears on his way to God's judgment hall, the glory is almost complete and the joy overwhelming until we remember Gerontius awaiting the moment of judgment as a low-lying clarinet climbs up a simply, questioning phrase; this is a part of the texture which many conductors seem not to regard as worthy of special attention, but given its place in the audience's consciousness by the slightest degree of emphasis, its effect is overwhelming. Percussion instruments mean less to Elgar than they did to Strauss or Mahler, and he never seems to have any special interest in experimenting with them.

According to Mahler, he and Strauss were tunnelling into a mountain from opposite sides and would eventually meet in the middle. At first, their sense of the orchestra at its grandest, their choice of themes and 'programmes' for their works and their loyalty to the doctrines of Wagner provided each of them with a starting point from which they diverged. Mahler's first big work, the first which he cared to acknowledge, *Das Klagende Lied*, was completed when he was twenty and revised in 1893 and again between 1898 and 1900, ready for a delayed first performance in 1901. It is scored for soprano, contralto and tenor soloists, a choir and large orchestra, all used with great effectiveness in what might be called a conventional post-Wagnerian style, though there are moments at which Mahler seems to seek out colour for its own sake. Professor Donald Mitchell, who has studied the unpublished original manuscript score of the work before its later revision, has pointed out that the revision moderates the adolescent composer's demands; possibly only devout Wagnerism persuaded young Mahler to demand six harps for *Das Klagende Lied*, for the revision, made when Mahler was a renowned conductor with a probably clearer sense of practicalities, is satisfied with two. The use of folk-song style melodies, which necessarily influence the style of orchestration, is an entirely unWagnerian influence, and it influences the scoring towards the woodwind. Mahler told his friend Natalie Bauer-Lechner (who earned the gratitude of all Mahler's admirers by piously reporting his conversation in detail) that his Bohemian background showed itself musically in the prominence of the upper woodwind in his scores, and in his love for their voices used in the most pungent, strong folk-music style.

Das Klagende Lied tells in cantata style the folk-story of the elder brother who, for love of a Princess, murdered his younger brother. A wandering minstrel found one of the dead boy's bones, and from it made a flute. Played at the marriage of the Princess to the murderer, the flute played and sang the story of the murder. Mahler's score, as its original demand for harps shows, displayed a grand disdain for economy. The style of orchestration suggests the fundamental orchestral principles of Mahler's later works, but it rejoices in the vastness and power a large orchestra could supply. Amongst his demands in the cantata's final part is an offstage band—though the work is not designed to be staged and would prove unstageable, Mahler aimed at drama—of three bassoons, four flugelhorns, two cornets, timpani, triangle and cymbals; the final revision did not alter the numbers of the offstage band because Mahler as a conductor knew that there is a considerable difference between the effect of a dozen players playing loudly and heard from a distance and half a dozen instruments playing more softly from nearer at hand; for the sake of practicality, one supposes, he turned the flugelhorns and cornets into normal horns and trumpets; the purpose of the unusual instruments, like the purpose of the offstage band itself, is dramatic effectiveness—a wish to separate the music of jubilation from the doom-laden atmosphere of the story which mentions it; the offstage band is meant to allow the composer the freedom to rejoice in the context of a melodramatic tragedy. Typical of Mahler, too, is that fact that he writes for the pert, penetrating E flat clarinet, an instrument which he was to use probably more frequently than any other composer.

Mahler completed his First Symphony in 1888, his Second in 1894 (after great difficulty in finding the right culmination and in bringing the work to an end) and he had begun to compose his Third Symphony before the Second was completed. The Third was finished in 1896. These three works in point of orchestration, are the most grandiloquent of his works, demanding huge orchestras with enlarged percussion sections and written at considerable length. The First Symphony has four movements only because a fifth, intermezzo-like movement was suppressed after some early performances. The Second Symphony has five movements, one being a gorgeous song for contralto and the fifth requiring two soloists and choir. The Third has six movements, the second and third being intermezzo-like, the fourth another *Lied*, the fifth a setting of folk-song words for women's choir and boys' choir, and the sixth the slow movement. During the period in which he composed the three symphonies, he composed twelve songs for voice and orchestra, the words taken from the anthology of folk poetry, *Das Knaben Wunderhorn*, which provides ideas and references for the Second and Third Symphonies, both of which use poems from the anthology. The First Symphony refers to the earlier song cycle *Lieder eines fahrenden Gesellen*. One of the *Wunderhorn* songs, telling how Saint Antony of Padua preached to the fishes, who thought his sermon magnificent but behaved just as badly when they had heard it as they had done before, is expanded into the Scherzo of the Second Symphony.

Mahler had no special devotion to the strings orchestra, not even as a comfortable support for a solo voice in the songs; it is as though Mahler's orchestration takes nothing for granted in the orchestral tradition, and in the songs the orchestra is used selectively, so that whatever instrumental voices are heard are deliberately selected for the sake of their colour and tone; the human voice, he seems to believe, is always as reliable and self-sufficient as any orchestral instrument and can hold its own even when his strongly played woodwind parts set themselves to compete with it in dissonant counterpoints. The strings are simply yet another range of colours and effects, not the foundation of orchestral style. In the Second Symphony, long passages in the first movement occupy brass and woodwind with few important contributions from the strings. The huge first movement of the Third depends on wind tone, with the strings more or less reduced to adding a range of effects; the first movement of the grim Sixth Symphony, a vast symphonic march, is equally dominated by wind tone, the second subject, which is at first lyrical and exultant, is the one moment of glory for the strings. The result never, not even in *Das Klagende Lied* and the First Symphony, coalesces into a great mass of gorgeous tone; Mahler's ideal from the first is an orchestra in which each contributing instrument makes us aware both of its thematic importance and of the colour it brings into the score, and when strings take the lead, it is because their voices and colour, often in Mahler yearning and emotional, is the right tone and colour for the passage. Mahler provided players with enormous difficulties of articulation and balance, but he never, after *Das Klagende Lied*, wrote impractically for them.

In the Second Symphony, as in the early cantata, Mahler added an offstage band to an orchestra which already included six horns and four trumpets. The offstage band consists of four horns, four trumpets, triangle, cymbals, side-drum and timpani; the final bars add an organ. The effect, inevitably, is overpowering, but the purpose of the massive orchestra, however, is not Straussian complexity but clarity; however overwhelming the sound of the final climax it is scored so that whatever has to be heard as important and essential stands out of the mighty sound with complete clarity.

"All my orchestra sings," Mahler told the invaluable Natalie Bauer-Lechner. "For me, even the bassoon, even the bass tuba, even the timpani, should sing." This, in a sense, makes all Mahler's instruments functionally almost interchangeable; in the opening of the First Symphony, one of the most glorious of romantic dawns is greeted by a fanfare, which suggests that trumpets should play it in a perfectly conventional way; it rejects convention and is heard from the woodwind. The austere funeral march section of the first movement of the Ninth Symphony ends in a brief violin fanfare. But trumpets, if they are robbed of typical effects which have become clichés sing long, emotional melodies, though one of the hallmarks of Mahler's style is the use of horn calls as peremptory calls to action as well as making them mouthpieces for long, solemn melodies. In the first movement of the Third Symphony, where a solo trombone propels a great deal of the action, it is given phrases marked 'espressivo', 'sentimental', 'piano', in Mahler's customary odd mixture of German and Italian.

In spite of what look like Mahler's aggressive, block-busting tactics—the impression given by the elaborate lists of instruments which fill his scores—his writing is always both expert and extremely subtle. If a note has to be repeated, and the second has to be heard distinctly as a repeated note, the composer arranges for it to be heard separately, the second note coming from second violins, for example if the first has been delivered by first violins, or in the voice of an instrument quite differently coloured from that of the first. If notes are to be detached from each other, the detachment is marked not simply by a *staccato* sign (a dot over each detached note) but by a change of voices. Xylophone, glockenspiel and tubular bells bring their own colours to his scores, but the colour is really the secondary reason for their arrival, the primary reason is that their new and unmistakable colour ensures the clarity and distinctness of whatever they add. The harp is, normally, an instrument notable for its surges and splashes of colour; Mahler demands the plucking of its strings by a plectrum more often than most composers; the plectrum gives greater distinctness to the notes that are heard. In the last ecstasy of the Eighth Symphony, a passage which Mahler felt to be an inspired revelation, harps sweep up and down long *arpeggios* in unison with the piano, so that the piano adds its clarity to the softer-edged wash of harp tone; Mahler's ideal was the maximum distinctness in scores where every note is functional and not simply employed to fill out the body of tone.

In the same way, his percussion is designed to play with a hard-edged definition. The Sixth Symphony, a vast, ultimately despairing work, wants dry-voiced side- and military drums and a whip, two flat pieces of wood which produce a dry, penetrating slap. Both it and the Seventh Symphony ask for cowbells, both 'deep' and 'high' sounding varieties are required though their pitch is not specified. Cowbells have a symbolic meaning to Mahler; they are the last earthly sounds to be heard by the mountaineer as he makes his way to exalted summits; they represent lonely exaltation of spirit above the confusion of everyday life.

In the finale of the Sixth Symphony, and nowhere else in his work, Mahler demands three loud strokes of a hammer upon a dull, unreverberant surface. The three hammer strokes, he said, are symbolic; they are the three blows of fate which would hit his hero, the human race, and the third of them "fells him like an ox". They are the three great punctuation marks of a movement in sonata form, marking the end of the major formal sections. Mahler seems never to have been satisfied with this effect, and he removed the third hammer stroke when he revised the work, though some conductors like to restore it.

Mahler's passion for clarity, which was at the heart of his fierce perfectionism as a conductor, was the prime motive of all his orchestral writing, and from the Fourth Symphony, in 1900, onward, it clearly dominated his idea of scoring. The Fourth Symphony is the only one of his works dominated by the strings, which seem to determine the course of the music in a way unlike any of his other symphonies. He described the Fourth as a work for small orchestra but although its score contains no parts for trombones or tuba, it demands xylophone and glockenspiel, and the clarinettists need instruments in B flat, A and E flat.

From the First Symphony onwards, Mahler had tended to work out much of the development of his music polyphonically, but the Fourth makes polyphony the entire essence of the work. There are no doublings, instruments do not run along together in octaves; later, Mahler seems to have decided that he disliked doublings so much that his performing editions of Mozart's *The Marriage of Figaro* and *Così fan Tutte* cancel out octave doublings with the flute deliciously playing an octave above violin melodies. The Fourth Symphony tends to discard every note which has no strictly functional purpose, achieving a great beauty of orchestral sound which is often disturbing in its lack of subordinate tissue, where two or three instruments each play important thematic passages in counterpoint that inevitably accepts strong dissonances for the sake of polyphonic logic. There are passages in which three or four voices are heard, with no cushioning from subordinate harmonies, each part occupied with thematic material. (*See* Appendix 2, No. 9.) The colour of such passages is often marvellously bright and striking, but their beauty of colour is a secondary product of their musical logic, because they are coloured only so that every strand of the argument can be clearly heard. There are passages of remorselessly crowded scoring in his later symphonies, but they are pages of involved, crowded counterpoint, like the complex double fugue in the first movement of the Eighth Symphony, in which soloists, double choir and a huge orchestra are working out the implications of two themes, each of which produces phrases to be treated separately in the course of the music. What is written is never beautiful padding but is strictly functional. The Eighth Symphony, although it is almost the most demanding music we have in regard to its demand for an army of performers, has pages in the Second Part (it is written in two parts, the second telescoping slow movement, Scherzo and Finale) in which the score on the page has unusual bareness because one or two instruments are occupied with what is essential, and until they have said their say they are undisturbed except, perhaps, by a single supporting voice maintaining the tonality of the passage with an extended pedal note. It is as though Mahler wants his vast forces to appear as a huge chamber orchestra, with no instrument speaking except when it has something strictly necessary to say. The second movement of *Das Lied von der Erde* begins with an oboe playing a plaintive, extended melody which, as it continues, evolves new inflections and new turns of phrase against which the contralto sings a melody which, too, evolves with the minimum of repetition, but in quite different rhythms and inflections from those of the oboe. The last movement, *Der Abschied*, begins with an oboe playing a lonely wisp of melody over repeated gong strokes, each of which is left to die away; to give a sharper edge to each gong stroke, cellos and double-basses play a *pizzicato* note, reinforced by a quiet bass drum to give clarity of attack to the gong; into this, the contralto voice enters with an emotionally neutral recitative-like narration. The end of the work reaches an atmosphere of such rarified quiet stillness that the quiet jangling of a single mandoline adds a new colour to the murmuring of strings and the embroideries of a celeste.

Mahler did not achieve the ultimate in summoning massed forces to his service; that was the achievement of Schoenberg, in his

Gurrelieder, an early work which predates his revolutionary compositions and is, in point of fact, more conservative in style than
Mahler's later music though Schoenberg became an ardent admirer
of Mahler's work and a friend of Mahler himself. *Gurrelieder* not
only requires solo singers, a speaker-narrator, a large choir and an
expanded orchestra but also chains to rattle during a passage in its
second part. The result, however, is never the bare, chamber
orchestral textures which demanded that Mahler employed a vast
orchestra for the sake of absolute precision and distinctness; it is as
lush, as flatly scored and as padded as any music by Richard
Strauss. It was the demand for clarity which led Mahler into excess,
if the demand for instruments which make their voices heard only
for a few bars in enormously extended works can be called excess.
The novelty of Mahler's orchestration was responsible for his
endless revision of his scores; the Fifth Symphony, for example,
was worked over and revised every time he conducted it, and only
the Ninth Symphony and *Das Lied von der Erde*, which he never
heard, comes to us as a first version; every revision meant a greater
sparseness of texture in the interests of unpadded clarity.

Mahler died at the age of fifty-one, so that it is hard to realize
that much of his career coincided with that of Debussy, who was
born in 1862 and was responsible for *Printemps*, his first big
orchestral work after he had left the Paris Conservatoire in 1887,
before Mahler had finished his First Symphony. Unlike Mahler,
and any other composer who had grown up in the Central European tradition, Debussy had no particular interest in the idea of
symphonic development, so that it is in a way surprising that
Mahler was one of the first conductors to realize the novelty and
importance of Debussy's orchestral works. Debussy's music vastly
extended the vocabulary of modern harmony, and his orchestration rapidly solved the problem of developing the new style which
was needed to exploit his new harmonic ideas. *Printemps* is a work
we know in an orchestral version revised by Henri Büsser, a
teacher, composer and conductor eleven years younger than
Debussy.

L'Aprés-Midi d'un Faune, a work of such originality that it still
surprises listeners, was apparently begun some years before the
composer reworked and completed it between 1892 and 1894. It is
a translation into atmospheric, elusive music of an elusive, atmospheric poem by Mallarmé. It is afternoon, summer, the weather is
hot, the faun is daydreaming in the sun and remembering; memories and daydreams pass through his mind; there is a great climax
with the strings delivering a passionate-sounding melody in block
harmonies; it has great power enhanced by the fact that most of
the work suggests and hints rather than states forthrightly. The

music is beautiful, sensuous, erotic and intangible, and it turns the traditional technique of formal contrast into an art of surprise. It begins with an exotic-sounding melody from a solo flute; horns and a harp *glissando* join the flute, the strings creep into the texture unobtrusively; a *crescendo* passage suggests that some action is about to begin but the moment of action passes and all that is left is an unaccompanied clarinet too warm, it may be, and too contented, to bother about movement. The climax is not built up, it simply arrives, for this is part of a dream, and Debussy succeeds in finding shapely and organized music for the arbitrary processes of the dreaming mind. Not a single instrumental idea is doubtful or misjudged; if the form and 'meaning' of the work are elusive, its sound, and its progress from sound to sound, is both beautiful and organized.

Debussy's orchestra is not the multiple, many-voiced instrument of the Central European composers but a collection of individual timbres and colours to be used when required, not in blocks or in familiar combinations of colour but simply when each is required for the sale of its individual voice. Oboes offer sharp, acid comments, flutes flash brightly in their upper register or cling plaintively to emotional statements low in their compass; the clarinets bubble and gurgle in their low chalumeau register but indulge in elaborate arabesques and trills when they are taken into a high register. Trumpets and trombones, open or muted, are sometimes deliberately strident and forceful, but the horns are a race apart, luxurious and dreamy.

The strings provide an inventive, detailed underlay to this; there are few moments of Debussy's orchestral scores in which they are silent, and the underlay they provide is often amazingly detailed, involving *pizzicato* and bowed effects played simultaneously by divided violins, violas or cellos. In *La Mer*, the only one of his orchestral works which approaches symphonic design and balance, with something like a symphonic disposition of themes, approached elliptically and by implication rather than direct statement; there is a section in which the first violins are silent while the rest of the strings, all divided, play figurations which seem to turn into music the multiple sounds of the sea as waves fall and pour themselves away on a shingle beach; it is not description, it is not (like the bird song of Beethoven's Pastoral Symphony) onomatopoeia; it is simply a conversion of natural sound into music. When Debussy designs a climax, the creation of atmosphere and the art of suggestion by which the climax is reached make its power and effectiveness enormous.

La Mer was written between 1902 and 1905, and it was followed by the set of three *Images*, composed between 1906 and 1912. It is

La Mer which remains Debussy's most explicit work. *Iberia*, the second of the *Images*, is masterly in its evocation of a hot Spanish night, of the burning sun, of a fiesta, but all these are conveyed by suggestion and the use of the Spanish rhythms and idioms by which French composers have always succeeded in writing convincing Spanish music. Idiomatic Spanish melodic phrases and rhythms, with an economical use of castanets, convey the rhythms of Spanish dance music. Always, in his orchestral music, Debussy exploits his art of implication and understatement, suggesting powers and passions we take for granted, creating an orchestral style which is completely unorthodox and completely convincing.

TEN

Twentieth-century Developments

By 1910, there was no musical point to be made by further enlargement of the orchestra and no new effect to be made by simply
extending its size. Mahler's remarkably extravagant economy had
led him to demand whatever instruments he had needed even if
they were to contribute only for a few seconds in a work that lasted
for more than an hour; the glockenspiel of the Fourth Symphony
plays in a tiny variation in the slow movement, and then is heard
no more; it is a case in point. The four saxophones of Strauss's
Sinfonia Domestica do not play an extensive rôle in the work, and
Germany had to be ransacked to find the necessary players; any
earlier composer, and most later composers, would reluctantly have
denied himself saxophones and probably distributed their parts
among the other instruments of a normal orchestra.

Havergal Brian, who was born in 1876 and continued to compose
until he was in his nineties, cannot have heard Mahler's Eighth
Symphony and had probably not seen that work in score when he
completed his Gothic Symphony in 1919. But reports of the huge
scale of the so-called 'Symphony of a Thousand' seemed to have
influenced the size and disposition of his forces. If Mahler began
his most grandiloquent work, we imagine him thinking, with the
Veni Creator Spiritus, why should not he end a work of comparable scale with the prayer for deliverance which concludes the
tumultuous praises of the *Te Deum*? But, after its first movement,
the Mahler work takes the huge orchestra to pieces, uses it
sectionally and only slowly builds it up again to the overwhelming
climax in which, he suggested, we are to hear the whole universe
singing together: Brian's Gothic Symphony deals in huge blocks
of tone, with the sections of the orchestra used antiphonally rather
than mingled to weave refined strands of colour, and even Brian
was applying Mahlerian orchestral scale to music totally un-
Mahlerian in outlook.

Few later works have risen to the scale of Walton's *Belshazzar's
Feast*, written for the Leeds Festival in 1931; it demands not only
a very large choir but also an enlarged orchestra with a great battery

of percussion, used with remarkable inventiveness, and two separate brass groups after the style of Berlioz's *Requiem*. These, the composer says, he owes to the advice of Beecham, originally booked to conduct the first performance though he eventually left that task to Sir Malcolm Sargent. Beecham, so the story goes, told the young composer that, as the work would never have a second performance, why should he not really enjoy himself and add a brass band? This, one feels, was Beecham's response to a score which, in its deliberate harshness and violence, did not appeal to his super-civilized taste, for none of the great conductor's other numerous prophecies proved to be so far from the centre of the target. But the mighty *Belshazzar's Feast* was written for the special conditions of a festival, to that some extravagance was not only permitted but welcomed.

A variety of causes both musical and non-musical were responsible for the recoil from the musically colossal. For one thing, apart from Brian who was, so to speak, using the Mahlerian scale for music essentially English in attitude, the colossal style was, at any rate for the time being, exhausted; the prospect of enormous orchestras and choirs did not immediately suggest to new composers the idea of works which would attract by their novelty and individuality; *Belshazzar's Feast* is, after all, a work which belongs to the Europe of twentieth-century violence, persecution and the great dictatorships which it prophesies. It has nothing to do with the spiritual triumphs, the yearnings and emotions of Mahler or the easy victories over purblind critics and the rapturous erotics of Strauss, but with intolerance, cruelty and destruction; its triumph is the total destruction of Belshazzar's Babylon. The colossal served for new purposes, that is to say, when the composer knew the new purposes to which it could be applied.

The aims and ideals of the immediately post-Mahler period were those of Sibelius, whose career began during Mahler's life—he had composed his first three symphonies, most of his symphonic poems on the *Kalevala*, the Finnish national epic, and his Violin Concerto, as well as a large number of smaller works, before Mahler's death, and he was to remain active throughout the 1930s although his last orchestral work, the Seventh Symphony, and the symphonic poem *Tapiola* were composed in 1924 and 1925.

The influence of Sibelius was due to the fact that he approached the symphony, and large-scale composition in general, in a new and logical way. In a sense, he foreshortened the form, presenting small thematic phrases as the substance of his movements and developing them into extended statements; his predecessors had presented the extended statements, analysed them and then rebuilt them. Exciting as his orchestral style is, it is a style of sternly black-and-white statements made with great austerity in his mature works, eschewing the harp, with its softness of timbre and neutralizing all the colourful woodwind. In Britain and America in particular, Sibelius became the example to composers, and even so individual a master as Vaughan Williams not only acknowledged his authority but, at times, shows his influence, whilst the First Symphony, with which Walton followed *Belshazzar's Feast* in 1935 (the first three movements were heard in 1932, but the Finale followed three years later) seems to find a starting point in Sibelius's symphonic procedures though its emotional world is anything but Sibelian. In America, the symphonies of Roy Harris, works of powerful intellectual and emotional appeal, show an even greater absorption of Sibelius's style.

Sibelius's rejection of the ostentatiously colourful does not avoid excitement. His strings weave interesting, unresting patterns as the basis of the orchestral texture; percussion is used with the utmost restraint and therefore with powerful effect when it is heard; the wind instruments enter with startling exclamations, and orchestral *tutti* are built up with great skill and equally great suspense, so that such climaxes as that of the Finale of the Second Symphony —still, perhaps, the composer's most popular work—is a magnificent example of the power to build up mighty climaxes over what, to either Mahler or Bruckner, is a limited time span. The later works are fundamentally calmer, less concerned with man and history, it may be, than with nature and time, but they have the same power more and more condensed and more austerely deployed, and the Fifth reaches a culmination as overwhelming as that of the Second.

At the time of Sibelius's mastery, central European music was working out the revolutionary consequences of the twelve-note system pioneered by Schoenberg to provide order in the post-Wagnerian world of extreme chromatic harmony. Far-reaching and influential as Schoenberg's new doctrines have proved to be, after 1908, when the Five Orchestral Pieces (*Op.* 2) included (as Number 3) a study in tone colour divorced from any real vitality of theme or progress in its harmony, Schoenberg's orchestral ideas were perhaps the one element in his style that remained conservative. A number of chamber works for mixed ensembles as well as for the classic combinations prove to be more unusual and more suggestive instrumental possibilities than his orchestral works, and the continuing difficulties facing listeners to his piano and violin concertos are due rather to the thick orchestral texture which baffles the listener than to their actual thematic or harmonic substance.

It was Webern, the second of Schoenberg's great Austrian disciples, who approached the orchestra as radically as he approached harmony and the use of themes. Five Pieces for Orchestra, developed from his Five Pieces for String Quartet, Op. 5, are so compressed that they play for hardly ten minutes. A tiny thematic germ twists and turns until all its implications are shown; each note can be presented by a different instrumental voice and in a different register from its predecessor with an effect that is bare and austere—rarely are three or more instruments speaking simultaneously. His Symphony for Small Orchestra, written in 1928, is scored for saxophone, clarinet, bass clarinet, two horns and strings. It is in two movements and is, so to speak, at an end before the unfamiliar listener has been able to gather its terms of reference. The material is spread out between the instruments so that only rarely does the same instrument play two or three consecutive notes of important material, with the result that themes appear in different octaves as well as different colours; a basic theme begins with the notes A, F sharp, F natural and G; at one point in the movement these are heard as A (a third below middle C) and F sharp a sixth higher, both played by the second horn, F natural, played by the harp, and G again played by the second horn; no other instrument speaks at the time, and rarely do three or four instruments speak simultaneously. To hear any continuity between these isolated tones, or to recognize their harmonic implications, demands unusual powers of concentration, but Webern's musical asceticism often provides the remote glitter that can be felt in the Five Pieces. The English composer, Sir Arthur Bliss, once described Webern's music as necessary to clean out ears that had grown clotted by attention to huge, busy orchestral masses.

In France, composers after Debussy (who died in 1924) found a new influence in jazz as it reached Europe. This, too, was a recoil from huge orchestral forces. Ravel, who was born in 1875, wrote his *Daphnis et Chloé*, the ballet score which is the largest of all his works, between 1909 and 1912, with a clear understanding of Debussy's orchestral music but with a panache and sensationalism quite unlike Debussy's musical thinking. By 1931, when he wrote his two piano concertos (the first in G major and the second "for the left hand"), he finished with the orchestra. The G major concerto, he said, is written in the spirit "of Saint-Saëns and Mozart"; he declared that a concerto "should be light-hearted and brilliant". But the light-heartedness and brilliance also involve jazz effects which appear in the score like apposite, witty quotations though they are quoted from no external source. The second concerto is the most deliberately powerful and impassioned of his works, but it adds nothing to orchestral practice while the jazz effects link the G major Concerto with the music of Darius Milhaud, his junior by seventeen years, who in 1924 wrote the ballet *La Creation du Monde* in a jazz idiom for a small, jazz-orientated ensemble. Jazz, French popular music and Brazilian music were among Milhaud's enthusiasms, demanding new orchestral effects and thus modifying orchestral practice while suggesting the sufficiency of relatively small orchestras. But at the same time, Milhaud was one of the most prolific of composers, responsible for ten operas of various dimensions, a dozen ballets, film music, four symphonies, a long list of concertos and miscellaneous choral and orchestral works, chamber compositions, songs and piano pieces. He was, too, a determined explorer of new effects, so that his incidental music for plays, for instance, find fascinating new uses for the percussion which became part of an 'orchestra of stage noises' for Paul Claudel's translation of Aeschylus' *Agamemnon, Choephori* and *Eumenides*, when they were produced as a cycle of plays in 1927, combining them with wind machines, natural incidental stage noises and the human sounds of laughter, wails and cries of pain or horror. Such effects, however, added little to the natural vocabulary of the orchestral composer and remain 'dramatic effects', more or less meaningless outside the context for which they were created.

Whilst composers thus recoiled from the high emotional intensity and orchestral massiveness of the end of the nineteenth century, there were other reasons, not strictly musical, for the passing of interest in the monster orchestra. So far, orchestral economics have lurked only in the background of this book. To some extent, however, they are a major factor in orchestral history, especially the history of English and American orchestras, in the twentieth century.

Had the impossible happened, and an Esterhaza prince found himself short of money with which to support his orchestra, choir and opera company, he would simply have dismissed the lot. The central European princes and noblemen who provided employment for so many composers and instrumentalists during the eighteenth century did from time to time need to reduce their musical establishments, and from time to time an orchestra was simply killed off. But the disappearance of such establishments, whatever hardship it may have meant for their members, was no hardship to the development of music. In the nineteenth century, these establishments gradually became national or municipal organizations, with 'public money' instead of a patron's private fortune to support them. They grew, of course, to contain between eighty and a hundred members, the numbers necessary to perform the music of Beethoven, Brahms, Dvořák and Wagner, for example, in concert halls of a size sufficient to accommodate enough listeners to make the sale of tickets worthwhile. The average European orchestra found that to cover its costs it needed about a quarter of its income from the box office; the other three-quarters came from a subsidy. A badly attended concert in Berlin, Munich or Vienna, for example, was a pity; in England and America, it was a disaster.

Thus, until the 1880s, the Philharmonic Society in London played most of its concerts in the Hanover Square Rooms to a 'select' audience of about eight hundred; the symphonies of Beethoven, and other works needing a Beethoven-sized orchestra, were played in a hall not really built to accommodate such numbers. Such a hall, too, could accommodate only audiences ready to pay high prices for tickets, and within thirty years of its triumphant foundation the Philharmonic Society was facing its first financial crisis. In 1852 it was faced, as well, with a new but powerful rival.

Part of the success of the New Philharmonic Society in its early years after 1852 was due to its use of the Exeter Hall, in the Strand, as its concert hall; a capacity audience in Exeter Hall was upward of three thousand people, and there was accommodation for a really large orchestra, so that audiences at Exeter Hall heard Berlioz conduct his own music with the type of orchestra for which it had been designed as well as more enterprising programmes than were offered at the Hanover Square Rooms at a lower cost than was demanded of patrons of the Philharmonic Society. The Philharmonic Society possessed greater social prestige, but the New Philharmonic Society, and the various later rivals of the old society often provided concerts which were musically superior to those of the original Philharmonic. But these concerts were indissolubly linked to the necessity of success at the box office; any music which deterred audiences from attending a concert was very unlikely to be played.

Throughout the nineteenth century, the orchestras involved in the various London concerts contained so many of the same players that it would almost be possible to describe each orchestra as a different hat worn by the same musicians. As the number of concerts increased, the Philharmonic Society's dependence on the orchestra of the opera diminished and players, engaged for a single concert but not for an entire season—let alone for a year—lived with no prospect of financial security, teaching and undertaking any musical odd job which offered itself to augment their unsatisfactory earnings; while their engagements were simply from concert to concert, with no guarantee that they would survive for a complete season, they were as badly off as the members of the average German or Austrian orchestra, whose pay was scandalously low. Charles Hallé, whose orchestra was founded in Manchester in 1858, found it relatively easy to recruit experienced instrumentalists from the Continent for his orchestra for the offer of a season's contract, the prospect of regular work for more than half a year, and the prospect of the contract's renewal season by season although their Continental engagements offered them security of tenure for life and not merely seasonal employment. But foreign musicians who came to London did so with grander ambitions than membership of the rank and file of an orchestra although not all these glowing ambitions were fulfilled.

The circumstances of the London orchestras, however, did not encourage players to feel any great sense of loyalty to an orchestra as an institution. Spohr, Wagner and other conductors from central Europe working with the London orchestras talked of the high quality of English instrumentalists but of the poor standard of orchestral playing. This was partly because conditions of employment encouraged the players to exploit the deputy system as an unalterable law of English musical life. The players could not regard themselves as members of an orchestra as a body with a continuing life of its own, so that they regarded themselves as free to accept any better-paid alternative contract which was offered them for the evening of a concert, even though they were already booked to play in the orchestra. The only necessity was that an absentee player should send a deputy. They had, of course, attended rehearsals for the sake of the rehearsal fee and provided a substitute if, through the demands of their teaching, they missed a rehearsal. As it was the key players who were most likely to be offered alternative engagements, it was most often the better players who sent substitutes to the concert. One German conductor engaged for a London concert noticed a player who had not, through the exigencies of other engagements or a busy teaching practice, missed a single rehearsal and thanked him for his diligence. "I'm sorry I shan't be at the concert, though," said the player, "but I'm playing somewhere else that evening."

The result was that when the Hallé Orchestra, an ensemble engaged for the season, its members always present at both rehearsal and concert, began to play regularly in London in the 1880s. Metropolitan audiences were amazed by its efficiency and discipline, its unity of style, its decision in attack and the extent of its repertory; unlike the London orchestras, it never sounded like a collection of good instrumentalists thrown together for a single event and not drilled into unity.

The concerts of the Philharmonic Society grew increasingly dependent on the support of wealthy patrons and the membership fees of associate members of the Society, elected for their wealth. The Society and its activities were still controlled by its own elected committee, but this could no longer be regarded as control by its musician members; the committee had become increasingly composed of academic musicians and organizers rather than of players whose membership of the orchestra was necessary to the orchestra's efficiency. The other London orchestras—or rather, the rival concert societies—were supported by private patrons or committees of private patrons who were, all other things being equal, prepared to arrange to make good any deficit on the season's accounts; but such patrons presupposed that such deficits would be small and that the orchestra would under normal circumstances succeed in supporting itself through the box office. London had no Charles Hallé, who from 1858 to his death in 1895 supported the Hallé Orchestra by his own (limited) fortune made from his piano recitals and by his own common sense and business ability. His profit on the first season's concerts amounted, he wrote gleefully in his *Autobiography*, to threepence per concert.

The opening of the Queen's Hall as London's principal concert hall in 1892 led to the formation, in 1895, of the Queen's Hall Orchestra, created primarily to play a season of nightly promenade concerts under the managership of Robert Newman, who combined musical knowledge with business ability. His concerts were to be conducted by Henry J. Wood, then twenty-six years old and already proving the unusual quality of his gifts. The Promenade Concerts were financed, at first, by a throat specialist, Dr George Cathcart; Newman later took over the financial responsibility until, in 1902, it was accepted by a syndicate of business-men who were musical enthusiasts, headed by Sir Edward Speyer. In 1915 Chappell and Co., the music publishers, who held the lease of the Queen's Hall, took over financial responsibility until 1927, when the hall became the responsibility of the B.B.C. The Queen's Hall Orchestra undertook regular concerts outside the Promenade series on Sunday afternoons, so that it remained in being throughout each year. In 1904 Wood refused any longer to tolerate the deputy system, with the result that a considerable number of his players resigned and formed the London Symphony Orchestra under their own management; the players themselves shared the financial risk and, through an elected committee of players, ran their own business affairs and chose their own conductors and the soloists who appeared at their concerts. Hans Richter took charge of their activities until 1911; his successors have included Nikisch, Koussevitzky, Mengelberg, Elgar, Beecham and Furtwängler. The years of the depression led to a lowering of standards, but the reorganization of the orchestra after the Second World War as a non-profit distributing company, its affairs still run by a committee of members and their paid officials, restored it to its old position as an orchestra of international class.

The London Philharmonic Orchestra, founded by Beecham in 1932, has a similar history. It was created as an orchestra of the highest virtuoso standards, and Beecham arranged that it should play for the Royal Philharmonic Society's concerts (the adjective was granted to the society on its fiftieth birthday), for the Courtauld-Sargent Concerts, sponsored by Mrs Samuel Courtauld, the wife of a wealthy industrialist and the young conductor, Malcolm Sargent (these were founded to present the best orchestras and soloists in the best programmes at a cost which the general public could afford), and also for the Children's Concerts supported by Sir Robert Mayer; in this way, Beecham planned to base his new orchestra firmly enough in London musical life to ensure its financial security apart from himself and his own wealth. His absence in Australia and the United States during the Second World War forced the members to save the orchestra from destruction by following the example of the London Symphony Orchestra and taking over its own management. The New Philharmonia Orchestra, too, developed along the same lines; created in 1945 as the Philharmonia Orchestra by Walter Legge, a power in the world of the gramophone record, its purpose was to be available for recordings of the highest quality with the world's best conductors; its recording and its concerts, with Guido Cantelli, Herbert von Karajan and Otto Klemperer were, apart from any questions of taste and preference, outstanding, so that when Legge decided that he could no longer be responsible for the orchestra's future, its own members became its management. Of London orchestras, only the B.B.C. Symphony Orchestra, created in 1930 and first conducted by Adrian Boult, had an external management with financial control and, therefore, a secure yearly salary with paid holidays and a way of life comparable to those of earners who are not musicians. After the Second World War, the provincial orchestras reorganized themselves and offered annual, and not seasonal, contracts to their members.

At first, a similar state of things prevailed in the United States. The oldest and most revered of American orchestras, though it was not the first to be founded, is the New York Philharmonic, which began its career in 1842 as an organization of musicians which set up its own committee of management and controlled its own affairs until 1908, when its parlous financial and musical situation led a syndicate of wealthy Americans to take over its management through a committee on which the players had their own elected representatives.

Apart from the Boston Symphony Orchestra, the famous American orchestras all came early in their lives to find themselves dependent on such methods of control and finance. Several of them

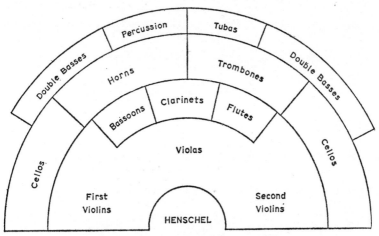

Boston Symphony Orchestra, 1881

began as self-governing ventures by groups of musicians which whetted an appetite for music and then died out to make room for new institutions with more effective means of finance; others, against beginning on the initiative of musicians, almost immediately found that finance through a syndicate of wealthy business men was the only certain means of survival. In Boston, however, the Symphony Orchestra was the creation of Henry Lee Higginson, a financier's son who had studied music in Vienna before deciding that a pianist's career was not for him and returning to Boston to follow in his father's footsteps. In 1881 he founded, organized and financed the orchestra in European conductors of his own choice to whom he gave complete artistic freedom, proving himself to be one of the most enlightened patrons in the history of music. Until he retired from business after the First World War, Higginson, who had spent an enormous fortune to keep the orchestra at the highest possible level of achievement, remained its sole financial support; then, realizing that after his death he could not endow the orchestra to any extent that would preserve its size and standard, he created a body of three hundred guarantors who would keep the orchestra afloat and maintain its standards.

The history of the New York Philharmonic runs in other ways parallel to that of the Philharmonic Society in London. Like its English pattern, it was faced after some forty years of steady existence by a wealthier organization with more up-to-date musical ideals, as the London organization was faced by the challenge of the New Philharmonic Society. This was the New York Symphony Orchestra, conducted by Leopold Damrosch, who had come from

M

Germany with some reputation as a conductor and already known in the musical world of Brahms and his contemporaries. The New York Symphony Orchestra was a salaried organization and not, like the Philharmonic, simply sharing the often exiguous profits of concerts among its members who were thus unable to regard membership of the orchestra as a major source of income. The Symphony Orchestra fell on hard times when Damrosch ceased to conduct it. Since no replacement of comparable musical gifts and personality was available, but though its concerts were suspended for five years until 1903, its sources of syndicated finance remained available for its future work.

In 1908, the struggling Philharmonic was compelled to accept outside help and control by a committee of sponsors, who co-opted representatives of the players on to a new committee of management, and appointed Mahler, recently resigned from the directorship of the Imperial Opera in Vienna, as conductor. Since then, the New York Philharmonic combined with the Symphony Orchestra and, like all American orchestras, has attracted support partly through a policy of appointing conductors-in-chief whose abilities and personality won the devotion of audiences. The qualities of a conductor as a personality are always important; in the United States they are a *sine qua non*.

In the years after the First World War, American governments encouraged generosity on the part of those financially able to support any artistic or generally cultural activities by exempting donations to such organizations from tax. The great foundations created by Ford, Pullinger and others played their part—the Ford Foundation, for example, has provided opera in the United States with vast sums, so that the danger of extinction which threatened several American orchestras in the 1920s completely receded. In Britain, the creation of the Arts Council to disburse public money to musical and other artistic enterprises, and legislation permitting local authorities to raise money to support artistic enterprises have eased the burden on orchestras, though the level of subsidies in England still leaves orchestras to play vast numbers of concerts every year to escape serious financial difficulty.

Thus, to return to the problem of performing music for a vast Straussian or Mahlerlian ensemble, the difficulty was that such music makes great demands on available resources. Enlarged orchestras need to rehearse, so that the initial cost of finding players for a performance involves extra rehearsal fees, which organizations permanently at war with an adverse financial situation prefer to avoid, especially as unfamiliar works are more likely to repel than to attract audiences. It took the secure finances of the B.B.C. as well as the inexhaustible musical enterprise of Sir Henry Wood to make possible a performance of Mahler's Eighth Symphony in London, in April 1930. The Mahler Ninth had its first English performance at a Hallé concert in Manchester in the preceding February, but while the so-called 'Symphony of a Thousand' could win a large audience impelled by curiosity to attend, the Manchester performance seems to have created singularly little stir and was not the signal for an outburst of enthusiasm for Mahler's music.

Even the more comfortably established orchestras of the Continent were not eager to incur the extra expenses involved in mounting colossal works; even apply subsidized orchestras have to work to a budget, and there was music enough to win and retain audiences without adding to financial risks at a time of Depression. Most composers, therefore, came to avoid the gigantic in spite of its special thrills because, even if they did not believe that Mahler and Strauss had exhausted the colossal style—a standpoint which would have been valid enough to deter them—there was the entirely sensible reason that works making great financial demands were unlikely to be heard.

The natural reaction, led by composers, against the over-expanded orchestra, was assisted by external circumstances, and the next notable extension of orchestral practice came from Stravinsky in 1913, with *Le Sacre du Printemps*, which more or less brought to an end the first stake in Stravinsky's oddly varied career. *Fireworks*, *The Fire Bird* and *Petrushka* had already established him as a major composer; they are music in the Rimsky-Korsakov tradition of Russian music, brilliant and glittering in colour, with a rhythmic *élan* and complexity that remain surprising and enlivening after sixty years. Their orchestra is not essentially larger than that of Tchaikovsky. Their melodies are characteristically Russian in their use of short phrases repeated and varied, pungently rhythmic, as though their sometimes folk-type melodies exist to articulate a rhythm rather than for any lyrical melodic purpose. In using them, Stravinsky could only give the orchestra a new tone of voice.

Le Sacre du Printemps, however, is a work completely governed by rhythms. The libretto is deliberately primitive—a human sacrifice is offered to the gods of fertility as the ballerina dances herself to death—and the music, for all the extreme sophistication of its means, matches the action in its insistence on rhythm. It is built from short melodic phrases, and sections grow out of their repetition and variation rather than out of any kind of development or contrast; they exist to identify and articulate rhythms. Only the opening melody for bassoon seems to exist in its own right as melody and, as the work puts all its elements under extreme tension, the bassoon is made to sing right at the strained top of its register.

Nothing happens which does not contribute to the effect; there is no deviation from the remorseless rhythmic urgency of the work; the powers and intensities with which it is concerned are entirely brutal in their manner of statement. Stravinsky writes for twenty woodwind: piccolo; three flutes (one changeable for second piccolo) and an alto flute; four oboes (one changeable for a second cor anglais); cor anglais; a piccolo clarinet (the player to use instruments in D and E flat); three clarinets (the players equipped with instruments in B flat and A) and one interchangeable with a second bass clarinet); one bass clarinet; four bassoons (one changeable for a second double-bassoon) and double bassoon. (See Appendix 2, No. 10.)

The brass is equally crowded: eight horns (two changeable for tenor tubas); one piccolo trumpet; four trumpets (one changeable for bass trumpet); three trombones; two bass tubas. The percussion section requires two timpanists; bass drum; side-drum; rape and antique cymbals sounding A flat and B flat; the strings naturally must be numerous enough to balance the weight of wind he prescribes. On the other hand, instruments like the harp, which lack incisiveness, are not required because they cannot effectively contribute to the task of forcefully marking rhythms. The orchestra becomes a rhythm instrument articulating complex metres with absolute decision and clarity, and even the work's harmonic progress contributes to these rhythmic procedures, throwing intense dissonances on to stressed beats which require special emphasis. Colour, as a means to orchestra allurement or as an element of some importance in musical structure, is rarely considered, just as melody exists only to outline and give memorability to basic rhythms.

Apart from *The Nightingale* and its offshoot *The Song of the Nightingale*, which exploit the Russian style, the works which succeeded *Le Sacre du Printemps* turn their back on the 'full orchestra'. *The Soldier's Tale*, completed in 1918, requires only a handful of solo instruments, three actors and a dancer but is a work of immediate appeal and vigour. Though the composer rationalized the work's apparent slightness as a response to wartime conditions which had brought him almost to pennilessness, it is not hard to imagine that behind that mundane practicality lay an almost instinctive wish to accept a sterner discipline than could in the twentieth century be applied to large orchestral works; the miniature stage work led him to a variety of impressive and completely realized pieces for 'small orchestra' or string orchestra. In 1920, the *Symphonies of Wind Instruments* make no unusual instru-

mental demands and the later symphonies, in C, and In Three
Movements, are works of deliberate moderation.

These works express Stravinsky's revulsion to what he called
"expressiveness", by which he chiefly seems to have meant any
addition to or exaggeration of a work's emotional qualities by its
performers; this revulsion seems to have made him aim always at
a hard, incisive orchestral tone. The *Symphony of Psalms*, composed in 1930 for the fiftieth anniversary of the Boston Symphony
Orchestra, omits the intrinsically 'emotional' upper strings—violins
and violas—from its score to obtain the firmest, most sculptural tone
that an orchestra can supply; for similar reasons he preferred the
sound of boys' voices to those of women in the choir of the work.

The deliberately remote, calm works for choir and orchestra
which came at the close of his career follow the same style, diver-
sified by what critics have called a 'Byzantine' style, by which
adjective they refer to an elaborately decorated vocal line. In these
works, Stravinsky seems to exhaust—so far as a style can be
exhausted—the possibilities of the remote, hieratic, incised music
of his choral works since the *Symphony of Psalms*.

The creative aspect of Mahler's orchestration, his use of an
expanded orchestra in an almost chamber-musical style where
every voice can be a solo voice, had to wait until the 1920s before
a new generation was able to begin to see its relevance to the kinds
of music they wished to write; a time-lag of a quarter of a century
between a new expressive development and its conversion into
standard currency seems to be a law of musical history. But interest
in works of less than full orchestral power continued. In London,
for example, the Boyd Neel String Orchestra was founded in 1933,
quickly adopted an eighteenth-century complement of wood-wind
and explored the eighteenth-century repertory while encouraging
composers to write new works for its concerts; similar chamber
orchestras grew up all over Europe, while Walton, for example,
became notorious in 1922, when he was only twenty, for the
original version of his *Façade*, a feat of great imaginative quality
and dazzling orchestral skill, written for a small, jazz-orientated
ensemble. The later, orchestral version, like Constant Lambert's
The Rio Grande, uses jazz idioms, and parodies them, with complete naturalness as though there were no cultural divide between
jazz and 'serious' music.

Jazz may have had some effect, through the inventiveness with
which it exploits percussion, on the chilling passage in *Belshazzar's
Feast* in which the soloist tells of the 'writing on the wall' accompanied by flutes, double bassoon, two harps, piano, cellos and
double-bass. The cellos play a quiet dissonant *tremolando* chord,
joined by the harps, which trill notes a semitone apart to achieve

the grating effect of a continuous minor second while *pizzicato* double-basses and double bassoons play an angular descending figure; against this very subdued background timpani, tenor drum, gong, castanets and cymbals, set up a harsh, grating pattern of sound (the flute squeaking like a slipping slate pencil) which seems to create the sound of the actual writing instruments scraping on the hard stone of the wall.

Any account of the remarkable brilliancies of orchestration to be found in twentieth-century music would offer little more than a list of names and titles. Many of these are the result of the exploitation of the orchestra in music like that of Bartók, which takes a fairly standard ensemble into music which uses it on behalf of a tradition with which it had not previously been in contact. Vaughan Williams, a composer who in his earlier works like the London Symphony, composed in 1914 and revised five years later, at first regarded emphasis as a demand for great orchestral weight (demanding great tact and finesse from the conductor if such passages are not to become disproportionately heavy in tone). Naturally, Vaughan Williams's later work proceed with a clearer, and therefore a more economical, sense of the orchestra. The rebarbative Fourth and the visionary Fifth of his symphonies (perhaps his finest purely orchestral works) create an individual orchestral 'sound-ideal' for the work. Late in his career, in the Eighth Symphony, Vaughan Williams developed an interest in sound as a thing in itself which his earlier music had never shown. The neglected Alan Bush, in his Byron Symphony, begins an eloquent slow movement with a long melody for strings, apart from double-bass, played not in octaves but in actual unison, creating an effect of great richness.

In 1936, so the story goes, Vaughan Williams protested against the unco-operative attitude of the orchestra when it was faced with one of the Festival's novelties, the song-cycle *Our Hunting Fathers*, by the twenty-two-year-old Benjamin Britten. The poems, some selected and some written by W. H. Auden, are about human attitudes to animals, and the virtuosity of its vocal line, its sparse orchestration and its use of unusual solo instruments, the spiky angularity of its themes and its deliberate satire may have suggested to the players that they were being asked to work hard with only a limited chance of personal satisfaction. Except in the third of the five songs—a girl's lament for the death of her pet monkey, which has a *ritornello* in which harp and strings are disposed to make a beautiful, subdued new colour—the orchestration is hard-edged and unsentimental. The last movement is a funeral march led by the xylophone, its dry tones never mollified by an accompaniment.

If audiences and players had been more familiar with Mahler's orchestral songs, *Our Hunting Fathers*, with its irony and wit, and its sense of parody, might have seemed less puzzling and less bleak, but in 1936 little of Mahler's music was known in Britain. The *Variations on a Theme of Frank Bridge*, which Britten composed in 1938, is the first of his work to exploit his knowledge of the string orchestra and manifest the inventiveness with which he uses instruments. The theme appears in varied styles which are sometimes grotesque, sometimes parodistic, sometimes high-spirited and sometimes emotional. A distorted Viennese waltz and a funeral march in which we hear the muttering of muffled drums which show Britten to be at home in the world of Mahler without modifying his own personality. English ignorance of Mahler's music in the 1930s must have added to the difficulties of those who found *Our Hunting Fathers*, with its satirical funeral march, its hard-edged orchestration and its solos for trombone and xylophone, beyond their immediate comprehension. A tough clarity of thought and sound do not immediately ingratiate themselves.

Compression and simplicity continued, and increased, in all Britten's work. The bareness of the last trumpet in the *War Requiem*, little more than a section for choir and brass interruptions and the jingling harness of the 'Driving Boy's' cart as it lumbers along on the heavy wheels of a tuba in the *Spring Symphony*, in the introduction to which a single chord in the unexpected voice of a vibraphone evokes the intense cold of winter, like the trumpets of "The Merry Cuckoo" which follow the frozen opening, the rival fanfares in the first scene of *Gloriana* or the ominous upsurge of the bassoon as Tennyson's Kraken wakes in the *Nocturne* —there are a multitude of other examples—show Britten enjoying the sheer brilliance of sound with its intensity augmented by the absence of any cushioning accompaniment.

To note the influence of Mahler on Britten's orchestra, his preference for clean, unclogged, muscular sound, athletic lines and spare texture, together with a gift for satire and parody, is not to suggest that Britten simply lives in Mahler's world. The *Sinfonia da Requiem*, composed in 1940, begins with a funeral march, entitled *Lacrymosa*, but though the funeral march is a very Mahlerian form this, unlike Mahler's ceremonial funeral marches mourning the fact of death, is entirely personal, an act of individual mourning. The second movement, the Scherzo, is called *Dies Irae*; its enormous violence is, so to speak, turns in on itself and disintegrates both substance and orchestra; it is as though the music has shaken itself to pieces, while the final, consoling movement, *Requiem Aeternum*, has a gentleness and serenity totally unlike anything by Mahler in its astringent beauty.

The international success of *Peter Grimes* after 1945 shows Britten's mastery of a large-scale orchestra handled with extreme discipline; the size of the forces involved assists rather than impedes a lean, muscular sound which is always functional and direct as well as beautiful. In the 'Moonlight' interlude—the entr'acte which leads into Act III—the surge and retreat of the sea (with the moonlight glinting on waves as they break) is a series of pulsating chords, rising and falling in the strings; Britten rarely writes in block harmonies of this sort, and the string harmonies of 'Moonlight' suggest a deep single line rather than an interplay of chords, while the menace of the sea, the disturbance of the calm rhythm of the strings, is evoked by the brass. The vivid and beautiful picture is evoked with great compression and simplicity.

The unprecedented success of *Peter Grimes* makes Britten's decision to write his next operas as chamber operas very surprising. Like Stravinsky explaining the tiny dimensions of *The Soldier's Tale*, Britten explained his turn to chamber opera in the most practical terms. The limited demands made by an orchestra of about twelve players and the absence of a chorus make such works more accessible to theatres in which the huge cost of full-scale opera spells something like ruin unless the operas are totally successful. Chamber operas can be staged effectively in theatres which can never accommodate a normal orchestra even for the Mozart operas. Like Stravinsky's, however, Britten's reasons for this turn to the small-scale may have had artistic motives which he himself did not completely apprehend. An orchestra of a dozen or fifteen players, all soloists, can play music which demands great subtlety of style with the most refined interplay of voices. Variety is assured in sound and colour by the mere fact that each member of the orchestra is a soloist.

In Scene II of *The Rape of Lucretia*, Lucretia and her servants fold household linen to the most exquisitely articulated web of sound; Tarquin rides from camp to Rome and his crime in a passage, the ferocity of which could not be increased by the addition of any number of instruments. In *Albert Herring*, the mourning of Albert's mother for his supposed death sets words of characteristic (in terms of the character created for Mrs Herring) banality to music of the most gossamer texture in which every instrument makes a vital contribution to the web; they colour the texture with harmonics; the flute plays a scale passage which is followed at half speed and in a different key by the oboe, which climbs a fifth and then curls back on itself, with a horn a third beneath. A harp glitters through the super-refined texture while the rhythm is marked by double-*pianissimo* strokes of a whip.

Britten's chamber operas delight in colour and delicacy although their orchestra is capable of violence and savagery. The procession in honour of Nebuchadnezzar's great idol of gold in the church opera *The Burning Fiery Furnace*, with a tiny instrumental group, succeeds in expressing barbarism and cruelty with frightening effect although nothing the instruments can do could make the music noisy. But the chamber orchestra of the Britten operas is not simply a vehicle of colour and dramatic effect. The dramatic turning point of *The Turn of the Screw* comes in the second act, where the children's governess left in sole charge by a guardian who has no time to attend to his wards decides that she must write to him and explain that the children are haunted by ghosts determined to corrupt them. The fact that she makes a decision simplifies the orchestra into what is virtually a two-part accompaniment to her voice, with agitated comments on the situation—the fear of supernatural evil and the fear of annoying an employer—and is conveyed in simple terms and coloured by instrumental doublings.

In the chamber operas, Britten's inventive use of the percussion is specially notable, but since his work for documentary films in the 1930s, when he composed from necessity rather than choice for small groups, inventiveness and ingenuity with a wide assortment of percussion has been one of his strong points. In Britten's work, all the indefinitely pitched drums, blocks, whips and so on are used, at times, to suggest melody by copying, so far as they can, its inflections. In *The Young Person's Guide to the Orchestra*, better known now as the *Variations and Fugue on a Theme of Purcell*, each instrument in turn plays a variation of its own on Purcell's sturdy dance theme; the percussion necessarily play as a group and present what is almost a text book example of how to get the best from modern percussion instruments needing to suggest the announcement of a melody. (*See* Appendix 2, No. 11.)

The most surprising of Mahler's disciples in the field of orchestration is Dimitri Shostakovitch, born in 1906. He established his reputation with his First Symphony, performed and heard before his twentieth birthday and is famous for the uneasy terms on which he lived with the Russian musical establishment, who found his work too intellectual, too personal and too exploratory at times to be regarded as orthodox communist music for the people; it is the Russian composer's duty to delight, inspire and entertain his listeners and to send them away with faith and confidence in the future. These were tasks which Shostakovitch did not always perform to official satisfaction.

Shostakovitch is often an ironist, given to satire and sarcasm; often, however, his use of long, lyrical themes suggests the huge, solitary landscapes and open spaces of Balakirev and the early Russian nationalists. The irony and satire of his works often appear as the obverse to a deep sense of tragedy expressed with great emotional power.

Shostakovitch's orchestration gives great clarity to his themes by colouring them separately from the rest of the orchestra. Vivid, and sometimes diverse, strands of orchestral colour are unwound against harmonies which have their own power and eloquence; often they evolve with great lyrical power and logic with an orchestra which makes everything clear and lucid through Mahlerian textures, so that what in other composers might appear to be orchestral freakishness, like the end of the Fifteenth Symphony, which leaves a group of indefinitely voiced percussion, wood blocks and the dryest sounding instruments, to play a rhythm, to die of exhaustion and fall to pieces without losing its sense of pace.

The extensiveness of twentieth-century orchestral practice provides any composer with a vast collection of techniques, so that composers not specially regarded as masters of the orchestra or inventors of new orchestral effects can find precedents and guidance for anything they wish to do. Subtleties abound, like the remarkable effects obtained by the Spanish composer, Roberto Gerhard, who settled in England; Gerhard developed the ethereal ringing tone which can be obtained from cymbals when they are stroked across the edge by a double-bass bow (which has thicker hair than a violin bow).

But in any age there are composers content with the materials they have been given and others whose musical instincts lead them away from whatever is conventional. In the late twentieth century, the revolution which Schoenberg inaugurated has led many composers to follow paths which seem to lead far away from any ideas from the past and thus from the standard orchestra as it has grown since the seventeenth century. Composers who are commonly regarded as progressive have little or no wish to create the full-bodied sound which was the ideal of most composers until, perhaps, the end of the Second World War. Even Mahler and Britten, who used the full orchestra comparatively little, have kept it always in reserve for the moments when its special power of fully saturated tone has been needed; but the composers who have carried the work of the Schoenbergian revolution much further than either Schoenberg or Webern anticipated have jettisoned not only the idea of essential themes and a style of harmony analogous to grammar in its obedience to necessary though elastic rules. To such composers, the order and sequence of notes and chords is something entirely subjective and internal, not subject to any formulae or conventional rules, so that to most ears their music sounds like a series of effects, delightful, exciting, banal or merely boring, assembled in what seems to be a purely arbitrary way.

Insofar as such composers regard the orchestra as a group of instruments selected specially for the work in hand and assembled for the colours they provide; these composers do not admit the necessity of certain types of tone, string, brass or woodwind. The works of Pierre Boulez, for example, are written for *ad hoc* groups of instruments, rarely many of them or particularly effective when heard as a *tutti*, altogether, but chosen entirely for their individual timbre. The result is, more often than not, a series of delightful, sophisticated sounds and sound patterns baffling to most hearers because there seems to be no essential relationship between the different stages of the series; form is discerned not through thematic repetitions, modulations or any of the formal signposts of the past but usually through the recurrence of different types of instrumental colours or patterns. In *Don*, for example, one of Boulez's works which takes its point of departure from the elusive poetry of Mallarmé, the orchestra functions not as families of woodwind, brass and string instruments but as three groups—of high-voiced, medium-voiced and low-voiced instruments irrespective of their colour, and the form of the work seems to be governed by the sections in which the instruments play in this lay-out. Messiaen, who was Boulez's teacher and whose music has had a vast influence on the rhythmic ideas and sound ideals of many younger composers, has not abandoned the idea of a theme with the determination of his juniors but calls into action vast numbers of tuned percussion—xylophone, glockenspiel, marimba and bells as well as tuned gongs—in music that has a range of expression from almost Straussian sensuality to austere remoteness. Karlheinz Stockhausen, a third extremely influential composer, likes to make music from the joint improvisations of a group of instrumentalists which he uses as raw material for transformation by electronic instruments which he controls while the instrumentalists are actually playing.

Among the works of interesting young English composers, like Peter Maxwell Davies and Harrison Birtwistle, there is little that approaches the conventional idea of orchestral music; they prefer to write works for ensembles created for the particular type of music they plan. Birtwistle's *The Triumph of Time*, his one major work for a more or less standard orchestra, however, gives proof to anybody who needs it that the more or less conventional orchestra can be used to great effect in the sort of work the composer wishes to write.

A search for new effects has led composers to write for woodwind deliberately overblown, to create arbitrary and unpredictable squeaks in the middle of coherent passages, to abandon traditional woodwind tone in favour of continuous flutter-tonguing, which deprives the tone of any steady 'body'. Brass players have at times been instructed to whisper, shout, sing, hum or yell into the mouthpieces of their instruments. String players have found themselves bowing their instruments between their bridge and their tail-piece, where an invariable cold, glassy squeaking tone is produced; a French cellist, after hearing strings played thus at a concert, is said to have wondered why he had spent the better part of a lifetime struggling to play the cello well.

Such effects, and the aleatoric, freely improvized music which stretched from Stockhausen's group-improvisations to works where a great degree of freedom is given to players of written notes, often demand new varieties of notation which give performers new problems of their own to solve. A score like that of David Bedford's *When I Heard the Learned Astronomer*, for tenor, woodwind, three horns, two trombones and tuba may look extremely problematical. (*See* Appendix 2, No. 12.) At times the singer and the instruments are working to conventional notation; at others they are set to play or sing in Bedford's own 'space-time' notation; some times, normal and 'space-time' notation are functioning together. In his 'space-time' notation, a heavy arrowhead is a signal to the conductor indicating the number of seconds that must pass (marked by a conventional number) before the next arrowhead is reached. The passage has the tenor singing in conventional notation in 5/4 time while the conductor's signals appear at five second intervals, so that the music can really be timed by the singer. Extended notes are open circles, like semibreves in normal notation, and they last as long as the horizontal line which follows them; open notes, like unfilled crotchets and tied by a horizontal tail, have no fixed time-relationship to the other notes; they are simply to be played in a very *legato* style and timed by the tenor's crotchets. Any number from two to a single crotchet to eleven to a crochet and a half appear in the illustration. Like the *legato* notes, the tailless black notes which indicate extreme *staccato* playing, are measured by the 'space-time' notation. *Legato* notes in the score of a companion piece for tenor and strings, *The Tentacles of the Dark Nebula*, are joined by a wavy horizontal line which instructs the players to make them either sharp or flat, as the player chooses, while diagonal lines leading up to or away from a note instruct the player to approach the note by an upward *glissando*; some are meant to take as long to cover a fourth as others do to travel an octave, so that the precise method of execution is left for the player to decide.

Such notations as these remain in touch with tradition, but more radical and unusual works have stranger forms of notation. There are scores which consist merely of a page or two of instructions, telling the player not what notes, but what type of music—slow or fast, high or low, *staccato* or *legato*, *forte* or *piano*—to play in certain circumstances which arise in the performance. Boulez's demand in his *Eclat* that the various sections of the work are played in the order which the conductor decides is obviously conservative compared to those of composers whose aim is to create no more than the circumstances in which interesting musical relations may be set up by pure accident.

Whether or not such works are opening the road which music is to follow in the future, or whether they are a temporary eccentricity, we do not know and cannot safely prophecy. There are influential musicians who wish us to believe that the orchestra and the concert hall are anachronistic survivals, museums for dead music (Boulez's description, a few years ago, of opera-houses), but it seems that reports of the orchestra's death, like those of Mark Twain's, are exaggerated. Music is never dead until it ceases to communicate with its audiences, and each year provides us with new music for normal orchestras as well as extreme new *avant garde* works. Not all the composers who work with and through a normal orchestra are elderly and rooted so deeply in the past that they cannot face the present; the orchestral works of the past also communicate as vitally now as they did at any time in the past. In a sense, they create the appetite they satisfy, and the mere fact that Bach, Beethoven and Brahms, for example, create new audiences for themselves year by year is a guarantee of their continued life until the music of the past ceases to be relevant to minds which have found their deepest and most cherished musical experiences in works by those who have traditionally been regarded as the great masters as well as by Mahler, Britten, Tippett and the composers of today. The orchestra will survive because it is the source of a musical nourishment we need, though it may have to survive with other stranger and less immediately approachable styles of music-making.

APPENDIX ONE

INSTRUMENTS OF THE ORCHESTRA

Wind instruments depend for their tuning on the note made or implied by the length of their pipe, and by its bore; the longer the pipe, the deeper the note produced. The length of a cor anglais gives it the fundamental note F, that of a clarinet B flat, A or E flat.

Modern horns are usually tuned to F—the fundamental note sounded by the length of their pipe, and modern trumpets usually are tuned in B flat. In the past, other lengths of horn or trumpet were available, but the development of valve horns and valve trumpets has made these instruments capable of playing in any key.

The slide of a trombone alters the fundamental tuning by as much as seven semitones; each extension of the instrument's slide lowers its fundamental notes by a semitone.

Those instruments—cor anglais, clarinet, horn and trumpet—which have their fundamental note other than C are transposing instruments; that is, the fingering of a scale of F for a cor anglais, or of B flat for a clarinet, is the fingering which needs involve no accidental semitones but is played on the natural notes of the instrument; the music of these instruments is therefore written down as though the key of B flat is that of C major—the key played entirely on natural notes. Therefore the music of an instrument in F sounds a fifth below the note written for it, and that of a clarinet in B sounds a tone below the note written for it. No key signature is given, in modern practice, for transposing brass instruments, but transposing woodwind instruments have their parts written in the key which compensates for their custom of playing above or below the note printed; a clarinet in B flat, to play in G major, has its part written out in A major; a cor anglais, intending to play in G major, has its part written out in C.

A piccolo is a transposing instrument, sounding an octave above the note written.

Double basses are transposing instruments, sounding an octave below the notes written.

Horn in
F

Harmonic series

written   sounds   Mahler: 6th Symphony

Trumpet
in B♭
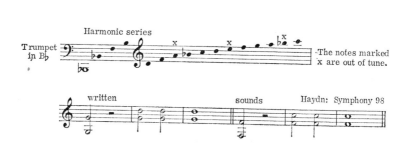
Harmonic series

The notes marked
x are out of tune.

written   sounds   Haydn: Symphony 98

Position
1.... 2.... 3.... 4.... 5.... 6.... 7
Trombone

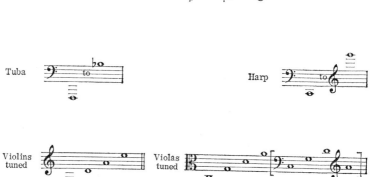

Tuba   to

Harp   to

Violins
tuned

Violas
tuned

Cellos
tuned

Double basses
tuned   or   or

MUSIC EXAMPLES

1. Bach, *St Matthew Passion*. Bach set out this chorus for two choirs and orchestras identical except for their flute parts. (*See* p. 41.)
(*Courtesy,* Bärenreiter-Verlag, Kassel and London.)

SINFONIA.

2. Handel, *Saul*, Battle Symphony. (*See* p. 53.)

(*Courtesy*, Gregg Press Inc., New Jersey.)

III

3. Mozart, Symphony 25, Minuet. The horns in B flat and G are transposing instruments; the actual notes they sound are identical with those of the first violins and oboes. (*See* p. 69.) (*Courtesy*, Heugel et Cie, Paris/UMP Ltd, London.)

4. Beethoven, First Symphony, first movement. (*See* p. 81.) (*Courtesy*, Boosey & Hawkes, Music Publishers Ltd, London.)

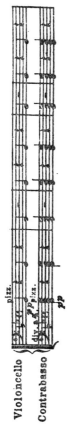

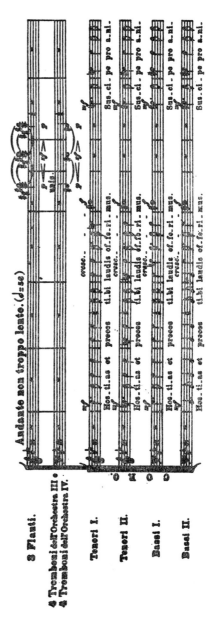

5. Berlioz, *Fantastic Symphony*, March to the Scaffold. Timpani and horns omitted. (*See p. 113.*) (*Courtesy*, Ernst Eulenburg Ltd, London.)

6. Berlioz, *Requiem*, *Hostias*. Strings omitted. (*See p. 111.*) (*Courtesy*, Broude Bros, New York.)

No. 8. Hostias.

Andante non troppo lento. (♩=56)

8 Flauti.

4 Tromboni dell'Orchestra III.
4 Tromboni dell'Orchestra IV.

Tenori I.

Tenori II.

Bassi I.

Bassi II.

7. Berlioz, *Romeo and Juliet*, Queen Mab Scherzo. The lozenge-shaped notes in the violin parts are the sounds produced by the harmonics, when the note is merely touched by the players and not firmly held down. The bottom two staves are violas and cellos (*See* p. 114.) (*Courtesy*, Breitkopf & Härtel, Leipzig.)

8. Wagner, *Tristan and Isolde*, Prelude. (*See* p. 127.) (*Courtesy*, Breitkopf & Härtel, Leipzig.)

9. Mahler, Fourth Symphony, first movement. (*See* p. 164.) (*Courtesy*, Universal Edition (London) Ltd.)

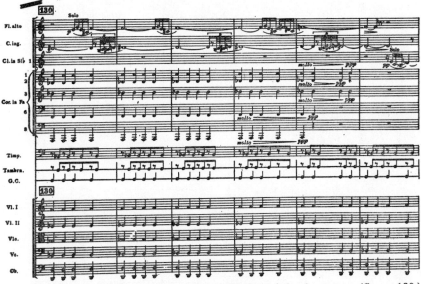

10. Stravinsky, *The Rite of Spring*, Ritual Action of the Ancestors. (*See* p. 180.) (*Courtesy*, Boosey & Hawkes, Music Publishers Ltd, London.)

11. Britten, Variation and Fugue on a Theme of Purcell. Strings omitted. (*See* p. 185.) (*Courtesy*, Boosey & Hawkes, Music Publishers Ltd, London.)

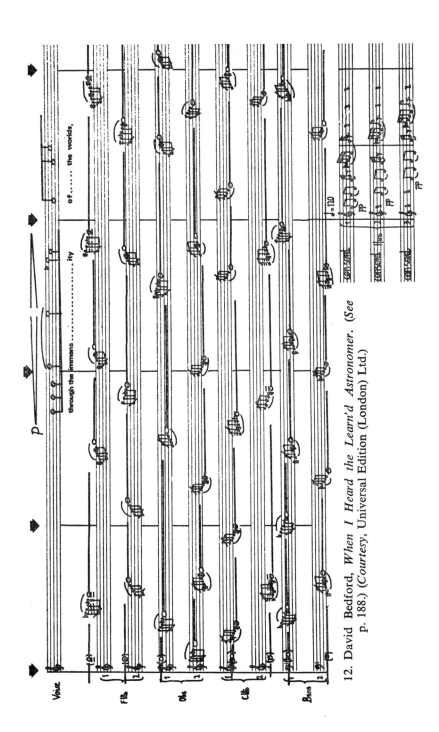

12. David Bedford, *When I Heard the Learn'd Astronomer.* (*See* p. 188.) (*Courtesy*, Universal Edition (London) Ltd.)

Index

Accademia, 34
Auber, Daniel Francois Esprit, *La Muette de Portici*, 106

Bach, Carl Philipp Emanuel, 38, 61, 62
Bach, Johann Ambrosius, 14
Bach, Johann Christian, 32, 58; influence on Mozart, 67; London concerts, 66–7
Bach, Johann Sebastian, 30, 36, 39–44, 48, 57, 61, 65; Leipzig orchestra, 40–2; professional duties in Leipzig, 38–9; Brandenburg Concertos, 47; Cantata 21 (*Ich hatte viel Bekümmernis*), 46; Cantata 71 (*Gott ist mein König*), 38; Cantata 160 (*Ich weiss dass mein Erlöser lebt*), 46; *Christmas Oratorio*, 29; Mass in B minor, 43; *St Matthew Passion*, 40–3; Suites, 45, 47
Balakirev, Mily, 152, 153, 185
Banister, John, 31–2
Barbirolli, John, 148
Bartok, Bela, 182
Basel, 14
Basset horn, 74
Bassoon, 13, 60, 90, 91, 107–8, 110, 162, 180; double bassoon, 86, 89, 90, 180
Bayreuth Festival Theatre, 124–5, 141
Bedford, David, 188
Beecham, Thomas, 139–40, 142–3, 144, 146, 148, 169
Beethoven, Ludwig van, 57, 68, 90, 94, 95, 102, 105, 128, 130, 143, 144, 147, 172; background and career, 78; conductor, 130–31; enlargement of orchestra, 84–6, 89, 91, 92; percussion, 86–7; popular appeal, 79–80, 96–8, 99, 101,
137; strings, 87–8; treatment of brass, 82–4, 92; trombone, 84–5; *Battle of Vittoria*, 85, 86; Choral Fantasia, 85; Fourth Piano Concerto, 85, 130; Fifth Piano Concerto, 89; Triple Concerto, 80; Violin Concerto, 80; *Egmont Overture*, 86; *Fidelio*, 86; German Dances, 80; *Ruins of Athens*, 89; Symphonies: No. 1, 68, 80, 81, 85; *Eroica*, 80, 82; No. 4, 84; No. 5, 82, 84, 85, 86, 87, 88–9; *Pastoral*, 82, 84, 85, 86; No. 7, 85; No. 9, 83–4, 86, 87, 88, 89, 91, 95, 100, 121, 133, 135
Benda family, 62
Bennett, William Sterndale, 96, 139
Berlin, 61, 106, 118, 135, 173; Philharmonic Orchestra, 143
Berlioz, Hector, 33, 101, 108, 120, 121, 122, 141, 150; background and training, 109; brass, 114–15; ceremonial works, 109–12; concerts, 117; conductor, 117–19, 134–36, 138, 140, 146; percussion, 115; strings, 113–14; technique of orchestration, 90–1, 112–13, 115–17, 127; *Childhood of Christ*, 112; *Fantastic Symphony*, 112–13, 114, 116, 118–19; *Harold in Italy*, 114, 118; *King Lear*, 118; *Requiem*, 91, 109–11, 112–13, 118, 134; *Romeo and Juliet*, 95, 114–15; *Symphonie Funebre et Triomphale*, 91, 109–10; *Te Deum*, 109–10
Bernstein, Leonard, 148
Birtwistle, Harrison, 187
Bishop, Henry, 99–100
Bizet, Georges, 150
Bliss, Arthur, 171
Bonn, 78
Boston Symphony Orchestra, 176–7, 181

DATE			
MAY 1 7 1979			
OCT 28 1982			
DEC 1 9 1997			